D0966448

PRAISE FOR *PAY PEOPLE RIGHT!*

"Pat Zingheim and Jay Schuster show the key role of pay in companies that are 'opening the books' and encouraging their employees to think and act like businesspeople. *Pay People Right!* is an up-to-the-minute guide based on good values and great business sense."

—**John Case,** executive editor of *Harvard Management Update*; author of *Open-Book Management* and *The Open-Book Experience*

"Why bother to get pay right? Simply because financial rewards are one of only three forms of motivation available to managers (the other two are a compelling vision and an appropriate organizational architecture). Zingheim and Schuster not only show how to create state-of-the-art rewards systems, they give practical advice about how to effectively link pay with vision and architecture and thus create a great company. Their invaluable six reward principles deserve to be posted on every office wall, right beside the company mission statement."

—**James O'Toole,** author of *Leading Change* and *Leadership A to Z*

"Pat Zingheim and Jay Schuster have written another great book in *Pay People Right!* It displays unique insights not only about pay itself, but also on how rewards relate to critical strategic issues. They provide a clear path for world class companies to follow that is innovative and strongly anchored in leading-edge business practice. I highly recommend *Pay People Right!*"

—**Richard J. Schonberger,** author of *World Class Manufacturing, Building a Chain of Customers,* and *Japanese Manufacturing Techniques*

"In *Pay People Right!*, Pat and Jay help you operationalize the often-used phrase 'people are our most important asset.' This important book shows how to build a foundation for capturing people's commitment to generating great work for your company. It is a timely read for today's high-speed global economy."

—**Skip Colbert,** Vice President, Human Resources and Public Affairs, Sony Electronics Inc.

"Pat and Jay have another hit! *Pay People Right!* is full of practical and creative solutions that apply to all types of enterprises—from manufacturing to e-commerce, from start-ups and fast growth to mature businesses. The six reward principles are truly a breakthrough in strategic rewards thinking. The concepts of ongoing value and the total employee experience provide solutions for issues facing us today as well as a framework for the longer term. I absolutely love it!"

—**Linda J. Salokas,** Director of Strategic Growth, Amazon.com

"*Pay People Right!* describes the roadmap companies should follow to enhance their ability to shift the workforce mentality toward enterprise, ownership, and sharing in the success they help generate. A must read for anyone contemplating reinventing rewards to add value to their business."

—**Tom Morelli,** Corporate Vice President, Human Resources, Solectron Corporation

"*Pay People Right!* transcends ordinary notions of pay. Pat and Jay offer total reward strategies that effectively aim toward bringing about a new 'better workforce deal.' The six reward principles and total reward components pull the entire topic together in one place. Leaders will see how they can go further to refine not only pay approaches but also the entire workplace experience. I recommend it for those who want to create sustained value through lasting partnerships with the people they lead."

—**Mark A. Speare,** Senior Associate Director for Human Resources,
UCLA Health System

"The only way companies will be able to compete in the future is by managing people effectively. Although pay is often the last thing that companies address, it should be among the first. For companies ready to address the issue, Zingheim and Schuster offer enlightened thinking and solid advice. The book is full of good examples, and they slice and dice the pay issue in every way possible. It's an enormously helpful tool."

—**Allan Halcrow,** Publisher/Editor-in-Chief, *Workforce*

"This book offers a world of experience and insight on how to align a firm's pay structure with its vision and strategies. Leaders need to read it, heed its message, and learn to do it right!"

—**Burt Nanus,** author of *Visionary Leadership* and
coauthor of *Leaders: The Strategies for Taking Charge*

"In *Pay People Right!* Pat Zingheim and Jay Schuster give us the tools to create compensation systems that make sense in the new economy. They show us how to integrate our reward systems fully with our business strategy in order to pay people for the true value they add. Anyone serious about managing, motivating and compensating people the right way should read this book and heed the advice these two experts have to offer. The chapter on rewarding scarce talent, alone, is worth ten times the price of the book.

"Here's a prediction. Companies that fail to learn Zingheim and Schuster's reward principles and adopt total pay practices will find it very difficult to recruit and retain the best and brightest employees. Zingheim and Schuster have produced an essential guidebook for CEOs, business owners, HR professionals, union leaders, indeed, for anyone seriously interested in the strategic use of pay and performance rewards."

—**Joseph H. Boyett** and **Jimmie T. Boyett,**
coauthors of *Beyond Workplace 2000* and *The Guru Guide*

"How people are rewarded can have a big impact on company performance. In *Pay People Right!*, Pat Zingheim and Jay Schuster provide solid principles for companies that are market leaders or wish to be."

—**Michael Treacy,** coauthor of *The Discipline of Market Leaders*

Pay People Right!

Patricia K. Zingheim

Jay R. Schuster

Authors of *The New Pay*

Pay People Right!

Breakthrough Reward Strategies to Create Great Companies

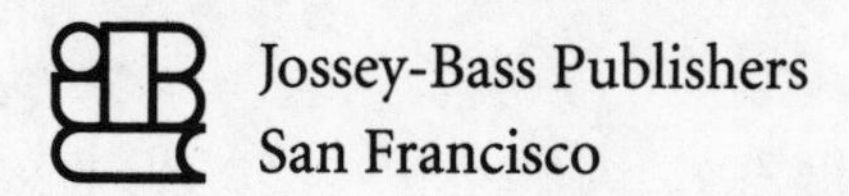

Jossey-Bass Publishers
San Francisco

Jossey-Bass books and products are available through most bookstores. To contact Jossey-Bass directly, call (888) 378-2537, fax to (800) 605-2665, or visit our website at www.josseybass.com.

Substantial discounts on bulk quantities of Jossey-Bass books are available to corporations, professional associations, and other organizations. For details and discount information, contact the special sales department at Jossey-Bass.

Manufactured in the United States of America on Lyons Falls Turin Book. This paper is acid-free and 100 percent totally chlorine-free.

Library of Congress Cataloging-in-Publication Data

Zingheim, Patricia K.
Pay people right!: breakthrough reward strategies to create great companies / Patricia K. Zingheim, Jay R. Schuster.— 1st ed.
p. cm. — (The Jossey-Bass business & management series)
Includes bibliographical references and index.
ISBN 0–7879–4016–X (hardcover: alk. paper)
1. Compensation management. I. Schuster, Jay R. II. Title. III. Series.
HF5549.5.C67 Z56 2000
658.3'22—dc21
99–050437

FIRST EDITION
HB Printing 10 9 8 7 6 5 4 3 2

The Jossey-Bass
Business & Management Series

Contents

To Squeaky Anne MacPherson

Preface

Change has made road kill of the futures of many companies and proud workforces. Who would have thought years ago that such companies as IBM, K-Mart, General Electric, AT&T, General Motors, Apple, Xerox, Advanced Micro Devices, Owens Corning, Westinghouse, and Disney would need to reinvent themselves to remain viable? Some of these enterprises met change and adapted; others are still struggling.

Gaining workforce support and commitment to business growth is a goal of most enterprises—some succeed and some don't. Often the difference can be traced to communications and the strength of the resulting workforce buy in. Newly developed approaches to rewards recognize change and position pay as a primary communications element of business performance.

People want to work for outstanding companies, and pay and other rewards are part of the formula that people look for. Pay can be the accelerator pedal for an enterprise to speed the business process and success. Pay can support company performance initiatives and make them real. Our purpose is to show how to do this effectively, consistent with your company's timetable and goals. This book is about how rewards can help a business be excellent in the eyes of its workforce and help ensure financial success and praise from customers.

The most important question about strategic alignment that a company's leaders can ask themselves is whether the firm can offer people the opportunity to share in company success or only in anxiety, lost trust, and discontent. This book is about fostering, sharing, and celebrating business success and about why your company should do so. This is a presumptuous foundation for a book on rewards. However, to remain (or become) great, companies must honestly communicate with their entire workforce to prosper jointly. Pay is a powerful communicator of values and directions. We believe it must be aligned with the business so it delivers the proper messages effectively. Pay too often makes an unfortunate statement of shortage—or plenty—when neither really exists. Aligning pay can be truthful and positive, and give both the workforce and the firm something to celebrate. We intend to show how pay can present an honest picture to people about what's expected and how this benefits them and makes them winners as partners of the company.

The foundation of this book is six reward principles that align pay and other rewards with business goals. We believe these principles create a road map toward making pay an effective tool of the business process. We intend to show how to apply these principles reasonably and practically to help achieve business results and also share success with the workforce.

We developed the reward principles from our consulting experience with a wide range of for-profit and not-for-profit organizations since the publication of our book *The New Pay: Linking Employee and Organizational Performance.*[1] The basis of the principles also resulted from our research on reward design, which focused on exploring contemporary business issues, for example, teams and team pay; skill and competency pay; rewarding scarce talent, salesforces, and executives; global rewards; and merger-and-acquisition (M&A) rewards.

The only way for a company to have effective total pay (base pay, cash and equity variable pay, recognition, and benefits) is to build an effective and understandable business case for changing rewards. *Pay People Right!* provides the tools to build the business case and shows how to apply the reward principles to link pay to the business case, thus creating effective total pay.

If your company's business situation and pay approaches are aligned, you may not feel it's necessary to read about aligning total pay with your business process. In this case, we suggest that some of our ideas about how to do things better regarding pay may be worthy of attention. Experience suggests, however, that the messages that pay gives and what organizations need to communicate are often not well aligned. If this is the case, don't be disillusioned. Pay approaches in use within a company are very hard to change because pay is an emotional topic and has an impact on everyone in the company. Pay gets people's attention. It can be an effective "heavy lifting" tool when an enterprise needs to change the workforce and culture to better align with business effectiveness and become an employer of preference.

You should select pay as the accelerator for the business process only if you're courageous, because it isn't a quick fix. Much of the popular literature on management and organizational change avoids issues of pay, perhaps because it's harder to address than many gentler and less powerful change tools the literature proposes. Changing pay requires patience and constant attention. One of our objectives is to help you know whether a business case for changing rewards exists in your organization. Subsequently, we suggest what to do about it and how to change total pay most effectively.

PAY AS A LEAD ELEMENT OF CHANGE

Pay People Right! defines the leading and communicating role of pay in business performance. Pay enjoys a critical role in helping companies and people enhance their performance. A number of important tools are available to improve pay design. We describe how people can add value and how your company can get from where it is now to where it would like to be.

Companies exist to satisfy not only shareholders and customers but also the workforce. People spend much of their lives working, and it makes sense to take reasonable steps toward making this time as productive, effective, and positive as possible. Most people clearly want to add value to their companies and are willing and able to do so. Since individuals work for pay as well as a number of other reward elements (such as development, the work environment, and the work itself), it's in the best interests of the enterprise to do whatever is practical and reasonable to make the work experience a desirable one. Pay and other rewards are strong symbols of what a company is about; they can help show the direction of change and encourage the workforce to become close partners with the company.

THE BETTER WORKFORCE DEAL VERSUS THE NEW WORKFORCE DEAL

We hear a lot about a *new workforce deal* that the workforce must learn to accept.[2] It began as a new deal of shortage, rather than of sharing. This new deal outlines a prospect of reducing people's expectations and having them accept more responsibility for their own performance. We don't agree with this concept of what a company can and should offer.

We believe companies can and must offer much more. We suggest that thinking companies can develop pay and other reward solutions that offer people the chance to share in the success of their company

—to do better as a result of making their company a success than they can do if pay is not changed. Our message is that a *better* opportunity and *better* deal not only are possible but should be a measure of success that the enterprise applies to make itself a more successful employer, a better performer, and a place where people want to work.

The New Pay introduced to pay the concept of "total" by optimizing base pay, variable pay, and benefits. *Pay People Right!* extends this concept to total rewards by including other rewards in addition to pay and addressing key business opportunities such as globalization, mergers and acquisitions, scarce talent, sales professionals, executives, and teams.

READERSHIP

Is your company struggling to make paying for performance real?

Are you losing key talent that's difficult to replace, and is this slowing the progress of the business?

Is your company doing well but looking for a way to enlist the help of the workforce to do even better?

Has your company moved to teams but is still rewarding only individual performance through base pay increases, such that people are slow to adapt to the team structure and team results aren't happening as quickly as expected?

Have you been involved in a merger or acquisition with a firm with a widely different pay approach?

Is your company going global?

This book helps you address these issues. Our primary audience includes executives, managers, business and union leaders, facilitators, advisors, change agents, human resource and compensation and benefit professionals, business improvement catalysts, and all workforce members who are responsible for or interested in company and human resource alignment, growth, and success. Readers are those actively seeking a way to involve people more closely in the business—to have the workforce make a performance difference and share in the success of the business. *Pay People Right!* takes a strategic, but very practical, business perspective to encourage using pay as an element of the business-planning process. Because we view rewards as potentially powerful partners with company performance initiatives, we believe that everyone who's been chartered to take a company in a new direction will be interested.

ORGANIZATION OF THE BOOK

We've organized *Pay People Right!* to help you browse for what you want, or to read in exploring issues to your depth of interest. We suggest that you first read Chapters 1 through 3 to get a framework for our message. Then, you can read individual chapters if you're interested in specific topics, for example, team pay, variable pay, scarce talent, sales compensation, global rewards, or M&A rewards. But we hope you'll read the entire book to get a broad picture of the potential power of rewards. We include a number of examples throughout the book. They may not be in the specific industry of your company, but we believe the information they impart is applicable to any situation where people can add value; we also believe you can generalize from the specifics of the example to your own situation.

Chapter 1: Total Rewards and the Six Reward Principles

In the opening chapter we introduce the importance of total rewards and describe the elements that make up total rewards to establish a context for the book. Although we start with a focus on total rewards because the broad perspective is important, the main focus of *Pay People Right!* is, as the title indicates, pay. We define the six reward principles that provide consistency of purpose and direction for the diverse pay topics we address throughout. The principles present a unifying theme and are universally applicable tenets that have proved effective in our research and consulting experience. The chapter describes them in the context of an enterprise's business, human resource, and total reward strategies. We suggest that moving your company aggressively in the direction of these principles results in a better way to reward people. Used in conjunction with your company's business case for changing rewards (a concept introduced in Chapter 2), the principles chart the path to get you from where you are to where you want to be.

Chapter 2: The Business Case for Changing Rewards

Why do something as difficult as change pay? Why change pay at all? Why not take an easier course of action, such as implement a new training program or modify the selection-and-hiring process? The only logical reason to change pay is to better align the workforce with the business process. In this chapter, we give you tools to help you diagnose where your company's business and its total pay solution are now. The tools also explore what the business prospects and opportunities are in the future, and how total pay may play an active role in getting you from where you are now to where your company must be to do well. Chapter 2 describes how an enterprise's business situation, business strategy, human resource strategy, and total reward strategy drive the business case for changing rewards; the chapter also includes some examples. We describe the better workforce deal and stress the importance of leading and reinforcing change with pay.

Chapter 3: Integrating Total Pay

Total rewards include more than total pay; they include the entire work experience and the better workforce deal. In this chapter, we discuss the importance of the total reward picture in determining a firm's competitiveness in the labor market. However, we narrow our focus to address the importance of each element of total pay for what it does best. It's clear that some elements of pay are best suited to emphasizing the value the individual adds to the organization. Others are best for recognizing results at the individual, team, group, business-unit, or company level; and still others do best when focused on supplemental rewards that are not directly related either to results or added value. This chapter reviews the possible pay elements and how and why some alternatives do things better than others. We discuss how to allocate pay dollars effectively to the total pay elements, to be consistent with the business case for changing rewards.

Chapter 4: Measuring and Managing Performance

It's important to measure and manage performance well because this is the cornerstone of sound pay and total rewards. The chapter discusses how business strategy and goals can best drive rewards to be successful. It introduces the importance of business-aligned goals and ongoing development and performance feedback. We believe that performance measurement and management should play a new and more positive role in the total pay process. Regardless of whether your company is measuring performance and capability effectively to add value, your shareholders and customers certainly are. This chapter discusses issues of selecting measures and goals, as well as skills and competencies, for use with pay. Performance measurement and feedback are the messengers for the firm's goals and competency requirements.

Chapter 5: Rewarding Individual Ongoing Value: Base Pay

Whether a company decides to pay individuals for the jobs they perform or for the skills and competencies they possess, it's critical that the base pay solution reflect value to the business. We define the concept of paying for an individual's ongoing value along three dimensions: (1) skills and competencies that the individual uses to get results, (2) the individual's consistent performance over time, and (3) the individual's value relative to the labor market. Ongoing value takes a broader perspective than just one year's performance; one year's performance can be meaningfully rewarded through variable pay or lump-sum payments. We show examples of how companies may emphasize one dimension over others and how they integrate the ongoing value of base pay with other pay elements.

Chapter 6: Building Infrastructure for Base Pay

The realities of the labor market are fundamental to effective base pay and total pay management. This chapter reviews the importance of the external marketplace as the basis for total pay, whether companies choose pay solutions predicated on jobs or the skills and competencies people have and apply to get results. The chapter reviews alternative structures for base pay, including grades and ranges, market rates, broad grades, and career bands. We explore banding as an infrastructure solution and suggest how, in combination with other total pay solutions, it may add value to your business. The chapter gives a framework for base pay in the context of total pay and, along with Chapter 5, defines the crucial base pay element.

Chapter 7: Rewarding Performance: Short-Term Variable Pay

Pay for individual ongoing value and variable pay are the one-two punch of effective total pay alignment with the business. Performance measurement and management guide the company to effectively define and communicate business goals to the workforce. Rewarding results has been and continues to be the focus of the move to new pay. Our primary interest in this chapter is in short-term variable pay (cash or equity awards in addition to and separate from base pay, and granted for a performance period of one year or less) because it's more nimble and flexible than other pay elements. It can reward team, group, site, business-unit, company, or individual performance. We review variable pay in its key forms and offer some information on how best to apply variable pay to communicate what's required to be successful and how to keep it refreshed. We propose short-term variable pay as a general approach to rewarding workforce results and suggest why it's such an important and powerful reward tool.

Chapter 8: Rewarding Performance: Long-Term Variable Pay

Companies measure success and provide feedback over extended periods of time. Although short-term variable pay measures and rewards results effectively over one year or less, a business is more like a marathon race than it is a 60-meter dash. Increasingly, companies are using long-term variable pay, especially stock options, for large segments of the workforce. This chapter discusses both cash-based and stock-based long-term variable pay as a reward tool not only for executives but also for key people, wherever they are in the firm. Broad-based stock options are an increasingly important reward tool, so we offer guidance on how and why this may be the case for your company. This chapter presents possible solutions and suggests how they can be combined with base pay and short-term variable pay to form more effective total pay.

Chapter 9: Recognition and Celebration

Treatment of rewards is incomplete without a discussion of how to recognize and celebrate success as part of the better workforce deal. This chapter guides use of recognition and celebration in a total reward strategy. Great companies recognize and celebrate. They don't all do it in the same way, but they all do it. Take a look at lists of the "best places to work" or "employers of preference," and you'll find recognition and celebration playing an active role in making the workplace special. In this chapter, we talk about the role of recognition and celebration and how pay design works best if it defines the change process to include having fun while accomplishing something. We include examples and suggest some possible resources for help and support on how having fun at work can generate value for the business and people.

Chapter 10: Rewarding Teams

Teams and teamlike organization designs are a central element in many company improvement initiatives. In this chapter we focus on small teams, such as project teams (established to achieve important business goals) and process teams (part of a company's basic organization design). Total pay solutions have traditionally emphasized the individual rather than collaborative effort. This chapter poses a challenge to individual pay and suggests that pay in small teams should be designed to make the team a success, not designed to erode team cohesiveness. This chapter addresses issues of measurement, skills, competencies, and results achievement needed to make teams work. We discuss team reward design and the issues surrounding the move to team pay.

Chapter 11: Rewarding Scarce Talent

Scarce talent represents a major challenge, even for the great companies. Because businesses emphasize growing by extending their core competency, the cost of attracting and retaining scarce talent is changing the playing field on which reward solutions must operate. This chapter addresses the short-term and longer-term challenges and opportunities in rewarding scarce talent and suggests some possible ways of designing rewards to be flexible and responsive enough to compete effectively. We discuss the shortage of information technology (IT) people as an example of what we may be in store for other areas of talent in the future. We propose ways to address scarce talent from a total rewards perspective and argue that as long as enterprises have an objective to grow rather than shrink, scarce talent is a continuing opportunity to change pay design and delivery. The chapter suggests ways to shape a better workforce deal for scarce talent—which can apply to all talent, for that matter.

Chapter 12: Rewarding the Salesforce

Sales compensation is an excellent opportunity to align the salesforce with everyone the company needs to design, build, deliver the product or service, and delight the customer. Few great companies have an unaligned selling capability that involves merely convincing customers to buy products and services. Although sales compensation is the subject of entire books, we believe in closely integrating the sales and marketing workforce into the company workforce. This chapter addresses the issues of sales rewards and argues for this strategy of inclusion. It discusses the changing role of the salesforce and how to construct pay to take advantage of changing designs and objectives in sales organizations. Increasingly, the selling process needs to be integrated with the overall business of the enterprise; we suggest how effective pay can support this.

Chapter 13: Rewarding Executives

One of the most controversial and attention-getting issues of total pay is how executives are paid. This chapter describes a positive role for how to pay leaders to add value to the business. Executives are important not only as champions of aligning total pay with the business process but also as role models for the pay change process. As with sales compensation, executive compensation needs to be part of the overall company's business process. This chapter suggests how to make this happen and the benefit it brings to company performance. We address some executive-compensation design issues and the importance of linking executive pay to business strategy. Stock options are a primary tool of executive rewards and have brought some criticism to the executive-pay process. We discuss options and how to better design executive rewards.

Chapter 14: Merger-and-Acquisition Rewards

In record numbers, great companies are joining forces. Merging and acquiring compete with growing your own as a way to expand profitably and increase shareholder value. Merging and acquiring enterprises have the chance to communicate new directions and opportunities in a positive, unifying fashion. This chapter suggests how your company may take advantage of this opportunity to better align rewards with business goals. Mergers and acquisitions involve combining different cultures, business processes, products, services, and ways of doing things. They involve joining companies or major organizational units within the same company, which may offer a challenge that's as important as joining corporate entities. Chapter 14 discusses the role of total pay during the turmoil of mergers and acquisitions. We suggest how an enterprise might best design rewards to encourage people to commit to making the merger or acquisition effective. The move to global mergers and acquisitions makes it important to consider both this chapter and the next (on global rewards) as partners in addressing tough pay challenges.

Chapter 15: Global Rewards

Globalization of business has created unique total reward opportunities. Although we acknowledge the importance of key global talent, we challenge current expatriate total pay practice and explore total reward alternatives that may better fit the needs of some global companies and their global talent. Global reward alignment with the business is critical. This chapter really tests the enterprise's ability and willingness to communicate consistent values and directions throughout its global workforce. We propose that a company's total reward strategy and consistent set of reward principles are important everywhere a company does business. We suggest how to implement the principles from a global perspective. During times when local taxes, local government regulation, and local pay practice strongly influence how pay is delivered, we describe how to apply the strategy and principles understandably and with local relevance. How to get the message through to people in New York and Singapore, or in Los Angeles and Mexico City, is a challenge many firms face; we suggest some possible ways to do this effectively.

Chapter 16: Making Rewards Work

It's not as important how well you do at the start of the race as it is at the end. This chapter tells you how to ensure lasting business value for a pay solution you've worked long and hard to develop. If a company is unable to communicate the logic of a pay change and educate people on what it takes to be successful to gain workforce understanding, acceptance, and commitment, the entire process is at risk. Unless a new pay solution is implemented and engages people, nobody gains from it. We emphasize workforce involvement and strong communications and education. Without them, effective change in pay is unlikely. This chapter addresses the communications, implementation, and continuous-improvement process and how best to communicate new pay solutions, implement pay change effectively, and provide lasting value from designing pay solutions through continuously keeping them reflective of what's going on in the business.

ACKNOWLEDGMENTS

Without friends and clients, consultants cannot exist. We've existed now as a business for more than 15 years, basically constituted as we started years ago. We have had a lot of fun being consultants for so long, and our sincere thanks must go to the companies that have given us a platform for our consulting and research. We learn something new from you every day. We've enjoyed partnering on projects together over the years and have considerable warm feelings for you. You're all throughout this book, some named and some not, but you are there.

Special thanks to Delene Smith, who's worked with us for many years. Her editing and assistance in getting this book to press was invaluable. Thanks also to the executives and professionals who commented on an early draft.

We enjoyed writing this book. It's a labor of love and helped us bring into focus many of the thoughts we've had for years. We dedicate this book to Squeaky Anne MacPherson, who inspired the entire work process, helped with the book as only she can, and brought major joy and entertainment into the book-writing process. We didn't use any ghostwriters, secret editors, mystery guests, or other people "hiding behind the tree" to write this book. Thus, whatever it is, it is.

Los Angeles
November 1999

PATRICIA K. ZINGHEIM
JAY R. SCHUSTER

The Authors

Patricia K. Zingheim is a partner with Schuster-Zingheim and Associates, Inc., a pay consulting firm in Los Angeles that she founded with Jay Schuster in 1985. She advises a wide range of companies on total pay and other rewards. A recognized expert on the role of pay in accelerating company growth and bottom-line performance, she is also coauthor of *The New Pay* (Jossey-Bass, 1996), which is acknowledged as a keystone work in linking pay with organizational effectiveness. She has published numerous articles and chapters for business and professional journals and magazines. She is quoted in management literature and speaks throughout the world on how companies can best align rewards with their business goals. She earned her M.A. and Ph.D. from Ohio State University and A.B. from the University of Michigan.

Jay R. Schuster is a partner with Schuster-Zingheim and Associates, Inc. He advises companies on aligning pay and rewards with business strategy. A recognized leader in the move to new pay, he has introduced many groundbreaking pay and reward innovations. His client list includes global companies that have successfully aligned rewards with their business. He is also coauthor of *The New Pay* and two other books plus articles in numerous business, professional, and academic journals and magazines. He speaks frequently at management and leadership seminars and conferences, addressing how companies, people, and rewards interact to add value to a business. He received his Ph.D. from the University of Southern California and B.B.A. and M.A. from the University of Minnesota.

PART I

Integrating Rewards

The Six Reward Principles

1. Create a positive and natural reward experience.
2. Align rewards with business goals to create a win-win partnership.
3. Extend people's line of sight.
4. Integrate rewards.
5. Reward individual ongoing value with base pay.
6. Reward results with variable pay.

The Four Components of Total Rewards

- Individual growth
- Compelling future
- Total pay
- Positive workplace

CHAPTER 1

Total Rewards and the Six Reward Principles

In *Star Wars,* the "droid" R2D2 has an electronic "key" that lets him translate codes and open locked doors with exceptional effectiveness. It makes things clear and available to the small band of space adventurers in their perilous travels through the galaxy.

Our R2D2 key is far less dramatic. It comprises six reward principles we have developed to serve as guideposts for *Pay People Right!*

We spent considerable effort choosing the words we use in *Pay People Right!* We have avoided using the words *employee* and *employer* for our protagonists in the process of changing pay. They just don't communicate the sense of positive community and shared destiny that companies and workforces need to be mutually successful. We tried to avoid repeating the words *workforce* and *company,* which are probably the best synonyms available. But in our view, these words, too, miss the boat. As a result, we have experimented throughout with labels for the players involved in making a business a success. We ask you also to think about the roles of those who work with you, in the hope that we might mutually come up with some better words that do right by everybody involved.

The principles are a bit like the satellite navigation systems on automobiles that help drivers find themselves when they come to a frustrating fork in the road. If you keep the principles in mind as you navigate through developing a total reward strategy, building a business case for changing rewards, and developing and communicating total pay to support your business, then it's likely, we believe, that you'll succeed. We propose that following even one of these principles helps; together they form a practical foundation for rewards.

REWARD PRINCIPLES

Changing how a workforce is rewarded is difficult and not for the faint of heart. Pay, which is one component of total rewards, communicates the business value of goals such as those associated with shareholder value, financial success, customers, market share, growth, product and service innovation, speed, and cost management. Although other messengers of change exist, pay is a highly consequential tool of business communications. Pay change isn't an initiative itself, but a way of putting meaning and momentum into other business initiatives. Pay is a way of gaining understanding, acceptance, and commitment of what people can do to help make a company a success. Few things get the attention of people in a company as well as pay does.

The reward principles that we've found to be useful and that make good common sense are outlined in Exhibit 1.1 as a reference.[1] Although these principles are discussed throughout the book, we want to get an early start on introducing them here.

Principle 1

Create a Positive and Natural Reward Experience

People who think can best accept what they understand. To gain workforce acceptance, support, and commitment, people need to be involved in the business and reward process. Extensive communications and education prepare the workforce for a new reward solution that supports company business goals. They help the workforce understand the business logic of the reward change, its impact on them, and the need for a balanced result to all stakeholders: the workers, the company, shareholders, and customers. Companies engage and involve people in determining how best to accomplish the goals and

Exhibit 1.1. The Six Reward Principles.

1 *Create a positive and natural reward experience.*

Leaders must take care, early on, to communicate and educate people on the reasons for changing rewards and the advantages to the workforce and company. Involve people in the change process to gain their understanding, acceptance, and commitment.

2 *Align rewards with business goals to create a win-win partnership.*

Both the company and people need to gain from the relationship. People who contribute to the organization's achieving goals share in the success. To ensure a balanced win-win partnership, the company must provide clear direction, people must continue to add value, and the company must acknowledge their value with rewards.

3 *Extend people's line of sight.*

Involve people in extending their line of sight to how they influence the results of their team, group, business unit, and company. Engage people in understanding how what they do affects the customer and how they can adapt to evolving customer needs. Ensure that everyone is a knowledgeable stakeholder in overall success.

4 *Integrate rewards.*

Use each reward tool for what it does best. Take an overall perspective of not only total pay but also total rewards when determining rewards for people. Create a customized better workforce deal from total rewards.

5 *Reward individual ongoing value with base pay.*

Use base pay to reward three dimensions of individual value: (1) the skills and competencies needed by the company and used by the individual to generate results, (2) the individual's consistent performance over time—whether individual contributions or contributions to team results, and (3) the individual's value relative to the labor market.

6 *Reward results with variable pay.*

The bottom line is that the company needs results to meet shareholder expectations and provide a compelling future. By rewarding the workforce for achieving results, variable pay (cash and equity) creates stakeholdership and a win-win relationship between people and the company so that both share in success. Variable pay is best suited to reward results because it is agile, flexible, adaptable, responsive, and able to focus on key measures of success.

objectives of rewards so that people—and the company—can be successful.

It's important that changes in rewards be made as positive and natural as possible to the workforce within the constraints of the business message to be delivered. Communicating, involving, and celebrating help the reward solution be better accepted. Focus groups or design teams are ways of involving people in the reward design process. The days of designing rewards in a black box and trying to sell them to leadership and the workforce on the back end are over. Building trust depends on making the reward change as positive as possible. This means truthful communications, worker involvement, and effective change management.[2]

Hewlett-Packard, Monsanto, GE, Microsoft, Intel, Southwest Airlines, and others have done a superior job of educating their workforces on the win-win, and of sharing success (or lack of success) with them. People understand the business and know their vital importance to the success of the enterprise. They extend themselves to make a positive business difference. Great companies are positive places to work; they've made total pay change positive and gained the loyalty and commitment of the workforce. Many others have done this successfully as well and reaped the resulting benefits. Other great businesses that emphasize positive work relations and effective communications are Coca-Cola, Gillette, Cisco Systems, Lucent Technologies, and IBM, as well as globally headquartered Sony, Royal Dutch, and Toyota.

Principle 2

Align Rewards with Business Goals to Create a Win-Win Partnership

Pay and other rewards are a powerful way to help communicate business directions and values. People become stakeholders as the company anchors rewards in the business and creates a win-win partnership. Once aligned with business goals, rewards can add value to business. This requires understanding how growth and profit benefit all stakeholders, extending people's line of sight to key company goals through education, problem solving, and real and meaningful empowerment and accountability. It means rewards emphasizing the external customer to optimize performance at the point where customers measure value. Because of the increasing need to collaborate, it also means deploying rewards to link the individual with team, group, site, business-unit, or company goals and results.

The win-win must be a balanced win in which both parties gain from the partnership. The company must believe it's getting value for the rewards provided, and people must believe that the company's expectations are reasonable for the rewards offered. The reality of the company's performance relative to competitors' performance and the labor market must also ground the win-win relationship.

Why is a positive win-win alignment with rewards and the business so critical? People often come to a firm with an expectation that the deal they make at the start is the one they'll have throughout their work career. Because this is no longer possible, businesses must do what is necessary to help people understand why rewards must change. People need to benefit from supporting this change. The better workforce deal is a win-win, and there's something for everyone in making the pay change. The old workforce deal was either paternalistic or highly adversarial. The next deal—the new deal—was one of the workforce coming more than halfway to be the company's business partner. The most recent deal, and the one we propose—the better workforce deal—succeeds if both the company and individuals get a fair shake from the business arrangement as it relates to total rewards. This better workforce deal is a cornerstone of *Pay People Right!*

Principle 3

Extend People's Line of Sight

The reason we use telescopes is to bring the distant close up for study and understanding. Company financial performance, and even external customers in some instances, may appear remote. Pay must be the telescope connecting the workforce to key measures of business success. We believe that people want to make a positive difference. They want to count and to perform effectively. They want to know what the company expects of them and how they fit into the overall plan for company success. This belief is reinforced time after time, in company after company. Asking the workforce to consider only goals that are a few feet in front of them creates a *dislodged* workforce. People are dislodged from understanding the business and the company's objectives in terms of the value they need to add to be successful and in terms of the goals that are necessary for the company to be successful.

When we talk about the concept of line of sight, we mean the business results people can influence as individuals or as members of a team. When asked what their job is, most people answer in terms of their specific duties and responsibilities. We suggest that great companies want the workforce to answer the question in terms of how what they do fits in with what the company is trying to do. This is extending the workforce line of sight to measures of business success that their performance influences. It renders company business and customer goals transparent to the workforce by making the measures closer and more real.

For example, people at Solectron (a Fortune 500 company and two-time Malcolm Baldrige National Quality Award winner) think in terms of running a business, not having a job. When a prospective customer asked an operator why she was picking up parts off the floor, she explained the six costs of scrap. This positive impression closed the deal and got Solectron a customer. Rewards help align operators with the business and enable them to see the fruit of their efforts by sharing their business's wealth.

Extending line of sight means interpreting what is needed to make the company a success in terms that can apply to the entire workforce. To communicate how people add value to financial performance, one electronics enterprise trained a multicultural workforce by means of a lemonade stand example. People learned about what makes their enterprise financially successful by first understanding the business of a lemonade stand: the implications of making a poor batch of lemonade, having a competitor open a stand across the street, and deciding whether to buy a table or lease one. Then they applied the financial principles they learned from the lemonade stand to understanding their own manufacturing facility.

In another example, an aerospace firm educated its workforce on return on net assets (RONA), a long-line-of-sight measure for variable pay, by engaging people in answering the question, "Who shot RONA?" Showing and engaging people in how their work influences measures of success such as quality, cost effectiveness, customer satisfaction, and delivery of products is the goal of lengthening the line of sight.

Extending the line of sight implies collaboration. In *High Noon,* Gary Cooper was forced to take on a band of outlaws single-handed. Though he prevailed, it would have helped to have some support from the townspeople he was protecting. Business is becoming more collaborative and interdependent. Both the broadly defined team and the individual are essential to company success, but people transferring performance emphasis from the individual to how the individual makes the team, group, business unit, and company more successful afford maximum advantage.

This is a difficult shift in the United States, where there's a strong and enduring sense of individualism and the go-it-alone approach is well established in the workplace. In the westerns, a John Wayne hero rides into town, defeats the bad guys with little help from the townspeople, and rides out in a blaze of glory, never to be seen again. But what makes a good western is not universally applicable to the workplace. It's true that the opportunity for individual recognition is critical to a feeling of well-being. However, this is often best done in a workplace where, to make the company perform well, people must become interdependent and effective performers in the context of the team, group, site, business unit, and company. This involves building a real and solid team-player mentality. Because skills and competencies often rest with individuals but no single person can handle everything required in terms of outcomes in a complex business, individuals are valued as contributors to team, business-unit, and company outcomes.

Clearly, we want to reward the exceptional individual performer effectively. However, the definition of a high-value individual is evolving in many organizations. The new breed of top-performing individuals contributes to the achievement of goals that others share and helps make colleagues more effective at the same time. If you can align the performance of every superperformer in your company with the interests of the enterprise, think how powerful this will be. If you can make excellence contagious to the rest of the workforce, think how beneficial this will be. If you can define excellent performance for the individual in terms of achieving shared goals, think of the value of a pay-for-performance solution that accomplishes this. We have a cartoon in which some large fellows are rowing on one side of a boat and some small fellows are rowing on the other. The bosses are standing in the front of the boat, not looking at the rowers, and saying, "We seem to be going around in circles." What would happen if all these performers pulled together to get the boat going straight?

Principle 4

Integrate Rewards

Total rewards offer a cornucopia when it comes to gaining alignment and commitment of the workforce to key business goals. You can take full advantage of this by using each reward tool for what it does best. It is not just a world of total pay; it's a world of total rewards. The company should consider and coordinate all forms of rewards when making a decision about compensating people relative to their overall worth to the company. This means a strong focus on the forest of total rewards rather than the individual trees, each representing one element of total pay and rewards.

As you'll see, total rewards involve many facets of worklife that are critical to building an effective enterprise. Developing and investing in people's future, offering exciting and challenging work, having excellent colleagues and leaders, and being part of the company's compelling future are all elements in total rewards. It's clear that people work for more than money. It is essential to integrate everything concerning total rewards, such that the combination (1) supports the role the company wants people to play in helping make the business a success and (2) defines how the workforce shares the results of organization success.

It's important to integrate rewards not only for the individual but also among people and worker groups. The integration occurs through business-aligned goals that ensure everyone—from the top to the bottom of the organization—is moving in the same direction. The third principle, extending line of sight, helps facilitate this integration.

Principle 5

Reward Individual Ongoing Value with Base Pay

What made Michael Jordan so valuable to the Chicago Bulls? It was his delivery of superior performance game after game, play after play. He brought individual ongoing value to the Bulls's business. He had not only "game" but also the "grit" to do it play after play. Jordan was not a flash in the pan. He was just excellent all of the time, probably even when he didn't feel like playing in a particular game.

What makes individual members of the workforce valuable? What makes people valuable over the long run—in other words, why do they have ongoing value? The same things that made Michael Jordan valuable. It's a combination of three dimensions: (1) the skills and competencies that the company needs and the individual uses to generate results, (2) the individual's consistent performance over time, whether individual contributions or contributions to team results, and (3) the individual's value relative to the labor market. All of these create an individual's ongoing value to the company, which is rewarded with base pay.

No one-size-fits-all pay solutions work. Emphasis can vary among the three base pay dimensions. Frito-Lay, Glaxo Wellcome, Aetna, BP Amoco, Champion International, and SmithKline Beecham, among others, focus on the competency dimension because competencies are the centerpiece of their human resource strategy. In our research of major information technology (IT) companies that depend for their business on the ability to attract and keep scarce-talent IT professionals, most granted base pay increases as soon as skills and competencies were acquired and applied. These IT companies couldn't wait for an annual pay review; people with scarce skills and competencies can move to other companies unless pay is kept at a competitive level for the value received.

The second dimension, consistent performance over time, differs from performance during only one performance period that the annual base pay adjustment typically rewards. Current and one-year performance and results are better addressed through variable pay because awards can be meaningful in size, rather than becoming an annuity for one year's performance. Ongoing value takes into account people's sustained performance trend relative to their current base pay level to determine if they produce more value than their current base pay warrants. Emphasizing this component strongly focuses on outcomes and results; goals cascade from the business strategy and operating plan to strengthen the connection between company success and an individual's ongoing value.

All companies consider the third dimension, value relative to the external market, but the emphasis varies. It may play a contributing role, or it may be the primary determiner—for example, when jobs or roles are clearly and similarly defined across the labor market and where variable pay is the predominant pay element. What's important in rewarding individual ongoing value is a change in logic from "I am my job, and my job is me" to "my value to the company counts and is defined by a combination of how I acquire and apply the needed skills and competencies and the contributions I make that help my company be a success."

Principle 6

Reward Results with Variable Pay

When all is said and done, companies need results to meet shareholder expectations and provide a compelling future. Because people make results happen, companies should reward them for achieving those results. Variable pay is flexible, agile, adaptable, responsive, and capable of rewarding a combination of individual and collaborative results as well as focusing on a host of measures and goals, from financial to strategic. Because people need to re-earn variable pay every performance period, it can provide a meaningful award for results achieved.

Variable pay is the paramount pay communications tool for linking the workforce to customer goals, extending workforce line of sight to what the company needs and values, and sharing in the success of the enterprise. Variable pay involves both cash and equity (such as stock and stock options). It not only functions as the primary reward element for executives, managers, and salespeople but must also serve as the key tool for the entire workforce. GE, Monsanto, IBM, General Mills, Herman Miller, and other market leaders have migrated to a reward strategy that invests in people's skills and competencies and then rewards the workforce with variable pay for achieving results. We view variable pay as a premier opportunity to focus on the results a company needs, when designed, implemented, and communicated in a fashion that considers the other reward principles.

Practical Business Sense

The foundation of these reward principles is sound business judgment, experience in many organizations, and research about what makes total rewards work. The objective of the principles is to help make people the "secret sauce" of company performance. It's important to determine how to get more value from the reward process. It's critical to continue to do this and remain flexible and adaptable. The reward tools may change, but the principles remain constant.

FOUR COMPONENTS OF TOTAL REWARDS

We view total rewards in any company as having four interlocked and directly related components; they are outlined in Exhibit 1.2. Two of them, total pay and a positive workplace, are at the foundation because how people are paid and how they view the work environment are essential to attracting and keeping individuals. However, these two components are not enough during times of stiff global competition and an imperative to grow profitably, and when companies must understand the value the workforce brings to the table of company success. Businesses must also consider providing the individual-growth component to make people increasingly valuable, and the component of a compelling future such that people have opportunities to continue adding value to the company.

Exhibit 1.2. Total Reward Components: The Better Workforce Deal.

Individual Growth	Compelling Future
• Investment in people • Development and training • Performance management • Career enhancement	• Vision and values • Company growth and success • Company image and reputation • Stakeholdership • Win-win over time
Total Pay	**Positive Workplace**
• Base pay • Variable pay, including stock • Benefits or indirect pay • Recognition and celebration	• People focus • Leadership • Colleagues • Work itself • Involvement • Trust and commitment • Open communications

Individual Growth

The first component of total rewards is individual growth. The people great companies require want to grow, learn, and become increasingly valuable. This creates the need for

- Believing that investing in people gives the company lasting advantage
- Making development and training active and continuing
- Measuring and managing performance effectively
- Providing challenging career opportunities

Compelling Future

The people whom great companies need also want a vision of the future of which they are an essential element. Xerox, for example, does this by communicating that the workforce is inventing the future of knowledge work. This component involves developing ways to make people stakeholders so they want the company to prosper, creating a work environment that provides a win-win opportunity over a sustained time period, and building a company that people can be proud of both internally and in public. This means an enterprise that is growing profitably as well as one that actively invests in people. In addition, company values are ones that people can appreciate and want to live by.

Total Pay

The total pay solution—base pay, short-term variable pay, cash and equity long-term variable pay, recognition, and benefits—must be attractive, be positive, and distinguish the company. The reward principles we introduced earlier in this chapter serve as the basis for total pay.

Positive Workplace

The people in great companies are positive and motivated to add value because the company believes they are important. This requires having an effective leadership team that sets the right examples, working with exciting and positive associates, and sharing accountability for delivering meaningful results by doing challenging and interesting work. It means creating an atmosphere of trust and commitment (based on effective communications and involvement) that keeps people in the loop.

Again, as with the case of the reward principles, we based the four components of total rewards on common sense, our research and consulting experience, and a business view of what makes a firm attractive.

TOTAL REWARD STRATEGY

A company's total reward strategy or philosophy describes the fundamental principles and parameters for designing rewards throughout the organization. Company leaders should consider the six reward principles as they develop the total reward strategy. Many factors affect the strategy. First, the business strategy clarifies the concept of the business and how this creates a compelling future. It specifies what business the company is really in (for example, a photocopying firm is really in the document management business). It also takes into account how the company addresses the business environment and competitive situation it faces. This business strategy drives the human resource strategy and organization design, which in turn drive the total reward strategy. The workforce influences the total reward strategy since the company must be sensitive to its needs to create a win-win situation.

In turn, the total reward strategy, along with the specific business conditions of the company or one of its organizational units, helps define the business case for changing rewards, which we describe in Chapter 2. This business case drives development of total pay and other rewards. This relationship is shown in Figure 1.1. Company business strategies differ, and so should the corresponding organization design and human resource strategy. Thus, the total reward strategy and the business case for changing rewards should be unique to an organization's specific situation.

Impact of Business Strategy on Total Reward Strategy

A company's business strategy offers clues to features of a total reward strategy, such as the core competencies of the company and how

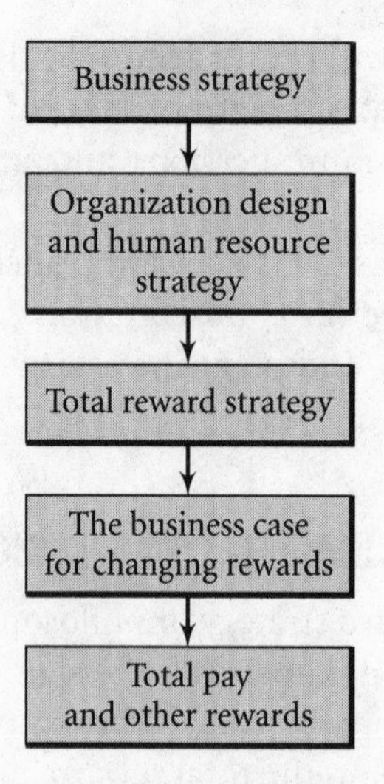

Figure 1.1. Alignment of Rewards with Business Strategy.

they're defined and evolving, the relative emphasis of reward elements, pay competitiveness, measures for rewarding performance, and the level of performance required. Organizations with differing approaches to the market have dissimilar total reward strategies. For example, low-cost producers may use lower base pay to keep fixed costs low, variable pay measures to optimize cost and quality, and ample recognition to celebrate successes.

A company that focuses on value-added may have a core competency of innovation or customer focus, which allows charging a premium price because of the value extended to customers. The same company may provide competitive base pay for the ongoing value of the individual in terms of contributions to the company and individual development that enhances value of the products or services. This value-added enterprise may also use variable pay to reward sustained value improvement—whether this is measured at the customer-team, business-unit, or company level.

Another familiar example is the Silicon Valley start-up before its IPO (initial public offering), where speed in bringing a unique product or service to market is critical. Here, total cash (base pay and cash variable pay) and benefits are less competitive and stock options are widespread because the company needs to invest its cash in product development, not pay.

Impact of Organization Design on Total Reward Strategy

Organization design also affects the total reward strategy. A highly centralized company may have similar reward solutions across business units as well as variable pay that delivers a strong message about overall company performance, more so than a decentralized company would. If a firm has organized around high-performance teams for a specific business reason, then it must create a meaningful award opportunity for team performance to reinforce the team structure and focus people on the needed team results. Perhaps a company has become a boundaryless or virtual organization. In that case, boundaries between the company, supplier, and customer are permeable and the interfaces change. Also, organizational units constantly reform according to business need, and roles constantly change with shifting responsibilities and lines of authority. In such companies, performance measurement and management and pay design are more flexible and based on the outcomes of a particular assignment.

Impact of Human Resource Strategy on Total Reward Strategy

The human resource strategy integrates rewards with other aspects of human resources. If the company believes that its differential advantage comes from people staying on the leading edge of technology, then it wants to hire, train, develop, and reward people who grow so they continue to add value to the company. Many human resource strategies now include contract workers, or an "outsourced workforce," working on a contingency basis. At Solectron and many other Fortune 500 companies, contract workers make up a large segment of the people counted on for their performance. The challenge is to have the entire workforce, including contract workers, on the same page addressing how pay can focus on building collaboration around shared goals.

Impact of Workforce on Total Reward Strategy

Developing a total reward strategy also involves consideration of the workforce. In the first half of the 1990s, more people were looking for work than there were jobs. Now supply and demand have switched, and in many areas more jobs exist than there are people looking for work. This is the case not only for knowledge workers but also for entry-level unskilled workers. What constitutes scarce talent at one time can change rapidly, even within a given company. Thus, agility is critical, and a reward solution that fits a specific company at one time may not during another as circumstances change.

To acknowledge a scarce-talent market as well as the increasing complexity of many people's lives, the total reward strategy is taking workforce needs and preferences into account more than before. The workplace has changed to allow flex time, job sharing, and telecommuting, with the twofold condition first that the company be able to accomplish its business and second that individual performance be at least satisfactory. Companies are directing more and more creative thought to how to attract and retain necessary talent. For example, a telephone customer service unit in the brokerage industry, faced with a tight labor market, actively expanded its search to include college-educated women who wanted to stay home with young children and who would work a certain number of hours by telecommuting from home.

Benefits to work/life balance such as wellness programs, sick child care, backup child care, and elder care are a win-win because the company keeps the individual at work and the individual addresses a personal concern. Convenience benefits such as casual dress, personal use of a company PC, and onsite concierge services also enhance the workplace.

Of the elements in total pay, recognition and benefits most address individual need and preference. Sound recognition that acknowledges outstanding contributions to the business customizes the award based on individual preference—for example, a sporting event for someone who likes sports, or choice in selecting merchandise or trips. Flexible benefits, PTO (paid time off), and 401(k) investments offer individual choice. Such benefits help with the flexibility needed by a diverse, multicultural workforce made up of generation Xers, baby boomers, and gray eagles. However, in a total reward strategy, the company must bridge differences to encourage forming a cohesive workforce that shares goals to accomplish results.

Impact of Company Culture on Total Reward Strategy

The company's culture plays a role in the total reward strategy as well. However, the intent is frequently not to try to reinforce the existing culture but rather to change it. Many enterprises want to move to a stronger performance-oriented culture with more information sharing and workforce involvement and accountability. IBM is an example where rewards reinforce the change to a high-performance culture involving winning, execution (speed and decisiveness), and teaming. Rewards at IBM changed to an emphasis on variable pay, less reliance on benefits, fewer job titles, market-driven pay, simplified job valuing with fewer bands (see discussion of bands in Chapter 6), selective use of stock options, and greater manager accountability and flexibility in managing pay.[3]

Stronger Link Between Pay and Performance

Most total reward strategies have a strong alignment of pay with performance as one of their key tenets. How this is accomplished varies by company, depending on the business strategy and all of the factors described above. It is this customization along with the company's ability to implement the total reward strategy that determines if reward programs are successful. Program success means that rewards facilitate the company's success in increasing shareholder value and whatever else is important to the company, as well as create a win-win for the company and its people. The reward principles help facilitate and magnify success because they cut across the differences in customized reward strategies.

CONCLUSIONS

The reward principles and the four components of total rewards are critical to effectively aligning rewards with the company's direction and values and are the foundation for each suggestion and alternative we present. As you work through the book, keep these concepts in mind:

The Reward Principles

1. Create a positive and natural reward experience.
2. Align rewards with business goals to create a win-win partnership.
3. Extend people's line of sight.
4. Integrate rewards.

5. Reward individual ongoing value with base pay.
6. Reward results with variable pay.

The Four Components of Total Rewards

1. Individual growth
2. Compelling future
3. Total pay
4. Positive workplace

It's been our experience that asking yourself *Does what I'm doing reflect these principles?* increases the likelihood that the approaches you select prove advantageous. The more the emphasis is on total rewards and the four total reward components, the more likely that design is effective. Although there is no one way to operationalize these principles or total reward components, they give you a framework to evaluate how your company's reward programs and reward change processes are likely to work.

Total rewards are important, whether a company is addressing issues of M&A rewards or global rewards, competing for scarce talent, or developing a base pay or variable pay plan. The reward principles and four total reward components make up a usable foundation for going forward. It just makes good business sense to do a bit of focused strategic thinking at the start of any undertaking as important as aligning rewards with business goals.

CHAPTER 2

The Business Case for Changing Rewards

Change vehicles have dramatically different "temperatures" depending on how intensely and quickly they get the attention of the workforce. The "hot" ones get everybody's attention quickly and strongly communicate new directions, priorities, and goals. "Cold" change tools may have an impact on people who are not now members of the workforce, or it may be that the influence of these tools is so slow-acting that the impact is gentle. Reward elements such as training and competency-based recruitment are cold communicators of change. Pay, on the other hand, is a hot change tool.[1] Pay change is not only hot but also "noisy." The workforce seldom comes to leadership and says, "Please change our pay to make it better aligned with company business goals." Instead, powerful, clear, and understandable business logic is necessary to gain the acceptance and commitment of the workforce.

Why should a company change how it rewards people? With everything else changing rapidly and continuously, why not leave pay alone and move on to something less controversial and potentially less threatening to the workforce-leadership relationship? These are questions of strategic importance. Many organizations approach the issue of changing pay and subsequently back off. Not because it isn't the right thing to do, because it often is. Rather, they back off because it's hard to do—it gets so much attention.

VALUE OF THE BUSINESS CASE

Because pay change is so attention-getting, any dramatic change must be strongly justified. The business case for changing rewards describes the current situation that necessitates change in how the company is to reward people. It also defines what the company wishes to accomplish in terms of new messages to the workforce. Without a clear and understandable business case, the chances of success in making pay effective are weakened. In this chapter, we focus primarily on the business case as it applies to changing pay, rather than to changing total rewards, because pay is often the most difficult component to change.

A business case is critical for a number of reasons.

Pay is a powerful communicator of values and directions. Pay should communicate and align with the most important messages the enterprise needs to deliver. If it doesn't effectively communicate the company's business concept, key business goals, and performance initiatives in understandable and actionable terms, the company ends up directing more energy toward overpowering unaligned pay just to get the message through to the workforce.[2]

Companies must make profit and increase shareholder value. Businesses are economic entities that want to deal successfully with other quality companies and excellent customers. Rewards should communicate fairly and honestly the company's expectations concerning people. The basis of the better workforce deal is a win-win relationship. Total pay is one way to share success with the workforce as well as communicate what's needed to adjust to a posture that adds value to the business. Even not-for-profit organizations need income to sustain their vitality; as the Roman Catholic sister who is chief executive of a prominent medical center said, "No margin, no mission." To afford a winning pay solution for everyone, the company must be financially successful.

Executives need justification to make change. Businesspeople need business reasons to change. This is especially true when they anticipate workforce noise as a result of the proposed change. The executive team must be convinced that a pay change is worthwhile to the business. The best way to demonstrate added value is to justify pay change in terms of a solid business case. Even though the existing pay approach may fail to add value to the business, new pay solutions must be built on a foundation that's explainable in business terms.

The business case justifies change to the workforce. Changing pay is very difficult; an enterprise is unlikely to be able to change pay without the workforce understanding and committing to the reasons for change. A business case creates a sense of urgency and commitment on the part of executives, other leaders, and the workforce that changing pay is necessary. Stakeholders must accept the fact that everyone is better off if pay helps to improve alignment of the workforce and the company with business goals and customers.

Changing pay (beyond just paying people more) is an attention-getter of the first order. However, pay can easily give negative messages that are hard to overpower through other forms of communication. It's just not possible to argue for pay and other reward change based only on human resource issues of fairness, competitiveness, and justice. These issues may be important, but pay and other rewards are business tools and need a business case for change.

THE BETTER WORKFORCE DEAL

Stephen R. Covey talks about a "win-win or no deal" arrangement.[3] This concept is important to the better workforce deal. It suggests that if the individual and the company cannot both win from the employment relationship, they should not make an employment deal. This prevents deals where one party is a winner and another a loser. Does the relationship suggest that shortage is what is to be shared, or is it abundance? The better workforce deal is a win-win, or else it's not a deal. It focuses on figuring out how the company and workforce can combine to share the abundance of success. It also implies that when the company isn't successful, stakeholders too should share in this reality. This is a major change for companies and their workforce.

The better workforce deal we advocate is at least the third in a series of "deals." Change may bring us back to one of the original deals, or it may create one beyond the better workforce deal. Exhibit 2.1 shows how the old deal, the new workforce deal, and the better workforce deal compare.

Exhibit 2.1. The Evolving Workforce Deal.

Factor	Old Workforce Deal	New Workforce Deal	Better Workforce Deal
Time	Through 1980s	1990s	2000 and beyond
Business environment	Number of jobs and people fairly well balanced	Reengineering, restructuring, more people than jobs	Invest in people, fewer people than jobs
Company plan	Business as usual; focus on quality	Layoffs, cost reduction	Profitable growth, speed
Culture	Paternalism, loyalty valued, people taken care of or treated like chattel	"Tough love," people accept accountability	Company and workforce partnership, more celebration and fun
People's trust	Satisfactory	Low	Rebuilding
Information sharing	Little information, top-down communications	Information about what people must do, some two-way communications	More open communications; extensive, ongoing information on company results and what people need to do to grow and add value
Base pay	Major emphasis, focus on internal equity, entitlement, steady increases	Base pay principally market focused, some skill and competency pay	Integration of market, skills and competencies, and consistent performance over time
Variable pay (cash and equity)	Small or not offered, not strongly performance-based	More, reward performance, cash variable pay often funded from potential pay at risk or base pay reductions, some use of stock options below management	Even more, reward performance, cash variable pay typically funded as add-on with achievable goals, deep and extensive use of stock options
Benefits	Liberal	Flexible benefits, offering choice with cost containment or reduction, 401(k) retirement plans	Stock purchase plans, work/life balance benefits
Employment	Job security, one employer for career	Insecurity, contingent employment, multiple employers, periods of unemployment	Choice by both parties
Development	Little	Individual responsibility to grow and learn, need to invest in self	Ongoing coaching and developmental feedback, more training and nurturing
Responsibility for career	Company cares for people, no individual responsibility for growth	Individual comes most of the way	Company and individual come halfway

The old workforce deal was one of pay entitlement; pay, other rewards, and continued employment based on tenure; and a view of the workforce focused on paternalism rather than value to the company. People "owned" the job they held—it was their "property." This all changed as a result of global competition and dramatic technological change.

These changes led to a new workforce deal. People had to adjust their expectations and meet the company's requirements in acquiring new skills and competencies and applying them to new definitions of performance. It was mostly a one-sided affair that only worked when more people than jobs existed and when businesses were more interested in cutting costs than growing profitably. No sooner did they realize that a strategy of growth, merger and acquisition, and globalization was the way to prosper than the talent shortage hit, and the deal was no longer one-sided. Companies couldn't go back to the old deal and couldn't stay with the new deal.

The better workforce deal is a healthy balance to build on. People add value, and companies make it attractive for them to remain, grow, and share in the success. The better workforce deal balances even better the equation between the company and the workforce.[4]

The better workforce deal addresses the ebb and flow of talent availability. More jobs are now chasing fewer people (although this most certainly will vary over time). Great companies view people as a source of strategic advantage. Knowledge workers have an increasing role and importance in business. All these things mean that this deal is change for the better. People aren't interested in sharing only in shortage and changing expectations for the worse. Talented individuals will not take on all the sacrifices involved in making the company a success unless the firm is willing to share in the future. Thus, the better workforce deal is necessary whenever the company needs to invest in the people required for success. This is a super deal for everyone.

BUSINESS REASONS FOR CHANGING REWARDS

Given our belief in a better workforce deal, what's the business case for changing rewards to help make this deal a reality? The business case includes defining the reasons for needed pay changes. It outlines the reasons the status quo is no longer acceptable and why change is important to the business and the workforce. No one business case fits all situations. The business case comes from what's going on in your company or business unit that makes it necessary for people either to do more of what they're already doing or to make changes in how they work and perform. It gives specificity to the total reward strategy by making the reasons for change meaningful to the workforce and including detail about operationalizing the strategy through specific pay approaches. It takes the total reward strategy from an altitude of 20,000 feet down to 10,000 feet; the actual design of the total pay solution then brings pay down to sea level.

Your Company and Its Business Case

To develop a business case for your enterprise, think about what's going on in your company. What is it about the business that is changing or will change? What will stay the same? How fast or dramatic must change be? What changes have occurred in the last few years? How has the workforce reacted to these changes? Is the way in which issues are addressed workable in the future?

Whether your company has been stricken heavily by adversity or remains on track with a viable business strategy, you'll find that things continue to change. Some possible business changes are that:

- The business climate requires a new view of customers.
- Business goals are changing, and adaptability is critical.
- Opportunities require formation of new business units or teams.
- Competition creates the need to refresh or change culture.
- Communications must be strengthened and consistent.
- Multiple complex goals require the workforce to collaborate.
- Flexibility and agility are essential.
- Performance and competencies must be refreshed.
- The speed of the business must increase to take advantage of opportunities.
- Cost management and effectiveness must improve for the business to remain competitive.

The Workforce and the Business Case

Look at how your company's workforce is doing relative to the changes that have occurred, are occurring, or will occur in your business. What are its strengths? What are the opportunities for improvement? How effectively are people dealing with changes in customer expectations, products, and services? Are any changes needed here? Now think about the messages your present total pay approach delivers in terms of the business challenges you have identified. Do any of these sound familiar?

- The workforce is the only customer for total pay.
- Internal equity is the primary focus.
- Central control is the approach to pay management.
- Conforming to culture, as is, is the test that total pay must pass.
- Paternalism is strong and lasting.
- The individual is the only focus of total pay management.
- Entitlement is entrenched.

The issue of making the business case for change is alignment of total pay with the business. If total pay already matches your business situation, you may not need to change. If it doesn't, then change may be in order.

Rick Seaman of Strategy Implementation tells a story we like. When he speaks, he asks his audience why at certain times of the year wildebeests migrate from one part of the Serengeti to another without concern for the extreme difficulty of the journey. After a short pause, Rick says, "They migrate because if they stay where they are they will die." He says that strong instincts drive the herd to accept the adversity of the trip in order not to starve or die of thirst. He continues, "This is why companies and their people must change and adapt as well."[5] Change is an issue of surviving and thriving; pay is a critical vehicle for suggesting why the enterprise should change, what makes it successful, and how to get it and the workforce to where they must be to be mutually successful.

The company needs to permit and help the workforce understand the business and how important it is to their future. The business case is the educational program for everyone and a key way for leaders to communicate with people. It can enlist help, feedback, growth, development, and performance. Understanding the business case is important to both people and wildebeests!

TOTAL PAY DIAGNOSTIC

It's now time to put your enterprise in context and decide what course of action is appropriate, based on your company's business situation, business strategy, and total reward strategy. Before articulating a business case for change, you need to be clear about your company's business and total pay situations. Exhibits 2.2[6] and 2.3 are diagnostic tools that present a spectrum of scenarios describing a company's business situation and total pay approach. You can use these tools to determine your business situation, both in the present and where it is going in the future, and the appropriateness of total pay to support it. As a result of evaluating where your company and total pay solution are now and where they should be, your company can decide what, if anything, it needs to do to align pay with its goals and directions.

Evaluating the Business Situation

Take a look at Exhibit 2.2, the business situation diagnostic, which shows some alternatives that may describe your company from a business perspective. Review this diagnostic to identify your present business situation—where your company is now.

The diagnostic raises some questions:

- Is your business stable and predictable, or constantly changing and thus requiring creativity and business acumen?
- Do you control your customers, or do they control you?
- How important is your workforce to company success?

Think about the workforce's role relative to your business situation:

- What must people do to add ongoing value?
- Should they do what they have always done?
- What messages do you need to communicate to the workforce?

A	B	C	D	E
• Competitive position is secure. • Many barriers to entry exist, preventing competitors from participation. • Industry is slow to change or is regulated. • Few quality competitors exist. • Few innovation opportunities are apparent. • Leadership style is historically successful and remains so. • Customers are secured, with few alternatives. • Change is scary rather than an opportunity.	• Competitive situation is becoming more changeable. • Dominance of past or closing in on competitor lead is less possible. • A number of direct business competitors are becoming more flexible, prospective about their challenges, and responsive to changing situations. • Market position is becoming insecure, and some customer loss is evident. • Existing products and services sometimes fail to provide their historical advantage, and new product or service entries struggle. • Change is apt to surprise company and lack of responsiveness is increasingly becoming a problem. • Leadership is struggling with making historical approaches work consistently.	• Position relative to competition for customers changes and varies in stability across product and service lines. • Competitors are improving steadily. • Market share is not consistently intact or assured. Products, services, and processes are in a state of change, and possibly revolution. • Change is persistent and dramatic—company may not always lead the change process, although it may try. • Leadership is performance-focused, emphasizes change, and is changing to match stretch-goal business strategy. • Time from concept to reality is accelerating—speed counts. Few customers are locked in.	• Market is changing, and share is hard to determine or predict. • Company needs process improvements consistently to stay in the race. • Customary and new competitors are becoming high-performance in attitude and results—business realities continually test paradigms. • Time from drawing board to execution is fast and accelerating. • Company depends on key capabilities and competencies to enter new markets and predict customer situation in future. • Company realizes it will live in future—and is getting there fast. • Leaders are changing processes and solutions. • People are becoming increasingly involved. • Customers have many quality options, and ultimatums about services are common. • Customers expect positive surprises and exceeded expectations.	• Market position is highly volatile and insecure, so dominance is short-term at best. • Many traditional and nontraditional competitors enter and leave the market. Some very good ones stay. Most are excellent. • Industry changes quickly and dramatically. • Processes, products, and services rapidly become obsolete; often leaders replace own leading products and services to retain position. • Innovation and breakthroughs are essential and a core competency. • Leadership style is active and responsive and moves strategy to tactics rapidly. • Value of collaboration is evident and expanding—involvement is important and adding value. • Customers are fickle as well as focused on quality, cost, and service and extremely hard to please, with ever-increasing expectations. • Customers drive the entire business.

Exhibit 2.3. Total Pay Diagnostic: Where Is Your Company's Pay Solution Now, and How Does This Match Your Company's Needs?

A	B	C	D	E
• Pay is centrally managed to ensure uniformity. • Job evaluation emphasizes internal equity. • Base pay increases may have transitioned from time-based increases to "merit" pay increases. • Pay communicates "fairness," competitiveness, and reflects historical practice.	• Pay is decentralized to business unit to recognize situational differences. • Job value is based more on external market than internal equity. • Some variable pay for nonmanagement and nonselling people diminishes traditional role of merit pay. • Benefits are cost-contained.	• Pay solution recognizes importance of communicating business-aligned goals and performance initiatives. • Managers have increasing accountability for pay. • Team, business-unit, and/or company performance measures introduced. • Variable pay is applied more widely. • Competitive total cash practice is prime consideration. • Pay experiments begin to reward individual ongoing value. • Banding may be used. • Benefit choice making is introduced. • Some workforce involvement in pay design. • Company is moving toward total pay integration.	• Pay solution communicates win-win business-aligned goals. • Company recognizes people as win-win partners. • Managers have considerable pay management flexibility. • Variable pay is becoming primary performance reward at all levels. • The external market is total pay foundation. • Individual ongoing value partners with job- or person-based pay. • Company may use banding, uses team pay where appropriate, and extends benefit choice making. • Total pay is business element in globalization, mergers and acquisitions, and other business opportunities. • Considerable workforce involvement in pay design process. • Company has integrated total pay and is moving toward integrating total rewards.	• Pay is business-focused and win-win and demonstrates business effectiveness. • Managers are immersed in applying total pay to their business needs. • Variable pay is primary performance reward for all or most of workforce. • Market realities as well as value added to the business determine total pay opportunities. • Individual ongoing value dominates individual pay process. • Team or group and individual share importance in pay process. • Benefit choice making is rule. • Total pay is key business element in globalization, mergers and acquisitions, and other business opportunities. • Pay design and day-to-day operation deeply involve people. • Total rewards are integrated.

Source: adapted from Zingheim, P. K., and Schuster, J. R. "Moving One Notch North: Executing the Transition to New Pay." *Compensation & Benefits Review,*

- Is their performance acceptable, or do you need something they are not giving now?
- Are new skills and competencies needed for them to add value and share in your success?

Now look at where your company will be in the next few years:

- What does the future of your business hold?
- Will current business solutions fit your vision of the impending future?
- What do you want your workforce to understand about the wildebeest migration?

This process should define not only where your company is now but also where it will be in the future. Because the business climate in general is changing, chances are that your business situation is changing as well. Review Exhibit 2.2 to evaluate where you think your company is going. In many instances, the business situation is migrating to the right, from the A side of the spectrum to somewhere at or beyond C. This evaluation of change and the amount of change are key to building a viable business case for changing total pay.

Determining Total Pay Alignment

Once you have determined where your company is and where it will likely be in the future, next you need to assess the appropriateness of your total pay solution. Look at Exhibit 2.3, the total pay diagnostic, to see what messages people are getting from your pay approaches:

- Does your pay solution communicate a sense of the realities of your business?
- If the business requires new skills and competencies, are they the foundation of your pay solution?
- What performance messages does total pay give?
- Do people need to work alone, or must they collaborate to achieve results?
- Is pay based on competitive practice sufficiently to match a market where one or more needed types of talent are scarce?

- Does total pay serve the business effectively in both good times and bad?
- Does it communicate with the workforce about what you want people to do more often and what they should stop doing?
- Where is your pay solution now, and does it fit with your just-completed analysis of where the business is now and where it is going in the future?
- Does this imply change, or more of the same?
- Do you think your current total pay approach adequately supports your company now?
- More important, will it be sufficient in the future scenario you have identified? If not, where does it need to be to do so?

Although each exhibit shows a continuum, we're not suggesting a direct correspondence between these two diagnostics such that if your company is at point C on the business situation diagnostic it should be at C on the total pay diagnostic. It's not like a thermometer, which tests your state of health and, if 98.6 degrees isn't the result, decrees that a repair job on your health is in order. If your company is now on the right side of the business situation diagnostic, or is moving there, then it may need to be more on the right side of the total pay diagnostic. However, this doesn't imply that all companies to the right of C in terms of the business situation need a corresponding total pay approach in the immediate future. But it does suggest that total pay at A or B will not for long support a business situation that shows an urgent or potentially urgent need for change. This analysis also suggests that the migration to more aligned total pay should begin now, since change doesn't happen overnight, and that the workforce should understand the extent of change.

What Should Your Company Do?

If your company remains in control of its business and customers, and if this situation is predicted to remain stable for some time, then staying put relative to total pay may be fine. The question then becomes, Should you initiate pay change to place yourself in a leadership position for future industry change? If your company and competitors are already in a volatile business environment, it may make sense to modify the roles for people and total pay in the future.

If your company has a number of people-based initiatives under way, and if the costs associated with pay must provide business value-added, then a new total pay design may be indicated. If there's a disparity with the present business situation, and especially with the future situation, then change is probably in order.

Most organizations find themselves transitioning from total pay in the A or B range to one from C through E in Exhibit 2.3 in order to align total pay with business and human resource strategies that affect how people act and perform. The diagnostics offer a chance to discuss the company's opportunities for pay design, given its business situation. This process is important in determining what the business case for changing rewards should be and how to communicate it effectively. The diagnostic is not only important from the strategic perspective; it's critical from the standpoint of communicating the business case.

ARTICULATING THE BUSINESS CASE FOR CHANGE

The business case for changing rewards takes the organization's business strategy and makes the total reward strategy more specific to the organization's current situation. The business case for changing rewards should be transparent and understandable. It doesn't make any sense to keep the business case a secret and expect the workforce to understand why pay must change. What can people do to create advantage? How can they influence company performance over the next few years? If a number of alternatives are available, which is most pressing? How simply can the message be stated so it communicates what must be said and is clearly understood?

The next step is evaluating the feasibility of accomplishing these objectives and determining what it will take in terms of organization design, capital deployment, and people. Are these objectives reasonable, or a bridge too far in terms of making sense to the people deployed in gaining the advantage?

Straightforward Message

When it comes to the business case for changing rewards, we often liken the need for understandability to an "elevator speech," a test of clarity and brevity. If you get on an elevator in a twenty-story building with workers who have no knowledge of the new total pay solution, can you communicate its key concepts to them by the time the elevator gets to the top floor? If not, there may be "too many notes," as the emperor admonished Mozart in the movie *Amadeus.* It's always more difficult to tell a story in a few pages than in many. During pay change, the workforce is impatient and wants to understand. The need for clarity suggests taking a major step away from deploying bureaucratic and overly complicated pay approaches, toward pay solutions that are direct and understandable.

Once the company has identified a strong business case and direction, it's essential to gain the agreement of the workforce that this objective is reasonable and attainable. This requires educating and reeducating people on the business case for changing rewards, why they must be involved, the role of pay in the process, and what's in it for them if they execute the change. The win-win for the company and the workforce is determined and communicated.

The next and most difficult step is involving the workforce in actually making it happen. People universally are more willing to accept something they have helped develop. It's a case of ownership, stakeholdership, and making the solution "theirs." Involvement is the key to real change, and total pay is a major communications element in this change process.

Critical Stories to Tell

The American Indian storyteller gains understanding by repeating the story again and again whenever the opportunity arises. The answer to "Why change pay?" requires the company to build and communicate a powerful and honest case for change. Here's how to start an effective change process.

1. *The why of it.* Tell the workforce why total pay must change. Provide real examples people can relate to. Communicating what makes pay an important element in the change process is essential.
2. *The present state.* What's the present business situation? What's the critical business challenge or opportunity, and where is the workforce in this process? What's the trade-off for executing the total pay change in terms of what people get if they support change and help make it happen? What's the win-win in the reward formula?
3. *The impetus for change.* What's the business reason for change? Does a "burning platform" exist in the company that makes changing

pay an urgent priority? Is the business case built on an opportunity for the company and workforce to have a mutually better future? Is it a course correction now so that major change isn't necessary in the future, similar to a spaceship making an immediate course correction that saves immense distance later? Or is it some combination of the company in distress and new directions? What's in it for the workforce to help? What are the risks and opportunities of changing as compared to business as usual?

Even though the form, substance, and urgency of business cases for changing rewards may differ, they cover the core elements we've outlined here. We've seen a host of business cases for changing rewards and have participated in developing quite a number of them. The business case for Ford differs from K-Mart's. Each starts from its own position in terms of the workforce and business, and it would be a miracle if the two were the same.

TWO EXAMPLES OF THE BUSINESS CASE FOR CHANGE

What constitutes a viable business case for changing rewards is clearly unique to a specific company, but they all start with a statement of the business situation, a corresponding human resource strategy, and finally a total reward strategy. Two examples help put what can be done in the context of your company.

Owens Corning

Owens Corning is a Fortune 500 company and a world leader in building materials and glass fiber composite systems. The company manufactures fiberglass and foam insulation, roofing and asphalt, vinyl siding, and fiberglass reinforcements at more than 100 plants in the United States and throughout the world. It's a 60-year-old company in highly competitive businesses where cost, quality, and service are vital to success.

BACKGROUND. Owens Corning wanted to enlist its workforce in improving performance. In large part, the workforce has been in place for a number of years. In the production areas, some plants are unionized and some are not. To help achieve the company's business plan of sales growth, profit growth, and global penetration, the company charged human resources with driving cultural change and implementing reward solutions to achieve the desired outcomes. The human resource strategy included using pay to speed implementation of the business strategy. This is the accelerator-pedal role for pay that we discussed earlier. It meant the leadership team and workforce working together. It meant changing union relationships and the union negotiation process to ensure that all parties can win. It meant significantly linking rewards and performance and evolving to roles that are more flexible than narrowly defined jobs.

The reward strategy for the primary manufacturing workforce included pricing skills reasonably in the external market and paying for skills used, not just acquired. The variable pay strategy rewarded performance at the plant level to support shared goals and a high-performance organization.

The primary workforce needed to change, and the change was to be made with dignity and without large-scale and indiscriminate reductions. This required a major communications-and-education process, first to get the message across so people could better understand the business and second to make it possible to acquire the capabilities and produce the outcomes needed to be successful. The overriding message was that the company wanted to share ownership, rewards, and risks.

Because the business situation varied among Owens Corning plants, they customized the consistent companywide reward strategy according to their specific business case for change in order to implement locally. Typically, either a course-correction or a burning-platform situation applied at the plant level, suggesting that plants must be viable now and in the long run.

ONE PLANT'S BUSINESS CASE FOR CHANGING REWARDS. One Owens Corning plant typifies the localized nature of the change. The plant's business case for change involved gross margin targets, labor cost reduction through productivity improvements, waste reduction, meeting customer delivery expectations, being accident-free, union-management cooperation, and becoming a high-performance organization. The plant leadership team and corporate human resources developed a business case that compared gross margin under the new approach with gross margin with no change or with some improved productivity. They related this to targets that must be sustained to make the plant worthy of continued investment from the company. They showed how eight global competitors of this plant compared in terms of total labor cost and total manufacturing cost. This plant was the second lowest on total manufacturing cost per kilo and the highest in labor cost.

The message to the Owens Corning plant was that as global competitors become more efficient in production, the challenge to be cost competitive increases. The objective was not to reduce people's pay but to make production improvements such that the plant would remain viable. The business case didn't stop with just presenting the situation; it presented a plan about how to get the plant to where it needed to be. For example, it included training to move the plant toward being a high-performance organization and backed this up by establishing a training relief pool that would give people the opportunity to develop. Over a five-year period, as people were trained and productivity improved, the training relief pool could decrease and the number of plant workers would be reduced. Plant reductions would respect people's dignity and occur through normal terminations and early-out packages.

The objective of the business case was to present the business situation to the workforce, show plans to make success real for the plant, and engage the workforce in making the plant successful.

Monsanto

Monsanto is a Fortune 500, globally integrated life sciences company comprising a variety of businesses. Each business is responsible for the financial, strategic, and tactical outcomes that add value to the strategic corporate business plan.

BACKGROUND. A companywide pay philosophy has evolved over several years to an emphasis on competitive base pay, deep deployment of annual variable pay, and competencies used for individual development plans. Monsanto values gaining differential advantage through people. Performance and individual development count, and pay is focused on the key measures of success required at both the company and the business levels as well. The company has effectively used reward designs at the level of the businesses to help develop an integrated performance-and-rewards solution.

ONE BUSINESS'S BUSINESS CASE FOR CHANGING REWARDS. This is an example of a business case that supports a better future. The Monsanto business in question marked an important milestone in developing an effective business case for total rewards throughout Monsanto. A few years ago, this business had successfully received approval from the Food and Drug Administration to commercialize a major new product that was unique in the industry and represented a significant change in how customers ran their businesses. The business had to move from being a research-based organization strongly focused on product development to a commercial organization responsible for introduction, sale, and delivery of a new commercial product. The business needed to change its culture and focus on acquiring and applying a new family of competencies. The leadership team of the business strategized that it was essential to base the win-win on a combination of business results and acquiring and applying the competencies that are required of a commercial business. A diagonal-slice design team developed a competency model that reflected the new business case for change and human resource strategy and served as the foundation for selection, training and development, performance management, succession planning, and pay. The goal was to focus the workforce on the new business initiative through a combination of pay design, competency selection and communication, and performance management.

The competency model developed by the business focused on delivering to market faster, better, smarter, and more efficiently. For example, one of the ten competencies, team orientation, communicates the importance of transitioning to an organization where research and development, marketing, sales, customer service, logistics, production, finance, and human resources must work with one another in multifunctional teams to solve problems and take advantage of opportunities. Customer focus emphasizes that people must be able to work with the customers to ensure their needs are met and to be able to improve the product from the customers' viewpoint. Functional proficiency is important to keep the business at the leading edge of technology. These competencies mean that research personnel can no longer function alone in an ivory tower; rather, they have to interface with customers and multifunctional teams to make improvements and address customer needs. The competencies also reflect the change from narrowly defined jobs to broadly defined roles, to encourage people to do what it takes to make the business successful.

The competency model came from the business strategy, so it helped communicate the business case for change. The design team developed the elevator speech, which communicates a continuous process involving business challenges and opportunities that must be solved (by the people who are the business's differential advantage). To address these issues, people must develop and then apply competencies to generate business results. Business results in turn create new business opportunities, thus completing the cycle. Rewards—both base pay and variable pay—reinforced the successful cycle.

This competency model, plus those in other businesses, evolved into a competency model throughout Monsanto that integrates all businesses with a shared focus on competencies and a commitment to development. The competency context is used as a unifying element. Success in aligning rewards with key business objectives in this business (as well as others within Monsanto) was a catalyst for continuing to fine-tune the overall corporate rewards strategy. This business's effort was important because it showed effective use of pay as a vehicle to communicate the need for the workforce to adapt, change, and move in a direction needed by the organization to be successful. This philosophy of an integrated development, performance management, and rewards program evolved throughout Monsanto.

WHERE THE REWARD PRINCIPLES APPLY

The reward principles introduced and defined in Chapter 1 apply consistently to all the topics we address in this book. At this point, we have our first chance to apply them; here, we direct them to the business case. In subsequent chapters, we relate the principles to the topic at hand, since they provide a unifying theme.

The Reward Principles and the Business Case

The reward principles apply strongly in the business case for change. For example, Principle 1 (create a positive, natural reward experience) is important because it's not possible to make people comfortable with change unless they see the value in it and understand the reasons behind it. The business case gives the information needed to make this a reality. It also articulates the business goals and outlines the win-win partnership (Principle 2) so people can see why total pay must change and what's in it for them. In effect, this principle *is* the business case for change because pay must recognize the realities of why the enterprise exists, while engaging and involving people in the business.

The business case extends people's line of sight (Principle 3) by showing them how they link to the measures, skills, competencies, and outcomes needed by the business to make both parties successful. It considers and integrates reward elements (Principle 4) so that rewards send people a clear message. Finally, the business case for changing rewards may include Principle 5 (rewarding individual ongoing value with base pay) and Principle 6 (rewarding results with variable pay) to accelerate a successful win-win partnership.

Critiquing Your Reward Message

Every reward principle is critical in the business case for change because the principles cause those who are building the business case to ask crucial questions:

- Does what you are doing create a positive, natural reward experience? Are people involved in creating a new culture that's attractive and characteristic of an excellent place to work?
- Are you creating a balanced win-win between the company and the workforce? Does the company get fair value for the rewards it offers? Do people share in the success of the company and receive rewards commensurate with their value? Is it a win-win all the way around, including other stakeholders such as customers and shareholders?
- Are you effectively extending people's line of sight so they understand the business goals of the company? Are you identifying the individual with team, group, business-unit, and company success? Are you adopting value-added customer goals?
- Are you integrating total rewards consistent with the business strategy, organization design, and human resource strategy? Do total rewards form a complete picture of what messages the company wants to reinforce?
- Have you built the logic for rewarding an individual's ongoing value with base pay? Is it associated with the individual's ability and willingness to perform, with their performance trend over time, and with their value in the labor market?
- Are results being rewarded with variable pay to facilitate making achievement of business goals a reality? Is variable pay the pri-

mary reward for achieving results for much of the workforce? Are the variable pay measures and goals important to company success, and do they reflect changing business needs?

Ask yourself these questions as they relate to your company's pay solution. How many of these questions can be answered positively ("Yes, we did that" or "Yes, we are doing that")? In most instances, best practice begins with positive answers to these questions.

CONCLUSIONS

An old song went, "The hipbone's connected to the thigh bone." The business case for changing rewards is about connectedness. It translates the business, human resource, and total reward strategies into total pay and total rewards, and the better workforce deal.

We are in at least the third generation of deals between companies and people. The first assumed that people would work for one organization for a full career and that the enterprise would take care of them. Then a new deal developed when businesses were flattening, delayering, rightsizing, and doing things that disenfranchised many of the world's best workforces. Major talent shortages and the need for businesses to grow ended this deal. People became more important to the enterprise, ushering in the demise of paternalistic "love" (the old deal) and "tough love" (the new deal) and starting a win-win relationship for both companies and workforces. This better workforce deal where everyone can be a winner represents change and needs explanation.

The business case provides the logic for the better workforce deal —why it's needed and what's the deal in terms of individual growth, compelling future, positive workplace, and total pay. It makes the total reward strategy clear and answers the questions, "Why are we doing this?" and "What's in it for us?" It's not a one-size-fits-all solution. Grounding the total reward strategy in a solid business case facilitates total pay and total reward change and explains it so people understand and buy in—and so it becomes part of the enterprise's fabric.

CHAPTER 3

Integrating Total Pay

A hammer doesn't do what a screwdriver does, nor would you use a screwdriver in the same way as a pair of pliers. This is how total pay works. Organizations choose where to invest time, money, and effort to get the most bang for the buck, and this applies to pay as well. Great companies increasingly get more from total pay dollars than others do. Selecting total pay tools judiciously, for what each does best, is important. This chapter emphasizes Principle 4 (integrate rewards), and in particular the total pay tools.

ABOUT TOTAL PAY

Pay People Right! is primarily about the total pay component of total rewards, but it is about total rewards too. Total pay helps an enterprise to strategize concerning how best to communicate the appropriate business messages. Sometimes total pay leads needed organizational change. Sometimes it supports additional elements that communicate required change. Both roles are potentially effective, but most companies that view rewards as a tool of effective communications are now using total pay to lead change. As the former chairman of Chrysler, Lee Iacocca, once said, "To succeed in business you need to lead, follow, or get out of the way." In our context, getting out of the way isn't an alternative for total pay. Unless total pay is in support of key company directions, it's unlikely to play a positive role.

BEST BUSINESS USE OF TOTAL PAY ELEMENTS

Each element of total pay does some things better than others do. Figure 1.1 in Chapter 1 shows the strategic relationship between total rewards and total pay; the figure summarizes our view of how best to align effective total pay. Taking a total reward view and improving on all four of the total reward components described in Exhibit 1.2 doesn't mean relying only on total pay to do the heavy lifting required to align total rewards with business goals. However, total pay can contribute mightily to effective communications.

Exhibit 3.1 outlines the best use for each total pay element. Again, the *total reward* picture counts, not just total pay. Alongside the cartoon in our office that we mentioned earlier is another showing a large fellow with a whip standing over a group of oarsmen sitting in a large wooden boat. He's saying, "I will be your incentive program for this venture. . . ." Not much chance that pay of any kind can overpower a "total reward" workplace like that!

Elements of Total Pay

The emphasis in *Pay People Right!* is on base pay, variable pay, and recognition and celebration. We addressed benefits in our previous book, *The New Pay.* Our views on base pay, variable pay, and recognition and celebration continue to evolve, but our views on benefits have not changed dramatically. To us, benefits just aren't an accelerator pedal to improve the chances of your company meeting its business goals or communicating effectively about the win-win that's required for the better workforce deal.

We don't want to shortchange benefits, because they are essential to effective total rewards. Refreshing and improving benefits design is part of the better workforce deal. For example, benefits dedicated to accommodating the virtual worker, 401(k) plans that provide a company match based on company financial performance, profit-sharing retirement plans that vary funding according to financial

Exhibit 3.1. Best Use for Total Pay Elements.

Element	Role in Paying People Right
Base pay (supported by lump-sum payments)	Primary reward for individual's ongoing value • Pay for skills and competencies used to generate results • Pay for consistent performance over time • Pay for value relative to labor market Increased importance to pay people right
Variable pay (cash and equity)	Primary reward for results • Team, group, business unit, company, or individual results • Quantitative or qualitative measures and goals • Flexible and adaptable • Win-win partnership • Short-term and long-term Increased importance to pay people right
Recognition and celebration	Primary celebration and fun reward • Celebrate and recognize individual, team, group, or business-unit achievements • Create atmosphere of acknowledgment and attention • Make outstanding contributions a winning occasion • Make enjoyment and positive rewards OK Increased importance to pay people right
Benefits or indirect pay	Supportive role in better workforce deal • Basic health and security foundation • Some talent retention value • Help make workplace positive Diminished role in paying people right

performance, and employee stock purchase plans that enable people to purchase stock, often at a discount, are among the key benefits. The last three are important because they create stakeholdership and ownership in the company—the win-win of Principle 2, particularly when assets in 401(k) and profit-sharing plans include company stock. Retaining a talented workforce requires reasonable benefits. However, once a workforce is in place, base pay and variable pay can fulfill the business communications role effectively.

Reward Principles as the Foundation for Total Pay

The reward principles are the foundation for integrating the elements of total pay. Combining the elements of total pay, emphasizing some total pay tools over others, and designing some in specific ways are all part of the total pay customization process. How the total pay formula is assembled is critical. Total pay design should communicate the importance of enterprise growth and financial success. We believe it's a good thing that the reengineering fad has died.[1] This chainsaw approach to improving company results did not help form effective company-workforce alliances. Furthermore, few if any businesses were able to "shrink to greatness." Instead, they engineered major staff reductions while robbing the workforce of hope and dignity. Effective total pay and total rewards, as parts of the better workforce deal, are positive ways to communicate the importance of profitable growth. They keep the workforce involved and share the success of the company with those who make it a reality.

CHOOSING THE RIGHT ACCELERATOR PEDAL

Experience and research suggest that using the total pay tools for what they do best applies to all areas, including team pay, global pay, scarce-talent pay, M&A pay, executive compensation, and sales compensation. We address these in upcoming chapters. For now, here are the primary total pay tools.

Base Pay (and Lump-Sum Payments)

Base pay does a good job of rewarding an individual's ongoing value to the company. As we detail in Principle 5 in Chapter 1, there are three essential dimensions to rewarding individual ongoing value: (1) pay for the skills and competencies that the company needs and the individual uses to generate results; (2) pay for the individual's consistent performance over time, whether individual contributions or contributions to team results; and (3) pay for the individual's value relative to the labor market. We believe that base pay and lump-sum payments best accomplish these.

Effective base pay requires that the individual continue to perform and generate results. Although lump-sum payments typically acknowledge short-term performance, base pay must increase only as the person continues to sustain individual performance. This means acquiring skills and competencies the company needs to be successful and applying them to perform the role or job. Additionally, the individuals must sustain performance to ensure generation of results.

We believe most people want to add value throughout their entire career and to continue to meet goals and produce outcomes. Paying for needed and used skills and competencies and the value of the individual's results over time suits base pay well.

Variable Pay—Cash and Equity

Principle 6 indicates that variable pay does the best job of paying for results. It's clearly the way to get a critical-change message through to the workforce meaningfully. Variable pay is a proven ally in making businesses successful and is responsive to necessary changes in direction. It communicates a range of measures and goals required to make the company a success and to reward the workforce accordingly.

Variable pay is the multipurpose reward for helping to generate needed business outcomes. It effectively addresses results at the individual, team, group, site, business-unit, or company level, and it can deal with both short-term and long-term results. Variable pay has proven effective for the entire workforce, top to bottom. The best variable pay solutions emphasize a few key measures, goals, and results. It can help extend the line of sight for the workforce and show how people's specific roles affect measures of company growth, profitability, and sustained success.

Recognition and Celebration

Recognition complements and magnifies the effectiveness of all other elements of total pay. It makes the better workforce deal a *big* deal. It gives a front-row seat to acknowledging that people are the primary source of competitive advantage. Recognition and celebration interject fun and deserved glory into the total pay and total reward solution.

Recognition involves more than cups, T-shirts, and wall plaques; it involves verbal and written recognition as well as cash. It calls attention to people making a positive difference and celebrates adding significant value to the business. Recognition and celebration are part of the solution to bringing excitement and attention to a company intent on becoming a great place to work.

Recognition and celebration aren't new, but they're playing an increasingly critical role in total pay and the better workforce deal. They partner with base pay and variable pay to communicate the message that a workforce aligned with the business is one that shares business success. Whether a company's climate is conservative or boisterous, recognition and celebration help the total pay accelerator pedal pump more gas.

Benefits or Indirect Pay

Benefits support the better workforce deal by laying a positive foundation of protection in the health and security issues that are of concern to any workforce. They're also of some value in retaining talent. But benefits simply aren't the accelerator pedal of total pay.

Benefits do provide the platform from which base pay, variable pay, and recognition and celebration can create the win-win. No one wants workers who have taken a job just because of liberal and extensive benefits. No company wants people who hide from business challenge so as not to lose benefits that are unmatchable by another firm. Organizations want a workforce that accepts the better workforce deal and total rewards. Waiting for retirement or wanting more vacation aren't characteristics of effective workforces that can stand the test of hard business times. It's the win-win that is important.

Summing Up Best Use

Total pay is like a mosaic that goes together in more than one way. Go back to Figure 1.1. The business strategy is the picture the company wants to compose, so the result can be significantly different in every case. Enterprises need to know what their picture must look like, and then they can put the pieces together. Organization design, human resource strategy, and the business case for changing rewards determine how the company assembles the mosaic. Total rewards and total pay are the pieces. The challenge is putting it all together; *Pay People Right!* is the guide to do it.

COMPETITIVE TOTAL REWARDS

Competitiveness doesn't mean just offering competitive total pay, but rather a company's definition of competitive total rewards and subsequently competitive total pay. It's impossible to conduct an exact survey of total rewards, or even total pay. Surveys of total cash (base pay plus cash variable pay) are also difficult to get for the general workforce. (Yet another of our cartoons shows a bridge that doesn't meet in the middle, and cars are falling into the river. The caption reads, "What the George Washington Bridge would look like if the engineering data were as accurate as salary survey data.") The fact that determining competitiveness is more art than science means the company must consider how it values each of the four total reward components in Exhibit 1.2, and address total pay as part of the formula. This implies subjective, but creative, business judgment.

Not How Much, But How

Being the top payer may not be the strategic answer. The chief executive of a once-famous merchant bank used to say his pay philosophy was "If you pay peanuts, you get monkeys." He believed a company needed to be the very highest payer of talent and defined his total pay strategy accordingly. He asked people to deliver significant results to keep their high pay up. As a result, they were among the highest paid in the financial industry. Unfortunately, the strategy caused them to take imprudent business risks to maximize profitability from loans. This practice brought the institution close to bankruptcy and forced its purchase by another major bank. The chief executive and all the highly paid members of the leadership team received attractive golden parachutes, but many other people were let go with no protection.

Those who take a total reward perspective assess competitiveness in terms of total rewards first and then each element of total rewards. This is an opportunity to develop the reward mosaic that matches the business strategy, total reward strategy, and business case for changing rewards. The idea is to consider everything the company offers in terms of total rewards. Consider how competitive and positive the total reward picture is and what the company is like to work for.

Questions for Your Company

The more positive answers you have for the following questions on each component of total rewards, the more competitive your company's advantage in recruiting and retaining talent:

- *Individual growth.* Does the company invest in people and provide a certain number of hours of business-relevant training per year for individuals? Do people receive feedback and coaching to enhance their performance? Do they understand how they fit in the organization and what work and growth opportunities are available to them in the future?

- *Compelling future.* Does the company have a vision and values that are meaningful and attractive to people? Has leadership articulated an exciting and achievable future that involves growth and plans for success? Does the company have a good image and reputation? Is it economically viable in the long run? Does the company offer a win-win and create stakeholdership?
- *Positive workplace.* Is the climate positive and supportive of the business and people? Does leadership lead? Are colleagues supportive, and do they help each other be successful? Is the work meaningful and challenging to people? Are people involved in making a positive difference? Is there trust and commitment on both sides? Are communications clear and two-way?
- *Total pay.* How competitive and positive is the sum of base pay, variable pay, benefits, and recognition? What about total cash? Are variable pay awards likely? How agile is base pay in keeping up with the dynamics of a changing market for skill and competency?

Balancing Total Rewards

Organizations with a positive workplace, exciting growth opportunities, and the promise of a strong future can consider these components in determining the competitiveness of total rewards. If the company is weak in one component, it needs to beef up another. Most of us can probably think of a company that has a negative workplace and that compensates by paying more competitively in the total pay component. Strength in more than one component results in fewer recruitment-and-retention issues.

What Great Companies Do

If you benchmark prevalent practice or look at a list of the best places to work,[2] you can see that many employers of choice[3] define themselves in terms of all four total reward components. However, the formula for success varies widely. Those emphasizing the individual growth component may not be as strong in portraying a compelling future. Others emphasizing a positive workplace may not be equally solid in the total pay component. No single solution fits all, but all of these companies have addressed the puzzle of total rewards and found the solutions that fit them. Because companies customize solutions to their situation, they work. What Kodak does may not work for Microsoft, and what Amazon.com does may not work for Saturn. Yet it all works because they use judgment effectively.

Total Pay Competitiveness

Once you determine an overall picture of total rewards in your company, total pay warrants attention—the total picture, not just individual elements. If base pay is strongly competitive or higher, a company may offer less competitive variable pay opportunity and benefits. A company with significant upside variable pay potential and a good probability of significant awards may be less competitive in base pay and benefits. The emphasis in total pay shapes the type of workforce the company attracts. A firm with a strong retirement plan keeps longer-tenured people. Strong base pay and exciting recognition retain people paid close to the minimum wage who are sensitive to small changes in base rate. Strong cash and stock option variable pay and good recognition with moderately competitive base pay and benefits attract people who accept risk and challenge and believe they can make a performance difference.

Great companies are in business to grow, profit, and increase shareholder value. They can't be highly competitive in all elements of total pay unless this practice provides business advantage compared to talent and business competitors. This means financial performance outstrips that of others by more than the level or amount of above-competitive pay. In large part, people focus principally on the competitiveness of base pay, or take-home pay, and managers responsible for managing pay also highlight what people are paid in terms of base pay. This presents an education challenge: making the workforce aware that there are other elements to total pay. In the final analysis, what makes a total reward strategy fit the company is much more than just how competitive base pay is.

Sometimes firms and people don't know what they have in terms of total pay. An oil services firm implemented long-term cash variable pay for a large segment of the workforce. The solution provided attractive payout opportunities at the end of sequential three-year performance periods. (We describe this approach in Chapter 8, on long-term variable pay.) After implementing the solution for two years, the human resource executive undertook a study of competitive pay because the workforce expressed feelings of gross underpayment. With the long-term projected payouts, total pay opportunity was much more competitive than at business competitors. The problem here wasn't base pay competitiveness; it was failing to look at the overall picture of competitiveness of all total pay elements. The company was not getting bang for its buck because people were unaware of the competitiveness of their pay. The solution involved communicating the competitiveness of total pay, including the value of long-term variable pay, to the workforce. Once the company did this, understanding improved dramatically.

Total Pay as an Investment

Few businesses opt for attractive total rewards with little hope of some kind of return. This means a company should choose the business message it wants to deliver as the starting point of pay design. Consider our emphasis on the business case for changing rewards and on the reward principles to align rewards with business. No one solution fits every situation. Thus, even though you may find benchmarking the practice of others interesting, the results probably don't exactly fit your company. For example, in scarce-talent markets you might emphasize competitive base pay and lump-sum payments to reward acquiring and applying key skill and competency to get desired results. If you're interested in pursuing a strong focus on achieving key business results, you may emphasize a combination of short-term and long-term variable pay to achieve those results. You may want to include the total workforce in some such combination of competitive and strategic total rewards, or you may wish to be more selective and spend where you believe you'll get the most value because you can't afford it companywide.

Justifying Rewards with Results

Consider the relationship between results and rewards in determining competitive total cash—for instance:

- Paying median total cash for median performance results or meeting goals

- Paying 75th percentile total cash for 75th percentile performance results or measurably exceeding goals
- Paying 90th percentile total cash for outstanding performance results
- Paying below-average total cash for below-average performance results

It's common practice, for determining the competitiveness of sales and executive compensation, to start with total cash competitiveness, determine the appropriate mix of base pay and target variable pay opportunity, and then determine competitive base pay. This approach is starting to take hold for professional or knowledge workers in industries where variable pay participation and opportunity are meaningful. As more and more companies use both short-term and long-term variable pay, they should start with total cash and move backward to define a role for base pay and variable pay. This means judgment calls because many conventional surveys don't measure the competitiveness of total pay or total cash below the level of managers or executives.

Strategic Total Pay

Sometimes people, skills, competencies, and roles are worth more to a company than competitive practice indicates. Some roles are so important to the success of the business that those who occupy them should be paid more or given the chance to earn more than others, compared to their respective competitive labor market. We call this paying strategically. People applying skills close to the core competencies of the business may be paid more competitively. An enterprise with leading-edge products and a core competency of innovation may pay key product developers at a higher competitive position relative to the labor market, or it may extend additional short-term or long-term variable pay opportunity. A study we conducted of corporate roles suggested that some firms paid strategically for certain roles (most commonly technology and strategic planning) that resulted in larger variable pay opportunity compared to others at the same organizational level.

Strategic valuing means emphasizing certain workforce areas or roles over others. During one time period, engineering and scientific roles and skills may be eligible for larger variable pay opportunity; at another time, other roles and skills such as IT may be worth more than what the market dictates. In the coming decade, strategy has to drive total pay practice.

CHANGING TOTAL CASH MIX TO MORE VARIABLE PAY

Sales professionals and executives have a history of being paid with variable pay. Pay of some sales professionals is 100 percent commission. Executives and senior managers often have a considerable portion of their total pay depend on such plans as stock options and long-term and short-term cash variable pay (which we address in Chapter 13, on executive compensation). What has changed significantly in pay over the last 10 years is the increased incidence of variable pay (cash and stock options) for the general workforce.

Reasons for Variable Pay

The move to variable pay for the general workforce comes for any of several reasons:

- *To communicate.* The company must get the attention of the workforce. Some critical measures, goals, priorities, skills, and competencies are essential to business success, and the workforce needs to become aligned with them.
- *To accelerate culture change.* The company wants to focus the workforce on a culture change or a performance initiative that requires people to be accountable for performance outcomes.
- *To share success.* The company wants to emphasize rewarding results and to share business success with those who helped create it.
- *To vary pay costs depending on ability to pay.* The company wants pay costs to be more closely associated with performance results and the company's ability to pay. As we indicate in Chapter 1, it doesn't want to provide fixed pay for one year's performance but instead wants people to work in each performance period to meet goals and earn rewards.
- *To acknowledge people's role in creating success.* Perhaps the company involves people in the business, shares information, and empowers them to make performance improvements. People

make performance improvements—and then they legitimately ask, "What's in it for me?" Variable pay responds to their question of why they aren't sharing in the success they help create.

Variable pay isn't meant to be a cost-savings tool; rather, it moves fixed cost to variable expense and aligns pay cost with the organization's success and ability to pay. More is spent, typically, but the performance results support the expenditure. In fact, the hope is to spend even more variable pay dollars, provided goals align with the operating plan, because it means the business is successful.

In *Pay People Right!* we specifically focus on the total workforce: professional, administrative, nonexempt salaried, and hourly people as well as executives and managers. Changing the total cash mix to more variable pay means a major change for people who are accustomed to pay solutions made up of only base pay and in which base pay adjustments have been regular and weakly communicated as dependent on differences in performance. If the business is to enlist the entire workforce, some portion of everyone's total pay must depend on business results. It's critical to get people's "skin in the game." When the company is more successful, total pay is more positively affected than when the company doesn't do as well.

We Are Stakeholders

All of us have more at stake than our pay if our company isn't a success. In fact, we may have our careers at stake if the company doesn't thrive and we don't invest in our own skill, competency, and performance improvement. Some pay solutions mask the realities of what is at stake. It benefits no one to make total pay look as if the workforce is not a stakeholder in the success of the organization.

The great pay lie of the last decade was that many companies encouraged people to emphasize only the performance of the duties and responsibilities that were close-line-of-sight and easiest to relate to. The workforce was told not to worry about company, business-unit, or other organizational performance—"that's management's responsibility." However, when company performance foundered, many people who stuck to their knitting lost their jobs, even after getting a so-called merit pay increase that communicated to the individual that all was well with them and the company. We believe that people should have more on the radar screen than just their own performance and should work toward making the organization a success, because doing so means they'll also be successful.

Is All Variable Pay At-Risk Pay?

Some say that any variable pay is pay at risk. We don't agree. Add-on variable pay permits earning more money with variable pay than without it, so variable pay affords only upside opportunity, not downside risk, from what the individual was earning before. Pay is really at risk only if people might make less in total cash if they're not successful in doing whatever the company has asked them to do as stakeholders in the future.

Two forms of at-risk pay are *base pay at risk,* in which a base pay reduction helps fund variable pay opportunity, and *potential pay at risk,* in which some or all of the budgeted increase in base pay that people have come to expect converts into variable pay opportunity. Another form of at-risk pay is when the company positions base pay below the competitive labor market and variable pay gives the chance to earn at least a competitive base pay level; in this case, the comparison group for at-risk pay is the external labor market. Considering all variable pay as at-risk pay reinforces an entitlement view of variable pay.

Not all organizations can merely add more pay cost on top of current pay levels without some sort of win-win that encourages stakeholdership. The move to at-risk pay occurred when inflation was low and the workforce was reeling from numerous reengineering, restructuring, downsizing, and rightsizing initiatives that threatened work security. The new workforce deal was a message of sharing shortage. During positive business times and in scarce-talent markets, at-risk pay needs to offer attractive upside opportunities in exchange for risk sharing. People become increasingly hesitant to accept at-risk pay unless they also understand what's in it for them. Workforces do not accept at-risk pay if they don't understand why they are being asked to change. The more likely it is that people have a chance to win in exchange for participating, the better the likelihood of acceptance and support.

Union workforces are typically more receptive to variable pay based on objective group measures than to merit increases based on subjective evaluation of performance. Competitive business pressures such as global competition and the desire to preserve union jobs increase members' acceptance of the move to variable pay. Add-on variable pay may be used in exchange for changes in work rules. Variable pay may involve potential pay at risk if business results need to improve to remain competitive.

Size of Variable Pay Opportunity

How much variable pay does it take to *start* to get people's attention? This question is asked a lot; for managers and sales professionals, the answer we hear most often is about 10 percent of base pay. However, variable pay averages around 8 percent of base pay for exempt workers and 5 percent for nonexempt workers across companies that offer variable pay.[4] These variable pay levels have been increasing and will probably continue to increase in the future as more companies emphasize variable pay in the mix of total pay.

Basically, to have support, variable pay should represent a balanced win-win in terms of what the company gets in exchange for what the individual gets. If not, one side or the other senses the imbalance. A company that doesn't think it's getting a good deal from pay in terms of business results tends to change it as soon as practical. People who don't see the exchange as reasonable tend to be less enthused about the opportunity.

Other factors also influence the size of variable pay opportunity:

- *Results achieved.* The value of the business results achieved provides funding. The better the results, the larger the award opportunity. The more that variable pay measures correlate with bottom-line financial measures, the larger the variable pay opportunity because the funding is available to pay for the awards.
- *Reasonableness of goals and line of sight.* The likelihood of the award actually being realized depends on how achievable and reasonable the goals are. In our experience, the more achievable the performance or the acquisition and growth of skill or competency, the more moderate the award size may be. The more stretch in the goal, the larger the variable pay. The more the goal is based on historical standards when business improvement is required to maintain competitiveness, the smaller the variable pay. The longer the line of sight of the goals, the larger the opportunity must be. The lottery offers huge prospects of award, but the line of sight is long and the probability of receiving the award is remote at best.

• *Change in total pay mix.* Variable pay opportunity is larger if some of it is built on base pay at risk or potential pay at risk, than if it's an add-on, since people have taken a stakeholder position.

• *Competitiveness of total pay and the total reward package.* The more competitive the rest of the total pay and total reward package, the less variable pay opportunity is needed (other things being equal).

Add-On Variable Pay

Add-on variable pay offers additional pay, usually in the form of a variable pay award or lump-sum payment, in exchange for some definition of performance or in recognition of acquiring and applying skill and competency. People make what they made before add-on variable pay was implemented, whether or not they meet or surpass the conditions that determine add-on pay awards. The majority of variable pay solutions involve add-on pay. The deal is that the company offers people the chance to get something more for accomplishing something more. The design issue for add-on variable pay is to develop a results-reward relationship that justifies the awards paid out while extending a large enough award opportunity to be meaningful to people.

Potential Pay at Risk

Potential pay at risk involves exchanging part or all of anticipated future base pay increases for one or more years for the chance to receive variable pay based on achieving goals or acquiring and applying needed skill and competency. Here are examples of the type of organization that might adopt this approach:

- Those in a low-margin industry where labor costs are a large percentage of total expense
- Those with some financial concerns
- Those wanting people to take a stakeholder position for the upside opportunity
- Those with high base pay relative to the labor market
- Those where just add-on variable pay awards wouldn't be of meaningful size because variable pay funding comes from performance results or improvements

EXAMPLE OF PART OF INCREASE BUDGET HELPING FUND VARIABLE PAY. Some companies take anywhere from 0.5 to 2 percent of the budget for base pay increases to fund variable pay. Blue Cross and Blue Shield of Arizona changed the mix of total cash for its general workforce over a couple of years by limiting the base pay increase budget and adding variable compensation opportunity. The variable compensation opportunity grew from 6 percent to 8 percent to 10 percent of base pay over a period of three years as the budget for base pay increases was limited. The goals of the solution focus on measures of customer excellence—something people can relate to and appreciate—and progress is posted on bulletin boards to track performance easily.

EXAMPLE OF FREEZING BASE PAY. Some enterprises may need to freeze base pay for a period of time. Valley Presbyterian Hospital is a prominent large hospital that faced the very reduced financial margins of California health care organizations caused by the strong influence of managed care. It wanted to change the culture to a customer and quality focus with people involved in making a difference in performance. The organization could no longer afford to continue its highly competitive base pay position in the labor market and needed to freeze base pay for a few years to move to a competitive base pay level. The pay strategy included sharing success with people through variable pay. A diagonal-slice pay design team (including the committed CEO and COO) developed and communicated the new pay solution, which involved variable pay, PTO, and no base pay increases.

The design team continues to deal with such issues as internal equity as new hires come on board, and other matters not directly connected with pay. In this example, extensive and continuing communications about the business and pay, celebration of success, the dedication of the design team, and top management champions made it work. All of these conditions are probably necessary to make the change work in a situation where pay is frozen for more than one year. Anything less probably won't work.

EXAMPLE OF LUMP-SUM PAYMENTS FROM BASE PAY INCREASE BUDGET. Other companies take some of the budget for base pay increases and use it for lump-sum payments for individual performance rather than for a separate group variable pay plan. OOCL (USA), an integrated ocean and inland transportation firm, faced low margins in a very competitive global environment. It had fewer dollars to spend on pay increases yet wanted to reward performance more strongly than in previous years. One year earlier, it had implemented a new performance management program that emphasized the feedback process and a combination of demonstrated competencies and individual goals linked to team or department and organizational goals.

OOCL (USA) led off the communications by reiterating that base pay adjustments are one component of a total pay package that includes competitive benefits and an annual bonus. They allocated the reduced base pay budget between a larger portion for base pay increases and lump-sum payments and a smaller portion for its all-star awards. The lump-sum payments under the base pay adjustment portion of the budget reward people whose base pay is above the labor market relative to their value.

All-star awards, reserved for top individual performers, constitute a meaningful variable pay award such that OOCL (USA) pays more for outstanding performance than it had in the past but in a way that doesn't become an annuity. The annual bonus, which line-of-business performance funds, is distributed with a stronger variation in award size depending on individual performance. This total cash approach enables OOCL (USA) to get the biggest performance bang for its buck. It also helps the company retain the stronger performers —the ones it most needs to operate successfully.

Base Pay at Risk

Base pay at risk means a base pay reduction and variable pay opportunity that allow people to earn back the reduction at a minimum as a result of surpassing one or more performance or capability hurdles. This typically happens in two situations. The first is when a company has severe financial problems. In this case, everyone's base pay feels the impact; acceptance increases if executives reduce their base pay by a larger percentage than that of other people. Variable pay should have high upside opportunity when the company is successful.

The second situation occurs when a company increasingly emphasizes variable pay in the total cash mix. The enterprise typically observes a specified transition period to ease the impact. In the redesign of sales compensation, for instance, to change the total cash mix to a smaller portion of base pay and a larger portion of variable pay, the sales professional may receive a guarantee for a period of time, or the old and new approaches may be run in parallel, with the individual receiving whichever is the larger of the two earnings levels.

An example of a combination of financial issues and increasing the variable pay emphasis in the total cash mix is a large medical group that needed to reduce the average total cash paid to physicians to reflect the reduced reimbursement levels of the managed care environment. Its objective was also to determine total cash strongly on the basis of performance and vary pay significantly according to difference in performance. Implementation of the new approach involved a three-year transition, with the first two years having a maximum percentage for total cash reduction and the third year having total cash fall to the level that reflected the physician's performance.

Less-Than-Competitive Base Pay

The less-than-competitive base pay approach involves positioning base pay at a moderately competitive or less-than-competitive level to manage fixed pay costs; in exchange, the win-win includes an upside opportunity to make a more-than-competitive level of total cash. A business may move to this approach once people see the payoff from a track record of variable pay. Also, greenfield operations may open under a different set of management principles, including workforce involvement, moderately competitive base pay, and larger variable pay opportunity.

Readiness Assessment for At-Risk Pay

A number of issues combine to determine how people receive and accept an at-risk pay solution:

- *Confidence and trust.* Trust and a history of leadership follow-through on promises to the workforce further acceptance. If pay at risk is one of a series of messages delivered honestly and credibly, the chances of this one working are good. If a workforce doesn't trust leadership, we believe the prospects for pay at risk are slim unless some remedial and effective trust building occurs. Communication about the business condition and the business case for changing rewards is a necessity.
- *Likelihood of win-win.* Variable pay should have a reasonable likelihood of paying off. The more reasonable and achievable the ob-

jectives, the more likely that communicating pay at risk can be successful. Remember, "Show me the money!" is important to building belief that the pay approach being adopted can really work.

• *Definition of risk as future potential.* Whether risk focuses on current base pay or future base pay increases is important to acceptance. Prior gains are tough to take away. Our experience with future-focused opportunities is remarkably better than when people have to give up what they have. This is true even when the workforce realizes that, historically, serious mistakes have been made in their favor.

• *Readiness factors that apply to any type of pay change.* Such factors as sharing a belief that people can make a difference in business performance, understanding what's needed to make a performance difference, fostering two-way communications, routine information sharing, having goal setting and tracking in place, and involving the workforce help make pay change successful; they're even more important when pay is at risk. However, companies can't wait for everyone to get on board before moving forward.

• *Measures within line of sight.* The closer the line of sight, the more likely the acceptance of pay at risk, other things being equal. Measures with long line of sight may seem too far removed for people to make a difference, so the upside variable pay opportunity must increase to make up for this. Business education and involvement help here.

• *Meaningful award relative to pay at risk.* The award must be meaningful for the type and amount of pay at risk. The size of reward must balance the performance and effort required to earn an award. The relationship must be truly win-win for both people and the company.

• *Personal circumstances.* It's important to anticipate what happens to the cash flow of the worker's family in the event of missing an award. Also, whether the transition is immediate or gradual counts in acceptance and commitment. People must go home and explain pay issues to someone. How this message reads at home is telling as to how it reads at work.

• *Pay history.* Prior experience with pay solutions in current or past company affiliations influences acceptance. What worked and what didn't are important; pay is a sensitive issue and memories tend to be long (especially if commitments weren't kept). How many times the company has blundered with pay change is an issue in acceptance. It's very important to do pay change right the first time, or the company may be hard pressed to get a fair chance again soon.

• *Early experiences.* Whether the workforce hits or misses in the initial performance period is important. If the goals are too difficult, or if it's impossible to acquire and apply the skill or competency soon enough to result in performance improvement, an early win may be difficult. In our experience, a win early on is a powerful trust builder. People can accept a miss if they've had a hit. However, a sustained track record of losses shows that something isn't going well.

• *Managing the change.* Will the company protect the workforce in some way initially to allow time to adjust? Pay change can be accomplished relatively quickly, but a transition period is essential. It's easier to transition if the opportunity to earn variable pay awards is concurrent with the timing of base pay change rather than, for example, having base pay limited or reduced and then waiting for the end of the year to earn variable pay. It may be worth considering having the new pay approach implemented in a dry run that doesn't immediately have an impact on pay. Speed of implementation, however, varies from one company to another.

The total amount of variable pay is typically a minimum of two times the amount at risk and preferably three times when base pay is potentially at risk, and up to four times if base pay is reduced. Three times the amount at risk means that if base pay is limited by 1 percent, then possible total variable pay is 3 percent of base pay. Variable pay opportunity depends on the factors described above. The more these factors are met, the smaller the total variable pay opportunity needed for acceptance by the workforce; if these factors are poorly met, then the larger the total variable pay opportunity needs to be.

Exhibit 3.2 describes a diagnostic that assesses conditions for variable pay design under the three approaches to changing the total cash mix to more variable pay. The exhibit shows the conditions under which these approaches can be used rather than representing actual prevalent practice or how they must be used. For example, line of sight can be longest with add-on variable pay, but these plans can also have short line-of-sight measures.

Formula for Success

The formula for success clearly depends on the situation surrounding the introduction of at-risk pay. People are never really ready for pay changes that don't result in pay increases or rewards that reflect their

Exhibit 3.2. Assessing Conditions When Changing Total Cash Mix to More Variable Pay.

Characteristic	Add-On Variable Pay	Potential Pay at Risk	Base Pay at Risk
Methodology	Variable pay is in addition to regular base pay adjustments.	Use some or all of anticipated future base pay increase budget to help fund variable pay.	Reduce base pay to help fund variable pay.
Business case	Ability to fund; reasonable base pay compared to labor market; wanting easy implementation with workforce acceptance and focus on business-aligned goals	Low margins and labor cost large portion of total cost; some financial concerns; high base pay relative to labor market; creating stakeholdership desired; ensuring awards of meaningful size	Severe financial problems; redesigning sales compensation; making other major total cash mix changes
Target and upside variable pay opportunities	Least	Medium	Most
Line of sight of measures	Longest	Medium	Shortest
Goal difficulty	Most	Medium	Least
Threshold	No	Maybe	Yes
Workforce readiness	Least	Medium	Most
People's current level of trust and confidence in company	Least	Medium	Most
Easing transition	Least	Medium	Most

Note: The characteristics show the conditions under which these approaches can be used rather than representing actual prevalent practice or how approaches must be used.

current experience. For this reason, the concept of *readiness assessment* makes little sense in determining whether people are ready for pay change. Pay change requires that company leadership initiate the change based on the business reasons and enlist workforce support and help.

ACCEPTING TOTAL PAY

If you wait for the best time to change pay, it will never come. Thus a need to communicate to gain understanding and acceptance faces you. Here are some of the actions you can take to communicate a strategy of total pay:

- *Communicate the business case.* One key positive action is always to communicate in terms of all total pay elements and how they fit the business case for changing rewards. Do what's necessary to create a positive, natural experience during pay changes.
- *Show value and win-win.* What's the total pay package worth? Show what is provided in terms of dollars and cents. Convert to examples of what is available—and remember the elevator speech.
- *Personalize.* People think of pay in terms of themselves and their families. If pay is changing, consider the family to be the audience as well as the worker. How do people describe the change when they get home? Is it a positive message, or does the person walk in the door and mutter "They're doing it to us again!"?

Total pay is a new way of thinking. But the company must lead the way to understanding.

CONCLUSIONS

The concept of total pay is changing. Business realities dictate that pay tools be assigned the responsibility for doing what each tool does best to communicate. Even though competitive total pay and total rewards remain important, it's sometimes difficult to assess because of blurring job comparisons, fast changes in the competitive market, and insufficient survey information. If this is the case, the company should make its best judgment. Enterprises need new ways to make themselves attractive, some related to pay design and communication. However, unless a company is a place people are proud of and where they look forward to spending their time, all the total pay in the world won't result in a positive work experience.

It is so important to strategize about pay in a total rewards and total pay context that focusing only on one element of pay without considering the rest shortchanges the reward process. Trying only to add variable pay without thinking about what this does to benefits is folly. Revising performance management while ignoring related pay solutions makes no sense. Our assumption throughout this book is that a company has a quiver of arrows that are total pay. One or more may be used at different times; however, the company is always aware of when and how it needs to use them all.

CHAPTER 4

Measuring and Managing Performance

We've all heard, in one form or another, the adage, "You can't manage what you can't measure." Without workforce performance measurement and management, effective total pay and total rewards are impossible. Even if a company isn't consistently measuring its performance in the form of results and competencies, you can be sure the customers are measuring it. Performance measurement and management involve setting and communicating goals, providing ongoing feedback and problem solving about how better to address performance expectations, and measuring results against goals. They support Principle 3 by extending the line of sight of the workforce to company business concept and goals.

In our view, to add value, effective measurement and management of performance must be continuous, developmental, participative, and just a regular part of "how things are done here." If a company is looking for something to institutionalize, continuous feedback and dialogue with people about what's going on and how they fit is the thing to choose. Measuring and managing performance is a major opportunity for discussion, exchange of ideas, and better communications. All the related tools and techniques in the world can only hope to improve, not substitute for, this important process.

MEASUREMENT DRIVES REWARDS

Regardless of the extent to which the outcomes of the performance measurement and management process are used directly in determining any element of total pay, their influence on the total pay process is significant. The outcomes can either help make needed results and required skills and competencies understandable and acceptable to people or make them muddled and threatening. Done effectively, the performance measurement and management process solidifies the better workforce deal and supports building trust, collaboration, and cohesiveness. Properly designed, the process can make managers into partners and coaches for workforce development and strengthen the individual growth component of total rewards described in Chapter 1. When done improperly, it can encourage procrastination and even undermine what's essential to people and their companies. We believe performance measurement and management are the foundation supporting effective total pay.

Wanting a total reward strategy that stresses a stronger linkage between pay and performance is a no-brainer. We all want performance to play a positive role in the company's pay process. Part of our formula for achieving this is to make company goals clear and communicate progress toward them regularly. This involves translating company objectives from the business strategy and operating plan into meaningful goals, skills, and competencies that people can understand and do something about. The other part of our formula is coaching, educating, and giving frequent ongoing feedback to build trust, understanding, and commitment. This means weaving feedback on people's progress toward goal achievement and skill and competency development into the fabric of the workplace, making it a natural part of day-to-day communications. This process needs to become part of the positive, natural reward experience of Principle 1.

POSITIVE, VALUABLE, AND WITHIN REACH

Our solution requires combining goals derived from the business strategy and operating plan with development feedback and performance feedback:

1. *Business-aligned goals.* They create the strategic connection with the business and customers, elicit leadership commitment and involvement, and focus on the future and what's required to be a successful company. This is how to communicate and translate vision, values, priorities, and initiatives from the strategic plan to the business unit, site, group, team, or other collaborative organizational unit.
2. *Development feedback and performance feedback.* Close-in feedback on individual results, skills, and competencies comes from the manager and possibly from internal customers, peers, direct reports, external customers, and other colleagues. It communicates relevant information for workforce development and constitutes a positive platform for learning. It combines managerial responsibility for workforce results, skills, and competencies with people's accountability to develop and continue to improve their value to the company and to contribute to organizational success. This is how managers communicate directly with individuals and coach and teach.

This process does not require formal implementation of a balanced-scorecard approach to goals, although for some this is a possible answer.[1] Nor does it require implementation of a sophisticated computer-assisted personal feedback system such as those associated with multisource or 360-degree solutions, although some companies may select this option.[2] But it does require that managers take responsibility for two of their key accountabilities: people development and leadership in accomplishing goals. Studies suggest that organizations providing regular feedback to their workforce outperform those that either use little active feedback or conduct only an annual performance review. As studies also show, at the largest and most successful U.S. companies that have transformed themselves the CEO is personally involved in setting prospective goals and reviewing the performance of the top 100 or so executives.

Speed Counts

This should not be a slow, painful, or agonizing process. Speed is what business is about. In the movie *Top Gun,* Tom Cruise is a pilot in air combat. He calls a nearby American aircraft carrier to launch more planes because he and his buddies in the air are outnumbered. The carrier tells him that the launch device is jammed, and they'll launch more planes in ten minutes. Cruise responds that the battle will be over in two!

Doing a perfect job of selecting measures, skills, and competencies is a worthy objective, but getting in the game with measures, skills, and competencies that work from the start and can improve over time is more critical. To develop supposedly perfect measures of results, skills, and competencies, many fine companies have endured lengthy and expensive undertakings, often so cumbersome and taking so long that by the time the metrics were in place the company was already behind the competitors. Our formula requires a faster process. Speed counts with customers, and the competition learns new things every day.

Combining Business-Aligned Goals and Feedback

The combined process for business-aligned goals and feedback on development and performance makes a complete framework for measuring and managing performance. Figure 4.1 outlines this performance measurement and management process. Business-aligned goals are tools of the strategist. Development and performance feedback is a tool of the social psychologist. The strategist often thinks of the psychologist as someone who works in soft, undefined areas. The psychologist views the strategist as someone who works with distant numbers and elaborate measures and goals. In fact, the two are at opposite ends of a continuum of essential performance management. They link strategy to the implementation of strategy through people. It seems obvious that these two processes are important individually and even more valuable when associated.

BUSINESS-ALIGNED GOALS

We use the term *business-aligned goals* because we believe goal setting throughout the organization should align with the goals of the company's strategic and operating plans. Goals are the announced

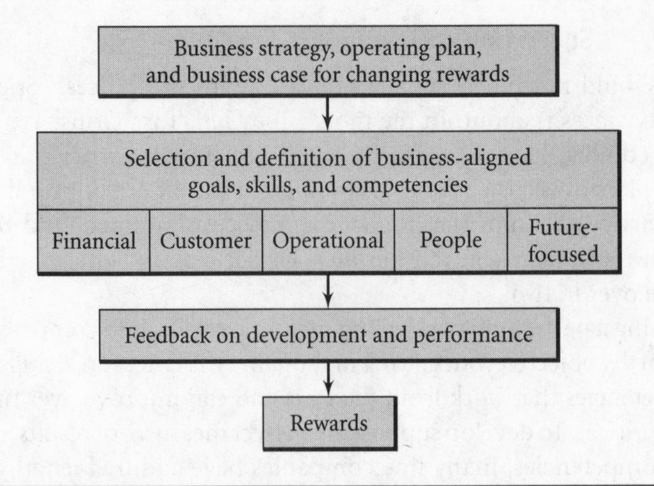

Figure 4.1. Alignment of Performance Measurement and Management with Rewards.

statement of how the company evaluates itself. They offer direction for the content of feedback on development and performance and stimulate redefining the skills and competencies people need. The goal-setting process starts by establishing the company's strategic goals; choosing the key drivers of company results; and determining, clarifying, and adapting as needed the factors critical to accomplishing goals. The process enables leadership to choose the best goals by which to help lead the enterprise, interprets these goals understandably, and generates the discipline to realize the goals (and to refresh them as required). The business-aligned goal-setting process can accommodate changes in direction by enabling discussion and revision of goals; it also opens up opportunities for new goals and results.

Goal Categories

Business-aligned goal setting involves selecting and using a package of strategically driven success measures, skills, and competencies to lead the business. Five categories suggest a starting place for customizing goal setting to your needs:

- *Financial goals.* Goals such as profit, earnings per share, revenue growth, EBITDA (earnings before interest, taxes, depreciation, and amortization), cash flow, economic value-added, and return measures (for example, return on capital employed, assets, equity, sales, investment).

- *Customer goals.* Goals such as service, customer retention, customer penetration, customer satisfaction, new customers, brand awareness, and market share.
- *Operational goals.* Goals such as process improvement, quality, efficiency, cycle time, delivery, cost, safety, and environment.
- *People goals.* Learning and development goals, reskilling, regoaling, value-added from skill and competency development, workforce satisfaction, workforce retention, workforce productivity, and implemented workforce suggestions.
- *Future-focused goals.* What the company and workforce need to ensure a compelling future, such as new products, new services, product and service line expansions, innovations, new markets, acquisitions, mergers, and globalization.

This isn't an all-inclusive or mutually exclusive list. We include the financial, customer, and operational goals as partners with the people and future-focused goals because they are all interrelated. Goals, skills, and competencies relative to people and the company's preparation for the future should generate financial, customer, and operational results. The enterprise should select goals according to how it can best get to where it needs to be. The executive team has to think outside of the box to develop the key goals, which are the drivers of results, skills, and competencies. They have to go beyond traditional financial results and think about the long run, not just this quarter or this year.

Leadership is responsible for setting a balanced collection of goals that optimize overall performance. We've all been involved in company situations where the goals weren't well balanced, and this universally created challenges. The primary driver in many instances is the CEO and the functional area the chief executive came from before becoming the boss. Financial executives try to drive the company on the basis of financial measures; operations executives favor operational measures; marketing and sales executives look to growth and sales measures; and engineering and scientific executives use technology and product development measures. Having the executive team together in the same room when developing the goals, skills, and competencies makes the actual goal-setting process more powerful and complete.

FINANCIAL GOALS. Perhaps the most common way to evaluate performance is with accounting measures of profit, asset performance, and the like. This involves communicating throughout the company financial goals that often entail a long line of sight. It asks those responsible for making financial goals how they will add value to the business. It's a retrospective process that looks at how the company did during the last quarter or year.

Complex organizations are finding that managing and enhancing performance requires more than just controlling a few major financial measures and pulling a lever if a financial imbalance exists. Communication is one shortcoming of this tactic. It's hard to tell a manufacturing worker or information technologist to "get out there and improve earnings per share" without translation. Additional measures must be the guides that lead to financial performance.

Financial accounting measures also tend to be short-term and focus on conventional management solutions, such as cutting cost or becoming a low-priced provider of products and services. Earnings performance, for instance, reflects how well the company executed a viable business strategy from the previous year, but it doesn't tell us whether the current business strategy is working. In this sense, financial accounting measures alone are likely to be backward sighted. Also, they often don't provide a way to operationalize midcourse corrections until it's too late. Thus, although important, financial accounting measures are insufficient as stand-alones for solid performance management.

It's impossible to run a complex enterprise by focusing only on cost and (as they say) squeezing the nickel until the Indian rides the buffalo. This might have been sufficient in a world driven by industrial-age industries, but it clearly is no longer a viable way to run a business. Harold Geneen did an excellent job of running ITT decades ago merely by squeezing the nickel, but this doesn't work if a focus on a compelling future is needed. When Geneen departed, he failed to leave a heritage of effective business strategy, which fact, some people say, damaged the company.

Eli Lilly, Coca-Cola, Monsanto, and others use economic value-added (EVA), a more forward-looking indicator than financial accounting measures. EVA measures after-tax operating profit in excess of the cost of capital and thus gets people thinking about generating a good return on the capital invested in their business.[3] However, this is a more difficult measure to communicate and track than profit, so people need significant education on EVA if it is to influence pay.

CUSTOMER GOALS. Customer goals are partners with financial goals, since without customers there's no revenue. Building a chain of customers helps people understand their relationship with external customers by making the line of sight to external customers transparent and uncluttered. Everyone in a company has a combination of internal and external customers. Some members of the workforce have principally internal customers, but ultimately these internal ones focus on external customers, thus establishing the chain throughout the company. For example, the manufacturing process may be organized in successive work cells, linked by the measures and goals required by the customer of each process. The second work cell in the process is the customer of the first work cell, and so forth. Everyone serves the next customer in the line stretching on to the external customer. The customer chain introduces measures and goals set not only by external customers but also by internal customers. This is a solid concept, so long as the company doesn't lose sight of who the real customers are and how to satisfy them (the external customers).[4]

At other times, external customer goals permeate the organization. The hotel industry is an example of this because the overall customer satisfaction score correlates highly with the number of stays. Still other companies, such as those with a process focus, determine the goals that people working in the process influence directly and that drive achievement of external customer goals. For example, an insurance company may measure not only customer satisfaction but also accuracy and timeliness of response to the insured as correlates of customer satisfaction.

We've omitted detailed discussion of operational goals since they tend to be specific to a company and an industry, and they commonly create less concern about line of sight than financial measures do. We've also left out people measures because we cover them throughout the book.

FUTURE-FOCUSED GOALS. Strategic companies look for what influences future financial performance. They want to invest in customers, products, services, innovation, and their workforce. They often believe that emphasizing only control measures (such as earnings performance and measures of revenue growth) tunnels the perspective of the future too narrowly. Instead, they require a combination of financial and other measures. Investments in technology, innovation, the workforce, customers, and other challenges mean expanding to consider more strategic indicators of success. Quality, cost, cycle time, and other conventional measures are insufficient. Concentrating only on the measures that others emphasize rarely yields competitive advantage.

Balanced Scorecard

Some companies use the balanced scorecard, a rigorous variation of business-aligned goals, for performance measurement and management. The balanced scorecard translates a company's mission and strategy into a set of performance measures that balance short-term and long-term objectives, financial and nonfinancial measures, lagging and leading indicators, and external and internal performance perspectives. Often communications of the balanced scorecard include a diagram that displays measures by type (financial, customer, internal, and innovation and learning), shows the interrelationship of measures by links, and tiers them by overall impact. This allows people first to see where they influence the company's primary measures and how their measures interact with others' and second to focus on their area of greatest influence on the business. It has a track record at Mobil Oil, CIGNA, Brown & Root, Chemical Bank, Monsanto, and elsewhere; the list is growing.

Setting Reasonable Performance Levels

Shareholder expectations and the business strategy drive the level of performance required for goals in the business or operating plan. Goals may also reflect a combination of recent performance, assessment of potential, comparison to industry standards, and comparison to best practice. Goals should have a reasonable stretch: not too much or too little. Because of increasing competition and focus on continuous improvement, most goals involve some kind of improvement. (An exception to this is performance at the world-class level, where merely sustaining performance becomes the goal.) However, goals can't be so high that what should be a win-win relationship becomes a win for the company and a loss for the workforce. Goal setting works best if people play a role in helping to set goals because it creates understanding of and commitment to the goals. People are especially knowledgeable about setting operational goals that drive the financial goals set by leadership.

Translating Business-Aligned Goals to the Team and Individual

Sometimes goals cascade all the way to the individual. Or the cascading may stop at some definition of team. However, even if goal setting stops at the team level, the team still discusses each member's role and the results it expects them to contribute to support the team's goals and work process. It also has some form of feedback process about the individual's contributions to team results. The organization may choose not to develop business-aligned goals for individuals for any of these reasons:

- The organization design is team-based, members work very interdependently, and the unit for measuring and rewarding results is the team.
- People are in flexible, broad roles where they do whatever it takes to accomplish team results.
- Individual performance is measured against performance standards in a job-based organization design.
- The focus is on the team or organizational unit achieving a goal that involves creativity and innovation, so the journey to that goal achievement has many possibilities and variations.
- The enterprise must respond quickly to changing business situations, shift directions frequently, and make rapid course corrections.

On this last point, financial goals typically don't change during the year, but the actions necessary to achieve the financial goals may change rapidly. Changing the goals and direction of a team is faster and easier than changing both team goals and individual goals. Time is spent communicating the change in direction, and in having teams solve problems to respond to the change rather than developing individual goals.

"SMART" Goals

Assuming the company wants to set goals for individuals, the business-aligned goals communicated from the company down through the team level need translation into individual goals so that people can add value to the organization. This involves providing a meaningful link between what people can do to what the organization needs to accomplish. Although it applies to goals set at any level in the company, one tool to facilitate the close-in goal-setting process is "SMART" goals. We've seen different words associated with the acronym, and the words can be interpreted freely to meet company needs, but SMART often means:

- **S**pecific: stated clearly, precisely, and unambiguously; something observable and verifiable
- **M**easurable: how well, what quantity, what quality, what speed or timeliness, what expenditure of resources
- **A**chievable or **A**daptable: realistically attainable goals, but with some challenge and stretch; a flexible goal-setting process where goals adapt to changing business situations
- **R**elevant or **R**esults-oriented: relevant to the business through the business-aligned goal-setting process; linked to the goals of the team, group, business unit, and company
- **T**ime-framed: specific time-sensitive boundaries; frequent monitoring of progress on goal achievement

Companies that are most successful in goal setting for individuals, we find, seamlessly connect individual goals with other business-aligned goals, thereby meeting the R (relevant, results-oriented) criterion. The process first involves communicating the company's and the business unit's business-aligned goals to the level of the manager's organizational unit, the team, or the work process. Subsequently, managers, leaders, or sponsors hold a group meeting with people in their unit at which everyone is involved in discussing the goals that have cascaded to the unit, and in setting and prioritizing unit goals that align with the business. They document the specific goals that have cascaded from a higher and larger organizational unit and are relevant to their unit, as well as the goals they develop for their own specific unit. This becomes a living, breathing communications document that the unit posts, uses to track progress and success, and modifies as direction changes.

From this document come individual goals. It's better if goals focus on value-added results rather than activities because results are more important and usually more easily measurable than activities. The goals of both the unit and the individual must meet the A (adaptability) criterion. The goal-setting process needs flexibility so goals can be modified to reflect the dynamics of most businesses today and to respond quickly to directional changes. A business-aligned goal-setting process facilitates understanding and acceptance of goals. Unless people understand, accept, and positively use goals to improve individual performance, no matter how SMART the goals are, they just don't add value to the business.

Value of Business-Aligned Goals for Rewards

For our purposes, the value of the business-aligned goal process comes from its educational capabilities. Because it emphasizes key goals and what causes their achievement, it's an excellent workforce teaching tool. Company leadership becomes an active trainer by managing performance. Leaders not only set strategy but also educate members of the workforce on how to add value. Beyond this, the business-aligned goal process is an opportunity for feedback not only from the top down but also from the bottom up. It's a way to educate the leadership team on what the close-in workforce knows about what is working, what may not be working, and what to do about it.

The business-aligned goal process helps translate remote strategy into actionable results and needed skills and competencies; it answers the question of where goals come from in the only practical way to address the line-of-sight issue. It's a global tool, a tool of teams, a tool of mergers and acquisitions, and most of all a tool to grow the business. This may require commitment to a new way of doing things, but one that has nearly all the features that total pay effectiveness needs from performance measurement and management. It supports Principle 3 (extending people's line of sight) by identifying the individual with team, site, business-unit, and company success and by adopting and communicating value-added customer goals in response to changing customer needs.

We believe that organizations should regularly communicate business-aligned goals above the individual level and progress on goal achievement through some form of internally publicized scorecard. Alignment requires widespread communications about company goals. Those who are concerned about the confidentiality of these goals and who fear competitor access should ask people to maintain confidentiality because otherwise winning is in jeopardy for all parties. Unless people know what the business is about and how they fit, it's unlikely they'll be very helpful in making the company a success.

SKILLS AND COMPETENCIES AND INDIVIDUAL GROWTH

The category of people goals that we discussed earlier includes value-added from competency development. Competencies are demonstrable characteristics—skills, knowledge, and behaviors—that the company needs or values in its people and that enable performance and improve results. For our purposes, there are four types of competency:

1. *Organizational competencies* make up the company's core competencies and represent the knowledge and skill the company has or needs to gain advantage. Examples are GE's competency of developing leaders and Sony's miniaturization competency.
2. *Strategic competencies* enhance business processes and supporting infrastructure. Process improvement may be a strategic initiative that can provide guidance on these competencies. Wal-Mart's distribution competency and Merck's ability to expedite FDA product approval are strategically driven and examples of the ability to convert strategy into action.
3. *Technical competencies* include breadth and depth of functional expertise. Examples of technical competencies are Internet or intranet development for IT professionals, electrical assembly capabilities for manufacturing workers, and financial analysis for financial workers. Hewlett-Packard, Microsoft, Intel, Eli Lilly, and Genentech are examples of enterprises that gain differential advantage from technical competency.

4. *Behavioral competencies* are the observable individual characteristics such as communications, teamwork, customer service, and innovation that permit the company to capitalize on organizational, strategic, and technical competencies to turn them into measurable results. Covey Leadership Center (now merged as Franklin Covey Company) is an example of a very successful business built on outstanding behavioral competencies.

As a company identifies behavioral competencies, it should avoid those addressing underlying traits and motives and stick with observable behaviors. It's hard enough to change observable behaviors; a 35-year-old person has spent 35 years perfecting their present behaviors.

People are the warehouse for the skills and competencies of the company. Nobody ever calls out to the jobs to learn something or accomplish goals; they call on people to help the company be a success. As high-performance organizations, process organizations, and delayered organizations broaden roles to become more fluid and dynamic and less narrowly and clearly defined, the skills and competencies a person has and uses become more important. But it's not enough to have skills and competencies; people must direct capabilities to get desired results.[5]

One of Several Definitions of Competency

We define competencies to include skills, knowledge, and behaviors. Some define competencies as only behavioral elements. Our definition is broader because the competencies described above are the capabilities that, experience suggests, businesses require to be effective. There are other definitions as well. Some view competencies as largely behavioral or strategic in nature and attribute them principally to knowledge workers. They view skills as operational and tactical and attributable to mostly hourly manufacturing or nonexempt service workers.

We believe that competencies and skills are part of the same formula that prepares everyone in the workforce to perform more effectively. Our view combines competencies and skills to unify the entire workforce around the same competency model. Throughout the book, however, we use the phrase *skills and competencies* so that all readers, regardless of their definition of competency, realize we mean all-encompassing. We include the term *skills* in the phrase to keep the attention of readers who have become disenchanted with competencies because of complex competency solutions that clumsily try to measure traits and motives.[6]

Where Do Skills and Competencies Come From?

Skills and competencies can be derived from the company's business strategy and values, customer input, executive interviews, high-performing individuals, and workforce focus groups. Each possible source of skill and competency deserves exploration to determine whether or not it offers advantage:

Business strategy. Core competencies and their definition and deployment are part of the strategic plan and values of many companies. Strategies that prove most useful are those that outline not only objectives and expected outcomes but also how the company prepares itself to achieve the required end results. This is our favored source of skills and competencies because it connects them to the business case for change.

Customer input. The customer is an ultimate source for determining needed skills and competencies. However, directly asking your customers what skills and competencies are necessary to serve them is only the start. The customer may send strong messages to the company about what's right or wrong with the business relationship. But interpreting this feedback in terms of core competencies, and subsequently into a performance management system based on skills and competencies, is a responsibility of the leadership team, accomplished by developing strategy concerning core competency and then interpreting this in terms of skills and competencies people must acquire and apply.

Executive interviews. If a business strategy derived from understanding the customer is the ultimate source of skills and competencies, then executives are best positioned to interpret the core competencies in terms useful to the workforce. This is critical because seeing core competencies from a strategic perspective often affords a longer-distance view, while development requires a nearer understanding of the skills and competencies needed. Executives should be both the interpreters of the business process and strategy in terms of skills and competencies and also the sponsors of the initiative.

High-performing individuals. Identifying the characteristics of these people may seem to be an obvious source of skill and competency, but this isn't always an accurate way to gather information on capabilities that continue to add value. This is because what constitutes an excellent-performing individual may change with the business situation. Undertaking change in culture and perspective often means changing the definition of what constitutes a high-performing individual. For example, a firm wanting to move strategically from focusing only on individual performance to the competency of collaboration wouldn't do well to interview the top solo performers to determine how best to communicate a capability involving collaboration. Nor would it be wise to seek competency information from an excellent-performing individual in a military technical area if the needed competency involves commercial rather than military businesses.

Workforce focus groups. After selection and definition of skills and competencies from the business strategy, it's useful to enlist people to carefully define and apply skills and competencies to the performance management system. But it makes no sense to ask people to make up what they think the skills and competencies might be unless they understand the business strategy and the business case for change. The value of having workforce members as participants in the skill-and-competency process rests in the high-involvement design and communications of a tactical human resource solution that reflects a business strategy.

Those who look to the past have little chance at high performance because the likes of Cisco Systems, Johnson & Johnson, Sun Microsystems, Pfizer, Wal-Mart, and GE are looking forward to the future. Thus, skill and competency must come from understanding the business concept and business strategy and translating customer input, not from a catalogue of competencies or from the enterprise as it is. If the strategy is future-focused, the development process must be as well. The objective is to encourage the workforce to acquire and apply the skills and competencies needed for success in the future—not in the past.

Exhibit 4.1 is from our study of competency use.[7] The results suggest that specific competencies are fairly common and that perhaps business advantage doesn't come from the actual selection of unique competencies but from how effectively they're implemented

Exhibit 4.1. Study of Competencies Used by Companies.

Competency	Frequency of Use by Companies
Customer focus	8
Communication	7
Team orientation	6
Technical expertise	6
Results orientation	6
Leadership	6
Adaptability	5
Innovation	5

Note: 10-company convenience sample.

and integrated into the company fabric. Great companies use competencies to raise the bar on performance expectations (not to establish the baseline of performance) and move expeditiously from building the competency model to application.

Value of Skills and Competencies

A company focuses on skills and competencies to gain advantages it believes it can obtain by emphasizing the individual rather than the job. These advantages include:

- Assembling a flexible and multiskilled workforce
- Having a workforce that learns and grows to continue adding value to the business
- Communicating how to achieve differential advantage in improving results
- Providing attractive growth opportunities for the type of people the company needs
- Encouraging a shared set of behaviors that reflect a newly emerging culture
- Moving to a focused learning environment where what people learn is important to the business

Figure 4.2 is an example of a competency model.[8] Competencies drive and integrate all elements of the human resource process such that staffing, training, total pay and other rewards, succession planning, and the performance measurement and management process support and emphasize a developmental perspective.

Development and Growth

As one of the four reward components, individual growth represents a shared responsibility on the part of people and the company. To ensure credibility of the development feedback process, managers are responsible for determining (1) what skills and competencies they need in their unit to expedite accomplishing their relevant business-aligned goals, (2) the gap between what they need and what exists, and (3) how to close the gap. They're also responsible for clarifying developmental needs to the people who report to them and discussing and mutually agreeing upon growth expectations with these people. The individual is responsible for preparing developmental goals and action plans and for identifying training and growth activities with the assistance of the manager or coach.

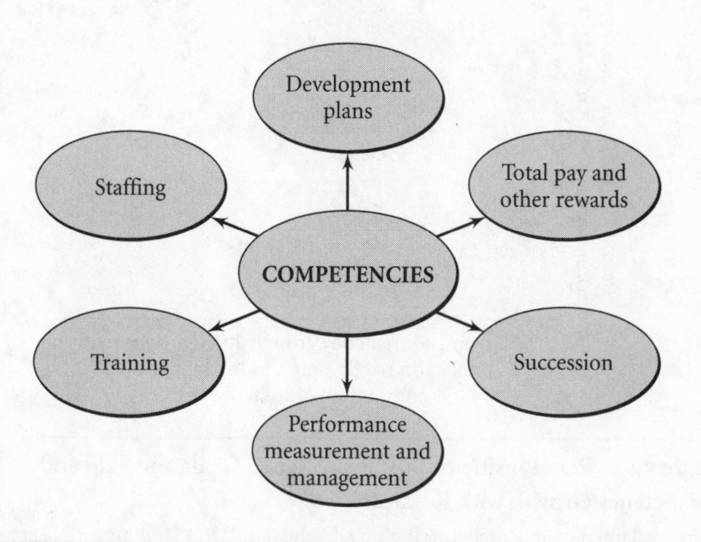

Figure 4.2. Competencies: An Integrated People Process.

Action plans help people enhance performance in their current role or enable them to perform additional responsibilities and identify how performance will change as a result of development. The focus of growth activities is on-the-job experiences, such as participating on a cross-functional team in a key role or as team leader, taking on a lateral assignment, or serving as a mentor for someone new to the organization. As the manager coaches and facilitates, people are responsible for managing their journey from the current state to where they must be in the future so that development improves performance.

Integrating Business-Aligned Goals and Skills and Competencies

Business-aligned goals and skills and competencies go hand in hand to create a total picture of performance. We believe that results from goals deserve the most emphasis, but that's a matter for companies to prioritize for themselves. We think of how people add value in terms of two dimensions, as shown in Figure 4.3. Because skills and com-

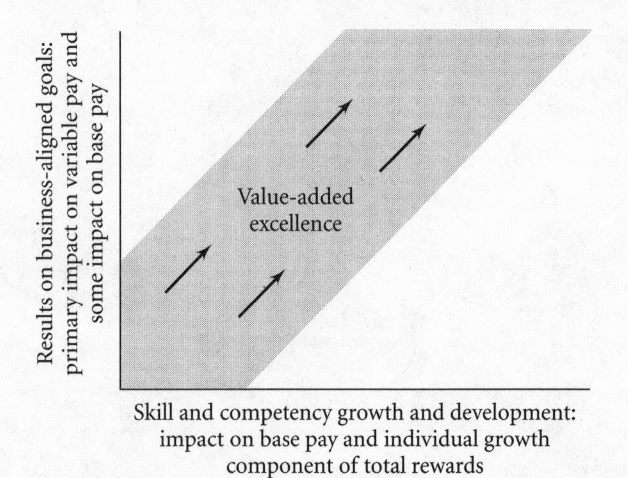

Figure 4.3. Relationship of Business-Aligned Goals and Skill and Competency Growth with Rewards.

Source: adapted from Zingheim, P. K., and Schuster, J. R. "Dealing with Scarce Talent: Lessons from the Leading Edge." *Compensation & Benefits Review,* 1999, *31*(2), 36–44.

petencies enable performance, the horizontal axis or independent variable represents the skills and competencies needed to generate the required business results. The vertical axis represents results measured in terms of outcomes that add value to the business. Both axes influence total rewards. On the vertical axis, variable pay rewards results, and consistent performance results over time play a role in base pay. The skill-and-competency horizontal axis plays a role in base pay and the individual growth component of total rewards.

DEVELOPMENT AND PERFORMANCE FEEDBACK

The objective of feedback on development and performance is to enhance outcomes by offering regular, ongoing input on performance based on the goals, skills, and competencies identified by the business-aligned goals. The objective isn't to design and complete forms for reviewing or appraising performance. Think of how a top-flight sports coach teaches and develops players. The coaching process doesn't happen once a year on a specific date, and it's unlikely that anyone fills out any forms at all. Rather, coaching and teaching happen in practice, in preparation for the game, during the game, after the game, and in every personal interaction between the coach and player. It's a continuous learning process, and this is what feedback on development and performance is about.

Feedback Example

Many organizations develop a procedure for feedback. For example, here's how an insurance company defines it:

1. Start with business and customer success measures and goals.
2. Interpret success measures and goals in the context of the individual.
3. Emphasize results, and then the skills and competencies needed to get results.
4. Provide usable feedback, coaching, and teaching.
5. Maintain continuous, honest, and timely communications.
6. Constantly adapt to the situation, and be flexible.

7. Keep involvement and dialogue at a high level.
8. Celebrate improvement and recognize results.
9. Make the feedback process positive.
10. Treat problems as opportunities to enhance the future.

The point this company makes is that continuous feedback, course correction, and teaching and learning avoid crisis-performance problems that are recognized only after considerable damage is done. This is what the development and performance feedback process is about: ongoing feedback, no surprises, and coaching and adjusting when needed as the process unfolds. It's much more difficult to make a late correction and still reach the target within acceptable performance tolerances. This means measuring and managing performance is anything but an annual event. Instead, it's part of the day-to-day work process necessary for the better workforce deal.

The meeting at the end of the performance period becomes a summary review of feedback and of the value the individual provided to the company; it is not the time for new feedback since feedback has already been ongoing. The manager and individual review what worked and what didn't, and they improve the measurement and performance management process for the upcoming year. Some companies separate the summary reviews of performance and development if they believe that discussing the two at the same meeting would cause the individual to downplay development needs. When this happens, chances are that there hasn't been sufficient ongoing feedback during the year and the meeting has instead become the annual appraisal event. During ongoing coaching, separating development feedback from performance feedback is difficult because the two are intertwined; the way to enhance performance often involves developing.

Multisource Feedback

A flatter organization design and meaningful workforce involvement necessitate feedback from more sources than the manager because the higher ratio of workers to managers means that peers, not the manager, may be continuously closer to the performance of an individual. Also, as work design changes toward cross-functional teams and people working on projects that are not under the direct accountability of their manager, the sources for feedback need to expand. The assumption in multisource feedback is that feedback to people is more accurate and appropriate if it taps into information from sources beyond the immediate manager. Feedback may come from peers, direct reports, internal customers, other colleagues, and external customers. Managers often find it useful to get input from a spectrum of people who have knowledge of the individual's performance and development because this allows wider and deeper understanding of how the individual is doing and a better opportunity for complete and objective feedback.

EXTENT OF WORKFORCE INVOLVEMENT. The degree of workforce involvement in the feedback-and-review process covers a range of levels. Exhibit 4.2 shows seven levels of involvement of individuals in measuring and managing their performance.[9] Level A, where the manager evaluates performance and informs the individual of the performance decision, is representative of a command-and-control management style. Very few businesses are at Levels A and B because

Exhibit 4.2. The A to G of Workforce Involvement in Feedback on Development and Performance.

Level	Involvement
A	Manager conducts the review and informs individual of results.
B	Manager conducts the review and listens to individual's comments.
C	Manager and individual provide input and participate in the review process; manager makes final review decision.
D	Manager, individual, and others selected by manager are review sources. Manager receives inputs from other sources, interprets and integrates results. Manager and individual participate in the review. Manager makes final review decision.
E	Manager/leader and individual identify multiple review sources. Both individual and manager/leader receive inputs from other sources, integrate results, and participate in the review process. Manager/leader makes final review decision.
F	Team and individual identify review sources and gather inputs. Team and leader communicate with individual. Leader is accountable for review.
G	Team and individual identify review sources and gather inputs. Team communicates with individual. Team is accountable for review; leader facilitates the process.

of the acknowledged value of moving at least to Level C, where self-assessment involves people's thinking about their own performance and development. At the other end of the scale are Levels E through G, where measuring and managing performance includes an increasingly strong multisource component. This part of the scale is representative of greater workforce involvement and use of teams.

We suggest moving one level along this scale toward G as part of continuously improving the performance feedback process. Performance management is a two-way interactive process. Given today's organization designs, managers should at least gather input from other sources and add this to their feedback for a well-rounded perspective.

HURDLES FOR MULTISOURCE FEEDBACK. Multisource feedback faces some major hurdles and challenges that can't be ignored. Not every company or workforce is ready for multisource feedback, and few are ready from the start. An alternative is to dabble with or pilot peer feedback processes. This may start with the executives and work down through the organization. Colleagues themselves may meet to give each other feedback when they are working in a more self-managing environment. Also, gradually integrating peer and customer feedback into the performance management process permits seeing how it works and whether it fits the company's needs. This often starts with technical performance and skills and later moves to behavioral competencies because technical issues are generally more objective and easier to discuss.

The criticality or inherent value of the work performed may help overcome resistance to multisource feedback. For example, registered nurses are often willing to give feedback to one another because the nature of their work involves speeding the healing process and saving lives. Although many roles can't offer such critical inherent value and the need to do things right, people are more willing to give feedback if they understand and support customer and business goals and depend on others to accomplish these goals.

USING MULTISOURCE FEEDBACK FOR DETERMINING PAY. We believe that, if Levels E through G are used for determining pay and not just for development, multisource feedback should be part of an ongoing process of honest performance feedback. People must be trained in giving and receiving feedback. We usually don't recommend a computerized multisource feedback tool of 20–50 questions done annually for determining pay because it acts too much like the stand-alone annual performance appraisal event or exam that most people come to dread. At a conference of users of computerized multisource feedback systems, we asked how many used the tool to help determine pay. Only one or two out of a hundred in the audience said they used it in this way. One participant drew the analogy that using the multisource feedback instrument for pay in the hands of an unprepared workforce is tantamount to using a "90 millimeter cannon at three feet." That is, if people aren't ready to give and receive feedback from anyone other than their manager, and if the pay determination process uses multisource feedback too soon, the results can be onerous.

On the other hand, some organizations dedicate considerable resources, time, and energy to developing a performance measurement and management approach based on some or all of the principles of business-aligned goals and multisource feedback. It's common for them subsequently to want to migrate at least eventually to using all the tools to help determine pay. Thus, finding some way to use multisource feedback in the total process calls for consideration and evaluation. We show you an example in Chapter 5 (on base pay) and explain how to use it in team variable pay in Chapter 10.

Getting Managers to Address Feedback

As we describe it, the development and performance feedback process is a continuing dialogue between managers and individuals, and managers must be willing and able to give feedback—and take some in return. This means managers, coaches, and team leaders need preparation and training in the feedback and coaching process. Feedback requires understanding, acceptance, commitment, and sponsorship. Although acceptance of the feedback process by the workforce is essential, acceptance and commitment by managers is critical. Because effective feedback is a continuous process and does not just occur once or twice a year, the role of the manager is becoming that of coach, trainer, facilitator, and even role model.

Getting managers to coach and give feedback varies in difficulty. Litton Industries, a Fortune 500 company in electronics, IT, and shipbuilding, developed a "charter" that included defining the role of the manager as coach:

- Have executive management champion the performance management process and lead by example.

- Encourage every individual to participate actively in the performance management process to make it part of the culture.
- Make sure managers coach, counsel, train, facilitate, and plan the performance management process.
- Emphasize the ongoing process of performance planning, feedback, coaching, and evaluating, *not* the annual performance review event.
- Educate managers and hold them accountable for all aspects of the performance management process, including giving accurate, balanced, specific, and factual review of an individual's performance, skills, and competencies.
- Educate people on the performance management process and hold them accountable for achieving goals, enhancing skills and competencies, and understanding how their role contributes to achieving business objectives.

In many companies the ability and willingness to give meaningful feedback has become a hurdle that people must cross before becoming managers. Coaching performance is an acquired skill. For some managers, a description of an effective process for coaching may be helpful. Once a manager has internalized one way of doing the important performance management process, changes of style and approach can improve the effectiveness of feedback. Exhibit 4.3 shows one possible process to consider at the beginning.

The managers who are most effective at coaching take on an owner/coach role such that they provide candid information about the business and how this is important to the workforce. Effective coaches don't wait for performance problems, or the chance to recognize and celebrate, to coach. They do it all the time.

CONCLUSIONS

Our formula for successful measurement and management of performance is based on business-aligned goals and feedback on development and performance. These ingredients translate company goals to goals, skills, and competencies that are relevant and meaningful to people and amount to a continuous coaching process that enhances goal achievement and development. No workforce can continuously improve its value to the company and contribute to business success

Exhibit 4.3. The Coaching Process.

- Communicate the company's and your unit's business-aligned goals to ensure that people understand how the unit adds value to the business. Discuss how your goals and the individual's goals need to link.
- Agree on results, skill, and competency expectations and define them in terms you and the individual understand. Agree on how continuous feedback and discussion will occur. Make communications comfortable and easy. Make it more than just scheduling meetings based on a calendar.
- Help prepare a development plan for the individual with goals, milestones, and expected results. The individual doesn't need to complete an elaborate form but documents briefly a description of performance, skill, and competency before and after development, resources needed, and a way to track and communicate about change.
- Make sure goals and messages are in key business-aligned goal areas. For example, if the goal categories are financial, customer, people, operational, and future-focused, determine if there is something meaningful for the individual in each area. Interpret everything in the context of the individual.
- Discuss how you and the individual plan to get past problems and roadblocks when they occur. Engage in a constructive problem-solving process, remove barriers, and get a positive focus on solutions, not on the negative. Focus on process improvement rather than on who is to blame or on making excuses about not achieving the performance.
- Define teamwork and collaboration so work with others gets done. Have a plan to show the individual how to combine skills and competencies with others to achieve shared goals.
- Agree on what to do about unreachable goals and what to do if priorities change midstream. Determine what resources and support are needed and will be provided.
- Customize the continuous feedback process to address the individual's needs. Will feedback be formal, informal, verbal, or written? Do you need regular meetings? How do you avoid the "just another meeting" syndrome? How do you make feedback part of the everyday work process? Who will be asked to give feedback, how will feedback be gathered, and how will this information be used?
- Concentrate on coaching, not the rating or scoring of performance if scoring is part of the company's process. Minimize discussing the "score" and focus on the development process and the value the individual is adding to the company. Be sincere, honest, respectful, and timely in giving feedback.

without understanding goals and objectives and what the members of the workforce can do about them.

But goals can't be so rigid and detailed that they inhibit breakthroughs that take the business to a new level. Enterprises are made successful not just by people doing the expected. Performance measurement and management and rewards must make it attractive for individuals and teams to create breakthroughs that test the existing business model and concept.

Measuring and managing performance is part and parcel of the reward process. The practical aspect of this is the need to review the total pay process together with how performance is measured and managed. Both give powerful messages and must align well and consistently.

In addition, it's increasingly important to hold managers accountable for coaching, workforce development, and performance measurement and management since people are a company's sustainable differential advantage. If managers are effective in this competency, they're in a better position to manage pay effectively.

PART II

Pay Tools: Accelerating Achievement of Business Goals

The Six Reward Principles

1. Create a positive and natural reward experience.
2. Align rewards with business goals to create a win-win partnership.
3. Extend people's line of sight.
4. Integrate rewards.
5. Reward individual ongoing value with base pay.
6. Reward results with variable pay.

The Four Components of Total Rewards

- Individual growth
- Compelling future
- Total pay
- Positive workplace

CHAPTER 5

Rewarding Individual Ongoing Value

Base Pay

Andy Grove, chairman of Intel, said, "Ask yourself this question: 'Will my skills matter in five years?'"[1]

Positioning base pay to reflect an individual's ongoing value is the most honest answer to this question, in terms of pay. Base pay is the largest element of total pay for most of the workforce; therefore, a company has a right to maximize value from base pay. People also have the right to expect base pay to represent accurately how they add value to their company. Base pay can and must become more business-friendly and effective; we propose that recognizing individual ongoing value is how your company can make this happen. We suggested this in Principle 5 in Chapter 1 and in Chapter 3, on total pay.

Because base pay is such an important element of total pay, *Pay People Right!* devotes two chapters to the subject:

1. *Individual base pay.* This chapter is about determining an individual's base pay—how people get increases. It's our "how to get and give a raise" chapter and suggests possible options.

2. *Base pay structure.* The next chapter is about determining the appropriate base pay framework for jobs, roles, and competencies or skills—the infrastructure for setting an individual's base pay.

REWARDING INDIVIDUAL ONGOING VALUE

Principle 5 defines individual ongoing value, which determines base pay, as consisting of three dimensions (also shown in Figure 5.1):

1. Paying for the skills and competencies that the company needs and the individual uses to generate results. These are the skills and competencies that the individual is willing to perform, and performs acceptably, and that generate successful business outcomes.
2. Paying for the individual's consistent sustained performance over time, whether individual results or contributions to team results. This means looking at trends in an individual's performance, not just the most recent year's performance. It may address how well the individual meets business-aligned goals or how well the individual advances the business.
3. Paying for the individual's value relative to the labor market. Being competitive relative to the labor market starts with total rewards and works its way down to making total pay and total cash, and then finally base pay, competitive. Individuals may contribute the same value as their closest match in the labor market (or more, or less).

Base Pay and Ongoing Value

In determining base pay, ongoing value reflects worth not at one point in time but overall, continuing, or sustained value; it doesn't reflect spikes in performance but addresses consistent performance trends. In contrast, variable pay rewards spikes in performance. Some companies emphasize one dimension of ongoing value over the other two. Others use different combinations within their own company.

Consistent with Principle 4 (integrating rewards), enterprises should emphasize an integrated total pay approach. This means base

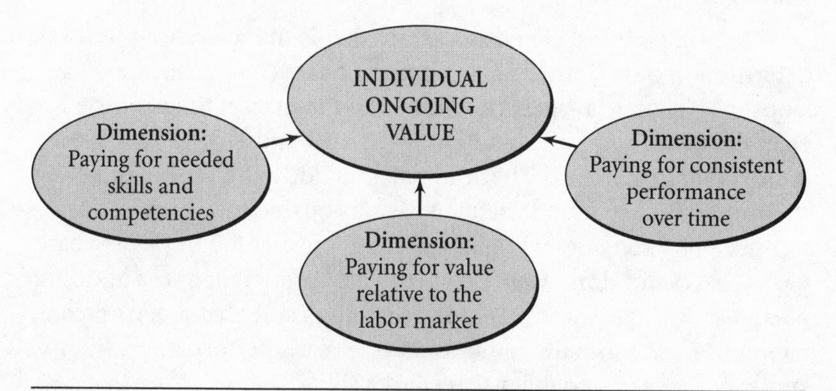

Figure 5.1. Determining Base Pay: Rewarding Individual Ongoing Value.

pay acknowledges an individual's ongoing value and represents the more stable total pay element. Variable pay in the form of lump-sum payments, cash or equity variable pay, and cash recognition is the primary reward for current performance. This allows giving meaningful awards for high performance during a specific time period but doesn't make awards for one performance period continue unchecked throughout the individual's career.

Base Pay Fundamentals

You may be asking, "Does this mean that base pay is a potential business accelerator? How can that ever be?" Our answer is that it can. However, it requires not only thinking outside of the box but also getting out of the box and doing something different about base pay. Where speed and agility come into play, managers can arm themselves with the business case for changing rewards and the dimensions that base pay should emphasize. Here's what it takes:

- *Manager accountability.* Managers are responsible for exercising sound business judgment in managing base pay and applying all three dimensions. They're allocated a specific budget to distribute among the people reporting to them. They're accountable for decisions about distributing the base pay budget to acknowledge the individual's ongoing value to the organization. They must do what's right for the business and take a business perspective in managing this budget effectively.

• *External market.* The external market is the reference point for determining base pay. It's a guidepost to start, not a hard and fast stop-or-go sign. Managers can vary from the market to acknowledge an individual's key skills and competencies and level of consistent performance over time. They can pay individuals at, above, or below the competitive market for any of various business reasons.

• *Emphasis on ongoing value.* Because most companies view base pay as fixed and don't want "pay cuts" to be a regular way of doing business, base pay must reflect the ongoing value that a person contributes to the company rather than one year's performance. Lump-sum payments or variable pay reward a single year's performance.

• *Only one part.* Base pay is one part of an integrated total pay approach that, along with variable pay, rewards total value-added. Managers should consider other elements of total pay to supplement and magnify the communications message of base pay.

Ongoing Value for Both Job-Based and Person-Based Pay

Individual ongoing value works well for both job-based pay and person-based (skill-based or competency-based) pay. Job-based pay typically entails numerous, very specific, narrowly defined jobs. Jobs have distinct boundaries, carefully prescribed and described activities, and levels often set primarily according to years of experience. People-based pay involves fewer, broad, flexible, and fluid roles, with levels (if any) based primarily on demonstrated skills and competencies or consistent value-added.

In today's business environment—one defined by global competition, emphasis on speed, and increasing customer expectations—it's difficult to maintain a rigid job-based approach because the lack of flexibility makes it difficult to respond to change. However, job-based pay can work if jobs are more broadly defined, boundaries are loosened, and levels are based on value-added, not just years of experience. Years of experience alone are not relevant beyond a learning period. That is, Person A has 10 years of uniform experience and Person B has 10 years of increasingly responsible or broader experience; each one brings different value to the company.

People-based pay works best in changing environments where workforce flexibility is critical. But some people-based solutions that elaborately define skills and competencies for each role can become overly complex and stall the organization in the process. For example, a large manufacturing facility created such a byzantine skill model for its production workers that the model generated a blizzard of paper and bureaucracy. Although computerized, it remained too intricate and cumbersome to maintain. A combination of job-based and people-based pay can also be complex if each job has specific competency levels identified and described.

As companies become more streamlined and business-focused, competency pay approaches that have as much structure and complexity as the old point-factor systems may not make sense. Less structured approaches are needed. This means that paying the person must be simplified from its most common form, and job-based pay must become more agile than is often the case.

EMPHASIZING INTEGRATION OF ALL ELEMENTS OF TOTAL PAY

The business situation, the business strategy, human resource strategy, and the business case for changing rewards anchor the use of the three ongoing value dimensions. This section and the three that follow offer examples of different ways of addressing base pay. This section describes companies integrating the three ongoing value dimensions of base pay with other total pay elements and allowing management flexibility and accountability to address base pay. In the following three sections, we discuss how to emphasize one of the three dimensions for base pay more than the other two. Exhibit 5.1 summarizes these four approaches.

Integrating Total Pay

Some companies integrate total pay elements to reward people: base pay, short-term variable pay, long-term variable pay, and recognition. Rather than addressing the elements in isolation, they create a total pay picture that reflects the individual's value added to the organization. They also hold managers accountable for effectively managing and distributing the base pay budget and other pay funding. The result is an effective performance management process (including the ongoing feedback that we discussed in the last chapter) as well as effective communication of the reasons for pay decisions to facilitate workforce understanding.[2]

Exhibit 5.1. Emphasizing the Dimensions of Individual Ongoing Value.

Characteristic	Integrating All Three Dimensions	Skills and Competencies	Consistent Performance over Time	Value Relative to Labor Market
Emphasis	Balance all three dimensions as well as other total pay elements	Reward needed skills and competencies acquired, kept up-to-date, and used to generate results	Reward performance trend, sustained track record, overall value added over time	Keep pay competitive with labor market
Business case	Integrate total pay; use total pay dollars effectively; focus on competitiveness of total pay, not base pay alone	Broaden roles, increase flexibility, and respond to changing technologies	Partner with other total pay elements to acknowledge performance; focus on consistent high performance over time	Retain talent when less supply and more demand in labor market; let variable pay reward results; define base pay competitiveness in total pay context
Conditions	Leaders are effective in making reward decisions and communicating the reasoning	Staying up-to-date with technical expertise; multiskilling; value from in-depth technical knowledge	More complex or less defined roles where differences in performance can lead to significantly different value	Large variable pay in total cash mix; well-defined roles or jobs; large labor costs relative to total cost
Pay approach	Total value pay	Skill pay; competency pay	Pay for sustained performance	Market rates

Total Pay at a Pharmaceutical Company

A pharmaceutical company provides an example of this integration. Performance management centers around frequent coaching and feedback discussions and on development without ratings or performance labels. The purpose is to encourage open and honest exchanges of information. Individual objectives translated from company strategies and objectives are monitored periodically and revised as needed when priorities change. Competencies such as customer focus, teamwork, and leadership communicate the behaviors that the company believes lead to success.

The head of each major business unit uses all the pay elements to communicate desired messages. Managers have three pay pools from which to reward people: base pay increases, individual variable pay with funding based on company financial performance, and stock options. For each pay element, there's wide differentiation in earnings opportunities at each role level. People who have had top performance during the past year may earn an average base pay increase, an above-average variable pay award, and an above-average stock option award. People whose base pay is below market and whose performance trend shows that they're continuing to add value but are not top performers may earn an above-average base pay increase to get them closer to market, a below-average variable pay award, and very few, if any, stock options. Key talent whose retention is critical and whose position relative to the labor market is appropriate may earn an average base pay increase, an average bonus award, and a significant stock option award. For this company, a combination of pay elements rewards individual ongoing value as well as recent performance.

Total Pay at IBM

As a result of its transformation, IBM is another company that has moved to integration of total pay and greater management accountability. The methodology for base pay increases switched from a grid of performance appraisal scores and ranges of compa-ratios (the percentage that current base pay is of the salary range midpoint) to giving managers a budget and a spreadsheet tool to use as they deem appropriate. Managers' alternative methodologies vary from ranking people on a variety of factors (both critical skills and results) to providing an explanatory comment of one or more sentences for each individual about the rationale for distributing the base pay increase budget. Managers receive coaching that basically requires differentiating the pay of stars from that of acceptable performers in order to retain the stars. The competitive labor market also plays a strong role because people's base pay must be within the market pay range for their position, within their band.

IBM managers are accountable for making sound individual pay decisions for the people reporting to them. The spreadsheet tool includes other pay elements. Managers integrate base pay decisions with decisions about other pay elements to create a picture of total pay. Individual performance determines the distribution of variable pay funded in proportion to overall company and business-unit performance. IBM built this variable pay opportunity partly from either reduced budgets for base pay increases or pay cuts to create stakeholdership. Top contributors in essential skill areas whom IBM wants to retain also receive stock options in the expectation of future contributions, not in recognition for past achievements.

This example shows how base pay doesn't have to take all the weight of rewarding individual performance. The program's acceptance shows that managers can have flexibility while being accountable for making sound pay decisions that support business needs and give appropriate rewards to people.[3]

Total Value Approach at AlliedSignal Aerospace

AlliedSignal Aerospace (now merged into Honeywell International) has an integrated approach to total pay that it calls the total value approach. Its base pay solution, called comprehensive pay decisions, requires managers to think beyond just recent performance. The factors used in the annual salary planning decision include past performance, pay compared to market, pay compared to others with similar jobs and skills, and potential for future contribution. This last item relates to individuals having a unique background or skill set that can influence future performance.

Managers use an automated pay-planning tool that includes market data to make their decisions. Although it's harder to get good market matches with a person-based design, market data are part of the information used to make the pay decision. Because of the emphasis on learning to improve people's skills and enhance their futures, the company encourages base pay increases or lump sums for lateral moves.[4]

E-pay

As organizations take an integrated approach to total pay, e-pay assists them. Managers improve their decision making about pay by using one spreadsheet that lists all the pay elements (base pay, variable pay, stock options, and recognition) of all the individuals reporting to that manager. This provides an integrated perspective on rewards, rather than each element in isolation, and facilitates addressing the overall value of the individual to the company. With this decision-making tool, managers can manage pay dollars effectively and test scenarios for determining base pay increases, variable pay awards, and stock option grants. The tool also totals each manager's decisions at the next higher level for reviewing and understanding the allocation of pay dollars and stock options; it also continues the roll-up to the top of the organization. E-pay doesn't replace oral communication between a manager and an individual, but it facilitates communications about pay plan features and speeds handling of administrative details.

EMPHASIZING THE DIMENSION OF SKILLS AND COMPETENCIES

A company emphasizes the skill and competency dimension of ongoing value if it believes people need to grow to continue to add value to the business over time. This is often the case in changing and dynamic industries where new technologies emerge frequently and staying state-of-the-art is important. A learning organization also emphasizes skills and competencies if it concentrates on flexibility, agility, and people's ability to move from one role to another.[5]

Skills and competencies may also drive individual ongoing value when the organization truly views people as constituting its differential advantage. In a company where, for example, customer focus provides the differential advantage relative to competitors, the competency of customer focus may drive an individual's ongoing value. Also, an enterprise made up of multiskilled workers and few roles may stress skills and competencies, as do businesses facing a scarce-talent situation.

Relationship of Skills and Competencies to Pay

Organizations that emphasize the skill-and-competency dimension vary in how they relate skills and competencies to pay:

- Some reward results only, use skills and competencies just for development, and don't link them to pay. They consider development as the precursor to results, and because results reflect skills and competencies they don't have to pay for these attributes directly.

- Some reward the outcomes of a learning or development plan that results in improved performance. This usually teams with variable pay, which rewards results.
- Some reward competencies based on an individual's ratings of competency along a scale. Behaviorally anchored rating scales (BARS) focus on observable behaviors. This often represents one side of a two-sided matrix of competency and performance.
- Some reward certification on skill or competency blocks, where each block represents a closely related set of knowledge, skills, or behaviors. This pay-per-skill approach is typically used for nonexempt workers in manufacturing or service organizations.
- Some reward achievement of skill progression (from entry to fully skilled to expert), where each level bundles a variety of skills. This is often called skill-based pay in manufacturing environments, or career ladders in professional or service environments.

Both Competencies and Results

Paying the person rather than the job is the core of paying for skills and competencies. But it's not enough to have the competency; people must also direct capabilities to get desired results. This is the foundation of individual ongoing value, using all three dimensions in some combination. With skill pay, for example, certification and pay at a skill level require some demonstration of efficient or effective performance. With competency pay, linking the competency growth to how it adds value to the business is critical. The reason competency pay alone is struggling is that it doesn't reflect an overall picture of individual ongoing value on its own; it's running into hard times because of the need to achieve results. Competency pay alone isn't encompassing enough to fit the business case for changing rewards.

As an example of the problem of paying for acquiring skills without paying for the outcomes, teachers take additional courses and earn additional degrees to receive additional pay. They aren't required to show how this learning process results in improved student educational outcomes. In this case, the performance dimension is missing. This isn't paying for individual ongoing value. This is paying for taking college courses that may or may not improve the individual's performance.

Development Focus: One Monsanto Business

Consider again the business that supported the evolving rewards strategy at Monsanto. It offered variable pay for business results and base pay for competitive ongoing value as a result of competency growth that added demonstrable value to the business. The design team debated whether to include individual goals in the base pay process but found that their team-based environment—with its many temporary cross-functional project teams; broad, flexible roles; and emphasis on speed—was too dynamic for continuing the individual goal-setting process for base pay adjustments. These concepts proved influential for Monsanto's overall reward design. Chapter 2 described the business case for changing rewards for this business.

COMPETENCIES AND DEVELOPMENT PLAN. Competitiveness, competencies, and development are the drivers of the base pay solution. The desire then was to communicate and reinforce the change in culture and to gain competitive advantage by having people grow and develop to increase their value to the business. The business encouraged everyone to prepare a development plan that charted a course for growth in a few key competency areas for a specific performance period. Individuals focused on specific competencies that were relevant to their role. This afforded the business a sophisticated competency model because it didn't require a person to grow in all competencies in every performance period. Development plans remain an important reward ingredient at Monsanto.

People were responsible for preparing their development plan with support from their manager. Coaches were also available for support throughout the process. The development plan described the current and desired situations, thus creating a before-and-(expected-)after description of the journey. Objective terms described the change: what work products and services would look like, what behavior would be like, and how performance would change as a result of the development so that feedback could be direct and clear. People were not "trained" and "developed"; they executed their own development plan. This included everyone in the business, from executives, managers, and professionals to technical, support, and nonexempt people.

PAY. To generate all increases or lump-sum awards from this process, the business used the percentage from the annual Monsanto budget for base pay increases. Completion of the development plan and competency development that resulted in role expansion or facilitated contribution to business results influenced the actual pay adjustments granted in the business. This later evolved into use of development plans for performance management purposes, base pay for competitive market practice and role changes, and variable pay for rewarding contribution to the business and individual development. This situation continues to evolve at Monsanto.

The developmental message is that Monsanto people are in charge of their growth, they should pursue more project roles that will broaden their skill base and lessen their functional orientation, and they must continue to become more valuable to the organization.

Pay-Per-Competency or Competency Blocks: PacifiCorp

PacifiCorp is a Fortune 500 global electric and gas utility that uses a combination of competency pay and variable pay to communicate values and directions. The examples we've chosen are two business centers, or customer call centers, reorganized around customer teams. One center is unionized; the other is nonunion. The competencies used as the communications vehicle include five application competencies (billing, customer service requests, credit and collections, energy efficiency, and team skills and service management) and three core competencies (business knowledge, technical or computer skill, and communication skills). Specifically defined for the call center workforce, these competencies extend the business strategy to the people the company believes are closest to executing the key competencies with the customer.

Centers comprise multiple eight-member teams with coaches who are participants in the pay system. The objectives are to move closer to self-management at the team level, emphasize career enhancement, and promote workforce flexibility so people can handle any customer question. Each competency has three blocks representing increasing levels of competency, so there are a number of breadth and depth competency blocks. The requirement is for the individual to move from the lowest, "contributor," level to the middle level, "pro," in all competency areas. The highest level, "champion," is optional and denotes a role model, trainer, procedure enhancer, and problem solver. Written material, a panel of experts, monitoring, and team members are all ways to assess or certify an individual on a competency. Each person has two opportunities to pass the assessment for a specific block.

Base pay starts at an entry rate. Each application competency block has an hourly monetary value; the three core competencies function together as a gate to pass through before earning pay for any block on that competency level. To earn the competency pay and the team variable pay, individuals must meet minimum performance expectations when assessed periodically. The objectives of team variable pay are to recognize teams for truly delighting customers, to motivate quality service and efficiencies, and to promote teamwork.

This example emphasizes the competency dimension of individual ongoing value, although it also addresses the labor market when setting the entry rate and total cash opportunity, which in turn set block values. One of the interesting features of this plan is the requirement that people successfully complete the middle, or pro, level on all competencies and that they certify on competency blocks within specified time periods. This requirement for people to go beyond the basics—and do it quickly—is important to becoming a high-performance organization within a reasonable period of time, but it also puts stress on the training program. Any competency pay approach involves an investment in training and development, but this solution tests the company's ability to provide timely training. Although the approach has the feature of blocks that make it look like skill pay, and it has the features described in the paragraph below on skill pay, PacifiCorp calls it competency pay because of the behavioral competencies.

Skill Pay

Skill pay involves paying only for the skills a person consistently demonstrates and uses to get results, not paying for the job or time or tenure. Rather than paying for any expectation that people have the capability to perform, as is the case with job-based pay, this approach pays after skills are proven with acceptable performance. Pay adjustments follow skill acquisition, demonstration, and application. Mastery is assessed or certified before paying for the skill. Company need, ability to perform, and willingness to perform are minimum requirements for paying for the skill.

RESEARCH ON SKILL PAY. Research on skill pay shows a track record of success when skill pay has the objective of improving workforce development and true empowerment, is consistent with other initiatives and management systems that are under way, has a feedback process that's perceived as fair and focuses on actual improvement, and offers sufficient training. Plans were terminated when they grew too complex and created unaddressable administrative challenges.[6] This has been our direct experience as well. In other cases, companies terminating skill pay believed it had become too expensive or that the work had changed such that skill pay was no longer workable.

SIMPLE AND FLEXIBLE SKILL PAY. This suggests that simple design and some flexibility and breadth in defining skill blocks or levels might work best. For example, certifying on a block means successful performance of the part of the process represented by the skill block regardless of changes in technology. Changing technology doesn't mean a new skill block. Blocks must be broad enough so that adding a new skill element doesn't necessarily argue for adding another block or increasing the value of the block. Before embarking on skill pay, a company must realize that it typically pays more per person in this approach, so it needs to design and evaluate the solution to ensure it derives value by improving efficiency or reducing the size of the workforce. When the objective of skill pay includes becoming a self-managing organization, the workforce reduction can come from reducing the number of supervisors and flattening the organization.

EMPHASIZING THE DIMENSION OF CONSISTENT PERFORMANCE OVER TIME

Emphasizing the consistent-performance dimension focuses on what results are accomplished more than how results are accomplished. A business may be or want to become a high-performance organization. Consistent performance over time reflects the individual's performance trend.

Assessing a Sustained Track Record

By answering certain questions, managers can account for this dimension in determining individual ongoing value:

- If people have individual business-aligned goals, do their goals meet the SMART criteria? Are their goals responsive to changes in the business situation? Do they consistently achieve more than one year's round of business-aligned goals?

- If the business-aligned goals stop at the team level, what's the individual's track record of contributing to the team's success over more than one year? Are the goals producing increasing value each year?
- Are individuals maintaining performance consistently at a level that meets requirements, standards, expectations, or goals on a sustained basis? Are they significantly exceeding requirements, standards, expectations, or goals consistently over an extended period of time? Are they failing to meet expectations because they're in an active state of learning or because they're not interested in or capable of meeting expectations?
- Are individuals consistently adding value to the business? Are they constantly enhancing the business?
- Is the individual's performance trend improving, staying the same, or declining (in the last year or two)? What about over more than the last two years?

It's difficult to determine consistent performance over time for new people because they haven't been with the company long enough to establish a track record and demonstrate performance trends. However, the available information can reveal if the individual's performance during the first year is trending up or down relative to what was anticipated when setting the individual's base pay at hire.

Variable Pay for Current Year's Performance

You're probably wondering about performance for the current year. Ongoing value takes it into account but really maintains a broader performance perspective. Lump-sum payments, individual variable pay awards, or recognition directly and effectively reward performance for the past year (particularly a spike in performance). Lump-sum payments, typically associated with the base pay budget, reward performance over an annual performance period. In contrast, the variable pay approaches we discuss in Chapter 7 fund separately from the base pay budget, may reward individual performance alone or performance of a combination of organizational levels, and may have performance periods other than annual. Individual variable pay also differs from lump-sum payments because the former typically involves setting prospective goals and relating variable pay opportunity clearly and directly to each of these goals. In contrast, managers frequently determine the size of lump-sum payments retrospectively at the end of the performance period. Compared to lump-sum payments, recognition is typically immediate and rewards a single contribution.

Communicating the Message of Change

Sometimes it's difficult to change people's mind-set from "merit" increases (which reward most recent performance with little or no consideration of their current base pay level) to base pay reflecting an individual's ongoing value. A large insurance company that wanted to communicate this change and didn't have lump-sum payments as an alternative implemented a base pay increase guideline with three performance levels, having the middle performance level ("consistently meets requirements") start at zero. This zero got the attention of the workforce and signaled the change to an individual's ongoing value determining base pay. Individuals who meet performance requirements don't receive an increase if they're already competitively paid for their contributions. Individuals who are paid high for the market value of their job or role are expected to perform well to earn that pay level. The performance level of "consistently and significantly exceeds requirements" entails base pay increases that start with an above-average increase because the company wanted to drive and reward high performance. This meant communicating competitive practice and what's needed for people to move from where they are to where they want to be.

An alternative way to communicate this message even more strongly might be to use lump-sum payments. People in the top performance category would receive significant lump-sum payments and anywhere from modest to significant base pay increases, depending on individual ongoing value.

Lump-Sum Payments

Lump-sum payments—rewards for current performance—are useful either when there's no other variable pay for the workforce or when people are eligible for variable pay that rewards individuals as a member of a group (for example, a cash profit-sharing plan). Lump-sum payments typically reward the current top performers and the contributors whose ongoing value indicates a small base pay increase or none. Awards for these contributors acknowledge their accomplishments; but since their base pay is high or acceptable for their ongoing value, base pay needs minimal change.

Funding for lump-sum payments may come from dollars in addition to the budget for base pay increases, or from part of that budget itself. Funding frequently equals 1–2 percent of the base pay budget. If it's 1 percent, for example, it can produce awards equal to 5 percent of base pay to about 20 percent of the population, or alternatively 10 percent of base pay to about 10 percent of the population. However, the actual size of awards usually varies according to individuals' contributions. Since lump-sum payments don't fold into base pay, the company must be sensitive to workforce concerns as the mix of the budget for increases in base pay changes from 100 percent fixed pay, if funding for lump-sum payments is not added on but instead comes from redistributing the current budget for base pay increases. Please refer back to Chapter 3 for this discussion.

OOCL (USA), discussed in Chapter 3, is an example of a company that uses lump-sum payments for an extra punch to the rewards for top-performing individuals. It allocates part of the merit budget to provide lump-sum payments to high-performing individuals. The pharmaceutical company described earlier in this chapter and IBM, as two other examples, distribute variable pay awards from a group variable pay plan based on individual contributions, to give an extra reward for current performance.

EMPHASIZING THE DIMENSION OF VALUE RELATIVE TO THE LABOR MARKET

We're unaware of any company that doesn't consider the labor market as the foundation for total pay, total cash, and/or base pay. In the next chapter, we discuss how to determine the market value of jobs as well as the increasing difficulty of assessing market value as roles broaden.

The Labor Market and Market Rates

Scarce talent situations accentuate the labor market component of individual ongoing value. Competitiveness must be maintained and timely to retain talent. The other two dimensions are also considered because the company may not be able to retain everyone with scarce talent and must determine who it is critical to retain.

An enterprise emphasizes the market heavily when using market rates or single rates for jobs or roles. There may be a learning or training rate, and a full contributor rate, or there may be very narrow ranges around the market rate to provide some minor variation in pay based on individual ongoing value. The company may use a go, no-go gate of individual performance to determine if a person receives a base pay increase. It may use lump-sum payments, variable pay, or cash recognition to reward outstanding individual contributions or results.

When to Use Market Rates

Market rates apply in four situations.

MEANINGFUL VARIABLE PAY. In the first, they're useful when variable pay is a large or meaningful component of total cash. Telesales representatives may have a single rate of base pay, with variable pay rewarding sales results and, perhaps, achievement of objectives related to sales skills and competencies. Executives may have market rates, with variable pay as the performance component. Market rates are broadly used across an organization when the enterprise wants base pay to serve the role that the words *base pay* imply: the *base* on which other total pay elements operate. This moves the focus away from managers and people negotiating on the fixed element of pay and onto the variable element of pay, where decisions do not have an impact throughout an individual's career. This change also helps facilitate attention to results and outcomes.

WELL-DEFINED JOBS. The second situation for market rates is when the job is well defined and variations in capability do not drive meaningfully different results. Think of the airport security guard who screens and checks your carry-on baggage for weapons and bombs. The job is well defined, the range of acceptable performance is narrow, and added skills and competencies don't meaningfully increase performance.

LARGE LABOR COSTS. In the third situation, a company needs to manage pay closely because labor costs are a large portion of expenses and the business may have low margins. For jobs with a large number of incumbents, the business doesn't want to be too far off the labor market. If they pay too low, they can't hire; if too high, they can't afford the cost. Registered nurses or physical therapists whose jobs are clearly defined according to licensing boards and who can easily work at another facility on their days off are examples of why organizations cannot vary too far from the standard of the labor market.

PAY NEAR MINIMUM WAGE. The fourth situation involves people paid near the minimum wage when the labor market is tight for this level of worker. Monitoring the nearby labor market closely can prevent losing people who might leave for a few additional cents per hour, particularly if there's no differential advantage on the other total pay elements or other total reward components.

Requirement to Maintain Skills

The important issue in using the labor market as the key dimension for base pay is requiring that individuals who have skills and competencies that are obsolete or need refreshment continue to learn what the company needs in order to justify keeping their base pay competitive. Both managers and workforce members work together to determine what skills people need to keep up-to-date and ensure they remain current. Managers must be active participants in this process because they're closest to what is needed to make their organization a success.

PROBLEM WITH BASE PAY INCREASES FOR CURRENT PERFORMANCE

Although variable pay can increase or decrease from one performance period to the next, this has rarely been a feature of base pay. Base pay increases that are predicated only on current performance end up paying an entire career for one performance period of results.

Detailing the Current Performance Problem

The difficulties with using base pay for current performance results rather than ongoing value are that:

- It takes a myopic view of performance in a pay element that should be the least myopic because it's fixed and often the largest component of pay.

• It creates a situation of overpayment for past performance results. It may also discourage improvement in individual performance results; if base pay increases are the only tool to reward current performance and the company is unwilling to increase base pay further when people are paid more than they're worth, additional performance or performance improvement may be discouraged.

• It may create overvaluing in the external market if people's overall value relative to the labor market for their role is not considered. A business can't afford to have pay dollars distributed ineffectively because of poor use of resources (both base pay dollars and the accompanying benefit costs that leverage off base pay) and workforce morale (to the extent that people are generally aware of this unfair allocation).

• It may discourage growth in skill and competency. The dimensions of labor market and skills and competencies combined with consistent performance over time determine the worth of an individual in the market. When the company considers only current performance, not performance trends, it doesn't encourage the workforce to continue to acquire and apply skills and competencies that the company needs (or will need in the future).

• It may create a vulnerable workforce in times of challenge. Ultimately, paying people more than their overall value has negative consequences because it renders them vulnerable in a downsizing or restructuring. It also makes them reluctant to seek something new on their own initiative because of inability to duplicate their current pay.

Lump-sum payments, variable pay, and cash recognition permit meaningful rewards for current performance. A broader perspective than just current performance is needed, though, for such an important element as base pay.

People Paid High Relative to Their Ongoing Value

People may have high base pay relative to their ongoing value to the company for a variety of reasons. In a job-based world, they may be "overpaid" because their job has been restructured and their accountabilities reduced. In this case, base pay is typically frozen until the range or market reference zone catches up with the individual's base pay.

Another possible reason is that in a person-based world or job-based world, the individual may not have kept up with new technology or may use a technology that's no longer valued as highly in the labor market as it was before. In these cases, the manager needs to have an honest discussion about what it would take for the person to be worth the value of their base pay. Managers may work with individuals to prepare a development plan to get them to the point of being worth at least the value of their base pay, or set goals whereby individual achievement would deliver the value needed by the organization.

PROCESS FOR BASE PAY MANAGEMENT

Here's the process for effective total pay integration and base pay management:

1. The company or business unit determines what dimension or dimensions it wants to emphasize in base pay, taking into account the messages that variable pay and recognition communicate. This may vary by type of job or workforce group.
2. The company or business unit determines a base pay budget based on competitive labor market movement, organizational performance, and affordability. As it allocates the base pay budget, it takes into account any differences in labor market movement as a result of jobs or roles being in scarce supply and high demand.
3. Managers use the budget they receive to grant base pay increases and/or lump-sum payments according to the base pay dimension or dimensions that the company has emphasized for the workforce group. Managers consider the interrelationships among the other pay elements to integrate total pay. They use the performance management process and any available information on the labor market to make a decision using good business judgment. They use a spreadsheet having all the total pay elements, to facilitate making sound decisions. They look at the ongoing value of all the individuals reporting to them to determine where ongoing value and base pay are most out of line, and then make corrections.
4. Managers communicate their decisions to individuals such that people understand the reason for the decision and how they can improve their value to the organization in the future.

As with other management skills, managers need training and good role models to help them hone their skills in managing performance and pay. In this era of growth and development, managers should subject these skills to continuous improvement, as they would any competency or business process.

Detailed Guidelines or Manager Flexibility

Organizations and people vary widely in their need for structure and consistency in base pay management. We prefer to have managers be responsible, enjoy latitude, document their decisions, and be held accountable for their decisions; but many companies need to have control (real or perceived) of the process. How much latitude also depends on the manager's competency in performing this important responsibility and the worker's level of trust in the manager's ability to make fair judgments. Union workers prefer the clearly delineated criteria typically found in skill pay approaches or market rates. Professional workforce members are generally comfortable with multidimensional judgments.

Consistency

Consistency is also an issue. Unless the company specifies another strategy for a group of workers based on the business case, the basic strategy about what dimensions to emphasize in base pay should be consistent among managers in the same business unit. The degree of consistency in application across managers depends on the company. Managing to a budget reduces some of the concerns about consistency and equity. But where people tend to be internally focused, more consistency is required because otherwise they'll think the grass is greener on the other side of the fence. Regardless of consistency among managers, each manager should be consistent in their own methodology applied to the base pay of their direct reports.

Ratings and Scoring

Some businesses have eliminated performance ratings or simplified the rating to one of pass-fail. Ratings tend to address current performance, not overall value to the company, and they tend to create labels that lessen meaningful discussion. Others, as in the earlier examples of AlliedSignal and IBM, provide principles rather than detailed guidelines or rules for managing base pay and hold managers accountable for effective pay management. This process moves responsibility for managing pay to those who know the business and situation the best: the managers.

Dollars or Percentages

The paradigm for base pay is shifting from a focus on rewards for current performance to ongoing value extended to the company. To be consistent, a business is better served if managers discuss base pay adjustments with individuals by concentrating on the new base pay level and the dollar increase, not the percentage increase. Percentages reinforce thinking about the increase relative to current base pay. The new base pay level emphasizes the individual's ongoing value to the company.

Secondly, communicating the pay change in terms of the dollar increase rather than the percentage highlights absolute rather than relative value. For example, with someone currently earning $38,700, you could talk in terms of the person earning $40,000 because that's the individual's ongoing value to the company and say that this results in a pay increase of $1,300 (rather than saying the increase is 3.4 percent). People who have relatively high base pay for their ongoing value become distracted by the small percentage increase they may receive. They often ignore the fact that it brings more absolute dollars than a person in the same role who has lower base pay and receives the same percentage or an even larger percentage increase. The absence of variable pay exacerbates this percentage problem since the organization can't take an integrated approach. Individuals may continue to make the translation to percentages on their own. However, if the company wants to change the paradigm, it must take the first step by not reinforcing the old paradigm.

Budget

Sometimes managers find it difficult to manage within a budget, particularly if they have very few people as direct reports. This occurs more commonly in hierarchical organizations than in those with flat structures. If it happens, the budget can be managed at a higher organizational level. Several approaches are available. For example, dollars may be shifted from one subunit to another. Or managers of subunits may work as a group with their unit manager to discuss how best to allocate and share the available budget. They may choose to discuss the ongoing value of individuals or the criteria used to determine distribution of the budget. The advantage of this approach is that it uses multisource input and increases the consistency of the decision-making process among managers, provided they're familiar with the individuals and the measurement criteria in the larger unit.

CONCLUSIONS

The future of base pay management is to pay what the individual is worth in terms of the value they add to the business. The definition of this varies from company to company. Whether a company remains in a job-based pay solution or migrates to one based on the person, base pay reflects the individual's ongoing value; variable pay, which can take many forms, rewards current performance. Determining an individual's ongoing value is increasingly becoming a multidimensional issue. One dimension is applying skills and competencies that the individual possesses to achieve results. The talent needs of the company's business largely determine this. Another dimension is a track record of successful performance and contribution to achieving business-aligned goals. The final dimension is the external market value of the individual. This is what the talent and job or role are worth competitively. The company provides guidelines concerning how individual ongoing value is to be defined and recognized, and the manager must be responsible for determining pay that represents the ongoing value of the individual.

The new approaches have several common elements: goals, skills, and competencies from the business case; consideration of the three dimensions; linkage to development and business-aligned goals; manager accountability; dialogue; feedback; flexibility; and continuity. These solutions differ from some of the existing skill and competency pay approaches that are too burdensome, bureaucratic, and vague to be the long-term answer. The new solutions also take a more integrated view of total pay and use all of the pay elements (base pay, cash variable pay, stock options, and recognition) for what they do best, to create a complete reward package that recognizes an individual's total value added to the enterprise.

CHAPTER 6

Building Infrastructure for Base Pay

Once you build a solid train, you need a sound track to run it on. In the last chapter, we described how to build the train; now the track needs attention. We showed, in Chapter 3, that it's important to start with the competitiveness of your company's total rewards. Once you determine where your company stands on all four components of total rewards, consider the competitiveness of total pay and then the competitiveness of total cash. Finally, at the end of the competitiveness chain is base pay. The competitiveness issue doesn't start with base pay; it ends up there, to ensure seeing the reward "forest" before the base pay "tree."

This chapter is about infrastructure, the framework for determining base pay levels. Like the plumbing in a building, it's essential and serviceable, and it plays a support role in making the architecture work. Infrastructure supports the opportunity to earn base pay; it doesn't communicate or determine actual pay for ongoing value and performance pay. Problems arise when a company uses the material covered in this chapter as the primary pay messenger. We believe salary structures merely provide support for something else the enterprise is trying to do with pay. They can help facilitate the pay change element the company wishes to implement, but they aren't a pay element themselves. Their role is to enable Principle 5, rewarding individual ongoing value.

DETERMINING MARKET VALUE

Part of establishing and maintaining a relative competitive position is to take the labor market into account. Most companies now use a market-based approach to determine value, in contrast to the internal-equity-focused, point-factor, job-evaluation approaches of the past. They just can't spend time focusing internally on whose job or role is bigger than whose when their concern should be external, on how to improve the business. Internal equity comparisons across functions (for example, marketing compared to finance) are no-win situations because individual perceptions dominate the discussion.[1]

Benchmarking

To determine market value, a company starts by market-pricing benchmark jobs (those for which survey data exist). But in doing so it may run into a catch-22. Although businesses are becoming more market-based and job-based compensation surveys are proliferating, some are finding it difficult to use such surveys because their jobs have expanded into broader and more dynamic roles, where people do what's needed to accomplish a process or produce a body of work. Definitions of roles often blur and are extremely fluid over fairly short time periods. People may have blended roles or hybrid jobs in which they perform a combination of the duties of narrower jobs. For example, the position of service associate in a medical center combines the duties of basic patient care, food service, environmental services, and patient transport.

Also, enterprises that have moved to paying people based on their skills and competencies have difficulty matching the skill and competency sets of people to benchmark job descriptions. Exceptions to the job-based surveys are IT surveys that base the match on technical skills and competencies—for example, data mining, computer animation, and network engineering. In the future, surveys might deal with competencies within a job family by performing multiple regression on the competencies, but this requires identification of common competencies and common definitions.

Survey Matches

Companies facing these survey-matching difficulties first determine the best-fit survey job match and then make adjustments to the survey data wherever the company's roles or sets of skills and competencies differ from typical benchmark job descriptions. A blended role may have a market value that ranges from one reflecting the weighting of the time spent in each of the jobs, to one valuing the highest job that the blended role performs, to a multiskilling premium.

Roles or jobs with significant additional responsibilities compared to the survey job description have their market data adjusted upward, while roles or jobs with significantly fewer responsibilities than the job match are adjusted downward. Enterprises relate skill and competency pay to survey information by starting at a lower competitive position or using entry market rate information or hiring information on college graduates for people who are learning and who have fewer of the needed skills and competencies, and by moving above the competitive position if people demonstrate all of the skills and competencies.

Typically, human resources makes the adjustments and gives the survey information to managers so they can make their own judgment about its relevancy and use it as one factor in determining an individual's ongoing value. To help managers make appropriate decisions, HR may provide them with more than one competitive position for a role or job. For example, a business with a median (50th percentile) competitive position may pass on additional information about the 25th and 75th percentiles for a role or job to give the manager an idea as to the competitive spread in the labor market, while maintaining the median competitive position overall.

More Transparent Market

Market pricing and survey information are becoming less of a black box created by HR and more of a tool for managers to use to make pay decisions. The responsibility is moving to managers to effectively manage what's often the largest part of their budget. Managers can make reasonable market judgments since survey data for the most part yield guidelines for specific pay decisions.

Also contributing to the demystification of market pricing are three factors that allow people to get in touch with their own market value: the tighter labor market with its greater job possibilities, online recruiting, and pay surveys on the Internet (even though self-report and sampling issues may reduce survey accuracy). This pay information is becoming increasingly transparent but at the same time misleading. Some organizations with mixed agendas may post misleading data, thus adding to the communications challenges. This is multiplied by blurring job definitions and the difficulty of comparison matching done by job title rather than content.

Slotting Roles and Jobs in a Market-Based Approach

With a market-based approach, whole-job slotting typically determines the band or range of nonbenchmark jobs and roles (jobs and roles for which there are no survey data). Companies compare the nonbenchmark job or role to those in a similar functional area on such dimensions as value-added, competencies, knowledge, skills, and accountability. The benchmark jobs or roles anchor the comparisons within a function so the slotting doesn't become inflated. An analogy to the slotting process would be to put the nonbenchmark job and a comparison benchmark job in either dish of a scale and find out which weighs more overall in terms of value to the enterprise.

Special Situations

This is the time to determine if certain roles or jobs have strategic value to the company and should have a higher competitive position than most others. Strategic value is typically reserved for roles or jobs that reflect the core competencies of the company. These roles or jobs may have a higher competitive base pay position relative to the labor market, have larger short-term variable pay opportunity, or be eligible for (or have) greater participation in long-term variable pay such as stock options.

Also, scarce talent in the labor market needs consideration. Businesses often address the competitive labor market for scarce talent more frequently than annually. However, the key issue is to determine which part of the market is scarce and which isn't so scarce. For example, as we write this book scarce talent includes IT people. But some IT competencies are scarcer than others. Companies are selective in adjusting for scarce talent—it isn't across-the-board in a given function. They first narrow their attention to the scarce-talent areas within a function and then identify which people in the scarce-talent areas are adding value beyond what they're currently earning. Some can't afford to continue to escalate the value of all their scarce talent and must determine who is critical to the business and who is less so. The critical individuals are those the company makes sure it addresses; as with roles or jobs having strategic value, different forms of pay (base pay increases, cash variable pay, and stock options) may be used.

The market is the starting point. The organization should define competitiveness and then let the manager make the decisions needed to generate the required business results.

STRUCTURE FOR BASE PAY

The base pay structure (the framework built around market information) specifies the spread in base pay that's available for a role, a job, or the skills and competencies of the person.

Which of the four basic approaches a company uses depends on its objectives and situation. We've already discussed one approach, market rates, in Chapter 5 because it can serve as both infrastructure and actual base pay. Here we turn our attention to the other three: multiple grades with salary ranges, broad grades, and career bands.

Multiple Grades with Salary Ranges

This is the grandparent of salary structures, where roles or jobs are assigned a salary range with the midpoint closest to the market value of the role or job. Grades and corresponding salary ranges generally number 20 to 50. Range spreads from minimum to maximum are commonly 50 percent for exempt jobs and 35 percent for nonexempt jobs.

Grades with salary ranges work in a structured, functionally focused, hierarchical company where jobs within one job family or career ladder occupy adjoining pay ranges, with one or more of these jobs anchoring the grade assignment through some relationship to the labor market. However, reducing the number of jobs, delineating very broad roles, or having a boundaryless organization model may mean that numerous grades don't send the right message. Grades with salary ranges continue to work when there is not a proliferation of jobs and job levels, a strong focus on internal equity, and a lot of requests for jobs to jump grades. The fewer jobs a company has, the better ranges work. They become a problem when job leveling and definitions are primarily semantic rather than based on clear and measurable differences. An organization can keep this form of salary structure if it continues to serve the purpose originally intended: to be the framework or foundation for making pay decisions, not the way to get pay increases. In fact, because it's just infrastructure, rather than concentrating on changing the base pay structure, the company might better expend effort on performance pay or improving the process for paying for ongoing value.

Broad Grades

Both broad grades and career bands are the newer kids on the block and have become popular pay infrastructure or support systems. Broad grades streamline the job-valuing and salary-structure administration process and reflect a flatter, delayered organization. Broad grades are in-between grades with salary ranges and career bands in terms of both number and spread from minimum to maximum. Typically there might be four executive broad grades, three or more other exempt broad grades, and four nonexempt broad grades. The spread from minimum to maximum is on average less than 75 percent. Generally there are no midpoints, but the company often creates more controls or guidelines for using broad grades than under the career band approach.[2]

Career Bands

Career bands reflect emphasis on individual growth and development as well as a flatter, delayered organization. They have the fewest number of levels, averaging two executive bands, three other-exempt bands, and two nonexempt bands. They have the largest spread from minimum to maximum, from 100 percent to 300–400 percent. There are no midpoints. Typically there are minimums and maximums but sometimes no maximums, and sometimes neither minimum nor maximum. (In this latter case, market reference points, market reference zones, or market clusters provide specific market information on roles or sets of skills and competencies.) They're called career bands because the focus is on the individual's continued growth to add value to the business.

MORE ON BANDING

For the rest of this chapter, we use the word *banding* to describe both broad grades and career bands since many of the design and implementation issues are similar for these "fat ranges." In fact, many times broad grades are called bands, so we settle for the word *band* unless we want to differentiate career bands from broad grades.

Reasons for Banding

Figure 6.1 shows a visual comparison of market rates, many narrow salary ranges, fewer broad grades, and the fewest (and widest) career bands. As you can see, just using bands visibly changes the look of the organization. Their message is a flatter, less hierarchical, more expansive opportunity for base pay growth to correspond with individual growth.

There are various reasons for moving to banding:

- *Accommodating rapid change.* Eliminating approaches that communicate values and directions that don't match new directions is often an initial element of change. Replacing multiple grades and salary ranges reinforces things that may have been inhibited before. For example, it can support redefining and broadening jobs to accommodate a new organization design, or encourage a new culture of workforce growth and development. It can help implement base pay solutions focused on individual ongoing value. Or it can merely simplify the administrative process surrounding pay management.
- *Supporting a one-company identity.* Global enterprises, those acquiring others, and businesses with many subsidiaries find that banding supports the one-company identity needed to promote synergy and remove barriers. The message of the type of roles or jobs in a band is consistent across the company. Yet there is enough pay spread to take into account local differences within each band, or else the bands can be valued locally if there's wide variation (for example, globally).
- *Delegating pay decisions.* Multiple salary ranges allow control at or near the top of the company or in HR, with centralization of the career and pay process. With more people and roles or jobs in the same band, responsibility for managing the pay process must be delegated lower in the company. This means local managers make pay decisions

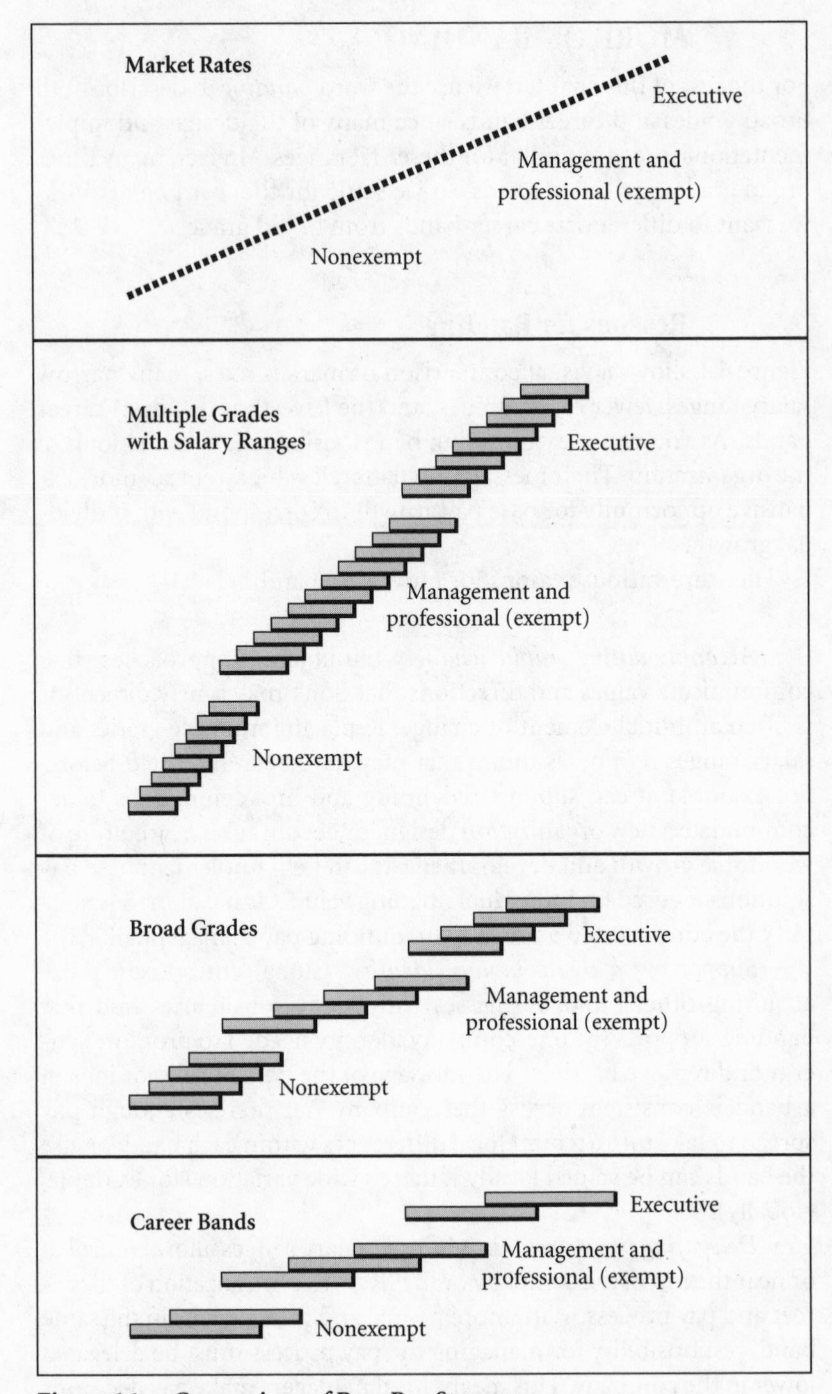

Figure 6.1. Comparison of Base Pay Structures.

on the basis of their diagnosis of the local situation. Companies often move managing pay budget and how the bands are used lower in the organization.

• *Symbolizing change.* Banding represents a message of change, a symbol as well as an item of infrastructure. It says, "We're loosening the grip of bureaucracy."

• *Supporting organizational flexibility.* In almost all instances, a company that moves to banding indicates doing so to become a more flexible organization. It does this in the belief that prior pay structures contributed to inflexibility and lack of agility. Often, users of banding had long histories with job-valuing systems that were highly detailed and administratively burdensome, and they wished to escape a bureaucratic pay approach that had a negative impact on the possibilities the company wanted to explore.

• *Reflecting a flatter organization design.* Having many grades with salary ranges often translates into many organizational levels and layers that may no longer match the organization design that best reflects the company's business strategy and direction. The belief is that banding helps delayer the organization and improve communications throughout. Combining people and jobs into fewer categories flattens the organization to expedite decisions and let information flow more readily. Banding permits eliminating job hierarchies (such as Analyst I, II, and III) and simplifies titling. Banding supports increased lateral moves and career development and decreased upward promotions, characteristics of a flatter organization.

• *Encouraging development and learning.* Banding places people and jobs that were separated by multiple grades and salary ranges into a shared band. Companies that encourage people to learn and grow their capabilities believe that banding focuses people on growing and adding value rather than jumping salary ranges. Without the semantic differentials that separate most job descriptions, actual growth and improvement in people can affect progression of base pay. Thus there's often a formal development or career planning process.

• *Emphasizing the person over the job.* Pay solutions based on grades with salary ranges and "merit" increases emphasize the job as the primary unit of organization design. A business wishing to focus on the individual and their worth to the enterprise tends to prefer banding. Banding can easily accommodate a pay solution that encourages pay growth based on how people acquire and apply needed skills and competencies to generate results.

• *Enabling organizational mobility.* When a company needs to have its people move from one part of the organization to another to fill a new or changed role, banding permits movement without emphasizing the grade number of the new role or job. To many minds, banding encourages the individual to focus on assuming the new accountabilities and looking forward to the new challenges and opportunities.

• *Supporting change in work design.* Some companies are finding it difficult to change how they're organized because of rigid and hierarchical job designs. The belief that "I am my job, and I do what's in my job description" makes it hard to change what people do, and expand their roles. Banding eliminates the bumpy ride people must take to assume more important roles in the company. The expectation is that changes in work design (such as from functional to process focus) are accommodated by eliminating many grades that imply only hierarchical career growth. Banding can reinforce dual career paths, where managers and technical and professional workers have similar individual ongoing value; banding can also enable movement between these roles without having it look like promotion or demotion.

Business Case Needed for Banding

Despite all these reasons for implementing banding, remember that it's an infrastructure tool that supports other changes. The reason for the change is the driver, and without the driver the banding solution doesn't make sense. Think about the business case for changing rewards, and see if banding fits. Banding doesn't deliver pay or pay messages by itself; it establishes the framework for pay tools to deliver pay. Banding depends on the pay tool it's partnered with to communicate, for example, what creates individual ongoing value or what results the company rewards with variable pay.

The reason for moving to bands must be clear, reasonable, and part of the business case for changing rewards. We've seen companies implement banding for a host of solid reasons and some questionable ones, such as "It was the easiest pay change to make" or "It made it look like we did something." Several years ago, a large utility company told us it wanted to retain a consultant to help move to banding. When we asked why banding was a priority, HR said the chief executive had read articles about banding and wanted to do it to "eliminate company bureaucracy" and "reduce pay costs" without the "hardship of changing the company pay system." When we suggested this might not be a realistic objective, the company hired another consultant, who implemented banding. Two years later, we read that base pay costs in the company had risen by 20 percent and that the executive team had been changed. These examples are clearly not the sound logic of a business case that is necessary for sustained effective pay change.

Integrating the Labor Market with Banding

Competitive pay remains an issue that must be managed under banding. Market reference points or zones, market clusters, or target pay zones for benchmark jobs can often serve as reference points for the entire solution. This gives managers guidance on competitive pay so they can take competitive practice into account in making pay decisions.[3] The manager has the chance to position an individual's pay at, below, or above competitive practice to reflect the individual's ongoing value or value to the business.

In Figure 6.2, the first example shows market reference points in a career band that covers entry, journey, and senior levels of a role or job that was formerly divided into three grades with salary ranges. Organizations disseminate this kind of market data regardless of whether they have moved to broader and more fluid roles or retained their job structure. Those with broad roles expect managers to make the translation between survey benchmark jobs and their broader roles when using the data.

A variation on providing market information is to cluster a group of roles or jobs within a band, as shown in the second example in Figure 6.2. Roles or jobs are clustered according to similar market value, and whole-job slotting places nonbenchmark roles or jobs into clusters. Managers receive the pay spread for each cluster as information to help make pay decisions.

The third illustration in Figure 6.2 shows how Fairlane Credit of Ford Motor Company, as an example, provides market reference zones for roles or jobs. Choosing a diamond symbol communicates that the largest number of people in a role or job should be paid near the fat middle part and fewer people should be paid at the narrow ends. The market is at the middle of the diamond; the end points can

Band for role or job family with market reference points

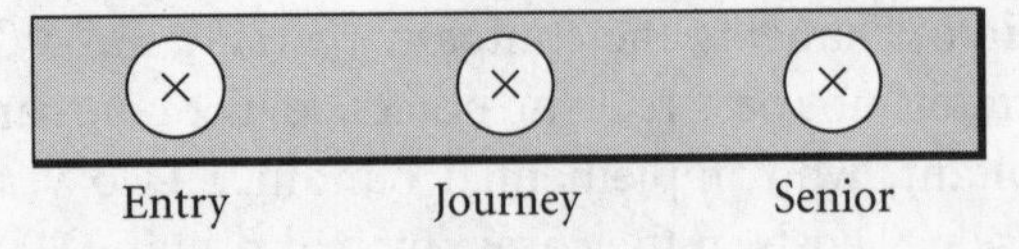

Bands with market clusters for a group of roles or jobs

Bands with market reference zones for roles or jobs

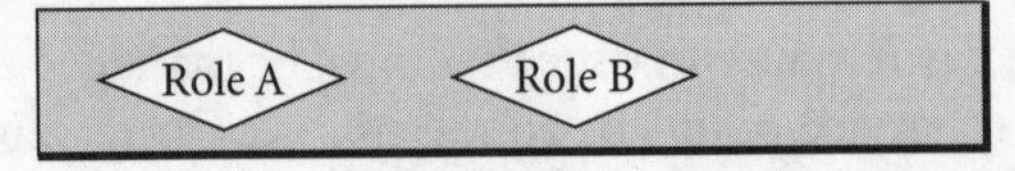

Band for job family with target pay zones and target highs

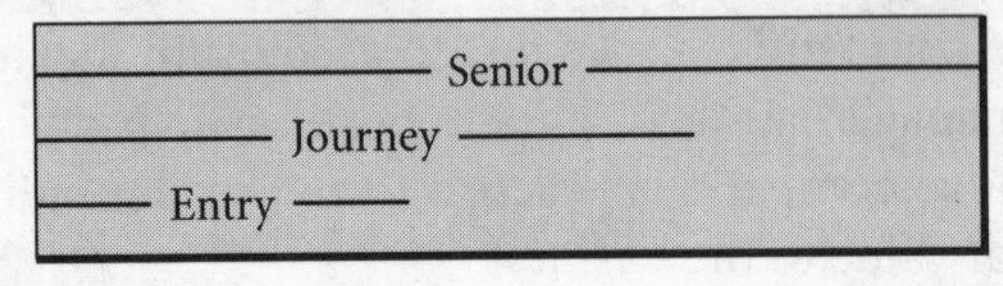

Figure 6.2. Examples of Integrating Market Information with Bands.

give information about either the relative spread desired or the common spread found in the labor market. This creates shadow ranges within the band, but the market information usually serves a guideline, not a rule.

The fourth example in Figure 6.2 shows how some organizations develop job zones that represent the spread to pay people in the same job if they keep the existing job structure. There are three levels in a job family, with overlapping job zones in the broad grade for entry, journey, and senior levels as well as target highs for each job. Job zones often do not overlap. They require clear definition of differences among the jobs in a job family. They look more like salary ranges than the first two examples, but in fact the spread in pay may be tighter for a job in a zone than in a salary range, particularly when there's no overlap between zones. A company tends to use job zones when it is moving to broad grades for purposes of simplifying administration or when clear criteria differentiate jobs within a family.

It's important to allow some flexibility. If the guidelines for administering banding (such as zones, shadow ranges, and market reference points) are indeed taken as hard-and-fast rules (as past structures were applied), the promise of a banded pay solution is likely to go unfulfilled.

The Logic of Bands

A critical issue is the message about how bands are defined. There are several alternatives.

CAREER STAGES. One approach—career development or career stages—reinforces the linkage between meaningful development and growth and the pay process. The approach describes the general stages people in all careers pass through, under the assumption that competency acquisition and application reflects career progression. It affords the opportunity for people to continue their growth, stop for a time, or stay at one career stage.

Career bands can be built on a career stage model, such as this one:

1. An individual with technical and team skills who is learning what is necessary to grow and add value
2. Team leadership, specialist, or full contributor to the company business
3. Contributing through others as a catalyst or guide to the business process
4. Leading through vision, championing, shaping the company and its future

In this approach to banding, the enterprise defines the developmental progress of people from one stage or band to another in the context of how they're actually growing.[4] Other issues to address include what the responsibilities of people and the company are regarding career growth and what happens if an individual doesn't progress beyond a specific stage.

A business unit that conducts basic research for a chemical company and that has a workforce made up mainly of scientists uses a career stage model for its banding. The scientists are responsible for initiating the process for moving into a higher career stage. When they believe they're ready, they present work samples and other materials to a review board that includes peers and that makes the decision.

COMPETENCIES. Like the first, another approach to the logic of banding—competencies—is used if a company moves to paying the individual, not the job, or has broad roles. Each band has a competency level, described for each of several competencies that the company believes bring differential advantage. Roles or individuals are placed in a band depending on how well the competencies required for the role or possessed by the individual match the competency descriptions for the band.

Alternatively, several related roles may be assigned to one band, within which competencies drive an individual's placement in the band. For example, the members of Frito-Lay's plant resource teams (resources, senior resources, and site resources) are in one band. The individual's placement in the band depends on their demonstration, on three levels, of four competencies that lead to being a good business generalist.

LABOR MARKET AND ORGANIZATIONAL LEVEL. If the reason for moving to banding is to streamline the salary administration and job-valuing process, the company may use the labor market, organizational level, or some combination of the two as the basis for bands. With the labor market as the logic, clusters of roles or jobs that have similar market value form the basis of bands. Sometimes broad grades under this market logic appear as if the multiple former grades were simply grouped and combined.

The importance of communicating dual career ladders of manager and technical expert may require the logic of organizational level to determine bands. For example, one band may include both leaders of functional units or departments with broad impact and scope and individual contributors who offer strong consulting expertise in highly technical or specialized fields. Another band may include leaders of functional teams with defined scope and impact and individuals who contribute project leadership and strong technical expertise.

SIMPLY ONE CONTINUUM. An example of how far banding can go is a business unit of a biotechnology firm. It developed a competency pay approach that was ready for implementation before they addressed the issue of grades or bands. After extensive discussion and careful consideration of the issue, the high-involvement team that was developing competency pay decided to have two continuums, one exempt and one nonexempt, with market reference points instead of several bands. The reason was that the team couldn't develop a workable, practical logic for multiple bands, given the organization's very broadly defined and fluid roles. They tried, for example, a career development approach but determined that it wasn't definitive because people might function in different stages at different times. Their decision reflected the fact that all issues of communicating pay progression, development plans, and the like were already addressed and pay could be managed without use of an infrastructure tool such as banding. Thus, the end point in the logic of bands may be effectively no bands at all.

If you assume you need bands, it's likely you'll get them, necessary or not. If the business unit had addressed the issue of banding on the front end of the design process, bands of some kind would probably have played an active role in the solution. As it was, infrastructure issues were not leading items in active change and communications processes.

Managing Pay Budgets

Although it's common for pay solutions based on hierarchical control, numerous salary ranges, and detailed job evaluation systems to be centrally managed, pay approaches accompanied by banding are not so managed and directed. One common change related to banding is that managers become more responsible and accountable for managing base pay within a specific budget for increases. Often, any budget for increasing base pay combines what was the former budget for individual merit increases with some of the budget that existed for promotional increases. Part of the promotional budget may be retained for movement between bands or significant lateral moves within a band; the manager is responsible for managing total pay movement under banding. Banding shouldn't inflate pay costs beyond what the company has been paying and what others pay for comparable skills and competencies as well as performance.

Banding suggests that actual management of the pay budget is a line management accountability and not merely a numbers game played by HR and the finance organization. Accountability also includes communicating to people the meaning of their increases. The challenge is whether managers can effectively administer a banded base pay solution. Companies and managers who aren't willing or able to manage the pay budget without the crutch of narrow ranges with which they may be accustomed don't find banding an effective partner to the pay management process.

To help managers be effective, the company must give them more than just infrastructure (banding) and accountability for budget management. It must also give them sound logic for how people get increases, such as the dimensions of individual ongoing value we described in Chapter 5. Examples of the problem that results from the absence of this logic are some of the large aerospace businesses in the 1980s that were very proud they'd managed the budget for a workforce of more than 20,000 without overspending. Close inspection, however, showed that they performed the pay increase process at the start of the year by forecasting the base pay increase each individual would receive by the end of the year and then actually carried it out by giving everyone exactly their forecasted base pay adjustment. The message to the workforce was one of entitlement and accurate forecasting of the pay increase budget, but nothing about adding value. Thus there needs to be more than infrastructure and the accountability for budget management; the enterprise must also provide an approach to adjusting base pay that supports the business. This is especially important to gain maximum advantage from banding.

Implementing Banding Successfully

To implement banding successfully, managers need training and preparation.

STRAIGHTFORWARD COMMUNICATION. Managers must communicate not only the reason for banding but also how people increase their worth to the company and thereby their base pay. Managers who don't talk straight to people about their individual ongoing value and career opportunities will have a difficult time implementing banding. Unprepared managers may precipitate the major drawback of banding: accelerated pay progression that's not justified by what people are contributing.

PAY GROWTH. Banding communicates the possibility of a growing base pay opportunity. It raises expectations and creates an opening for communication. People whose base pay progress has been stymied because they're paid near the maximum of their salary range often view banding as extremely good news because they now believe they'll finally be paid as highly as they feel they deserve. One key with banding is how to inform people about why they're not paid at the top of the band. Bands describe the full range of base pay for a group of roles, jobs, or competencies that have similar value to the company. Thus, not everyone can or would move to the top of the band. The discussion leads to identifying reasons for band placement closer to issues that make the individual more valuable in terms of skills, competencies, and consistent performance over time. This also commonly results in the need for managers to communicate about what people have to do to add more value to the company—for example, how they can expand in their role and have a more positive impact on the business.

PROMOTIONS AND LATERAL MOVES. People may also be concerned that they have fewer vertical promotional opportunities than under a job-and-salary-range system. This is true, and the company needs to acknowledge it. They often have more lateral career opportunities than in the past, which in turn lead to greater individual ongoing value. In moving to bands, the company should communicate if it transfers part of the promotional budget to the budget for base pay increases for individual ongoing value.

TITLING. If titling is changing, this also is a workforce concern. Titling serves as recognition with no direct financial cost. But continued delayering of organizations, and the move to broader and more fluid roles, simplifies and reduces titles. Some firms allow people to develop their own internal titles (as long as the team approves it and they don't assume officer-level titles). Others draw up a list of acceptable titles for each band. Still others use titles on business cards for customers who want to identify decision makers. Finally, some companies just put the business unit, not the job or role title, on business cards.

In spite of these potentially difficult issues, communication about banding typically shows the company's willingness to share information with people about how pay decisions are being made.

BUDGETS. Banding works best if the company doesn't reduce the budget for base pay increases during implementation because the objective of banding is usually workforce flexibility and development or streamlining of the salary structure, not reduction of pay cost. Also, try not to reduce headcount during implementation, since this usually leaves little time for people to develop and train. Remember that the issue is not only the move to banding; it's whether banding adds value to other things the company wants to do to improve pay and the messages pay delivers.

Selecting the Lead Pay Element

The lead element in a pay transition can't be banding. Our review of the banding literature[5] suggests that the reasons for moving to bands and success or lack of success with bands aren't all attributable to banding, but rather to the real reasons for changing total pay elements or organizational design. Banding supports the actual tool doing the communicating.

For example, banding doesn't create a flatter organization but supports the outcome of organization redesign. Skill development and flexibility result from specific training and development, emphasis on the skill-and-competency dimension of individual ongoing value, or changes in the reasons for base pay increases. Lateral development more likely comes from job or work redesign. Both variable pay and performance management are closer to supporting business goals than banding—variable pay by rewarding goal achievement and performance management by communicating specific goals. Although banding helps support many of the reported objectives and benefits, they are not the direct result of banding. Other things are more essential to helping companies realize the results reported in the literature than is banding.

CONCLUSIONS

Competitive practice must be the basis for pay. Beyond this, one of the infrastructure design tools is banding. Banding provides the plumbing so that the other lead pay designs linked to business initiatives can operate effectively. If variable pay, pay for individual ongoing value, performance management, and other essential aspects of your new pay solution make up the engine for the communications message, then banding may be the road that base pay runs on. But base pay can work just as well with or without bands. If pay change has any cool elements compared to other hot elements, banding is clearly a cool one. Perhaps it has become popular because—of anything we discuss in this book other than recognition and celebration—it's the safest and easiest thing to do. Still, we should not be taken in by banding testimonials. The real issue is what brings the most business advantage, rather than whether or not banding does it.

Even though banding may clearly increase flexibility, the vital question is, Flexibility to do what? Reward individual or team results? Improve development opportunities? Increase skills and competencies? Something else? Our bet is that even though banding is important, "something else" is more of a foundational element than an infrastructure issue. We suggest that what creates advantage is a new communications message that includes all the issues and total pay and total reward elements we discuss. If a company plans to spend six months considering, studying, developing, implementing, and communicating a new set of company priorities through pay, where do you think we believe it should principally expend its time?

If you guess that we believe the company should spend most of the time on the business case, developing a high-involvement design process, designing and implementing pay solutions that reward individual ongoing value and encourage growth and development, and designing and implementing workable results-driven variable pay, you're right. After these issues are addressed, banding becomes important as a possible support tool. It should align with whatever else base pay is doing. Banding is a trailing element in a major pay change, not an effective lead element.

CHAPTER 7

Rewarding Performance

Short-Term Variable Pay

Hollywood is one of the holdouts on variable pay for the general workforce. But director Steven Spielberg is thinking about it: "A recession inside the film business . . . would get Hollywood to figure out some way to cut costs, like issuing some kind of common stock among the profit participants, dividing up the pie better so we're all in it together."[1] Some people would say such a change might also strongly introduce the concept of performance pay to an industry that isn't exactly known for basing pay on results. In a host of industries, many companies have moved to variable pay, the primary reason being not to reduce costs but to accomplish other important goals.

THE VARIABLE PAY MENU

Variable pay is the "Chinese menu" of total pay—and you can have it with or without MSG! In an old Buddy Hackett comedy routine, the "rules" were that the patron of a Chinese restaurant could get only one food choice from Column A and two from Column B. The gag was that the patron always wanted to take two choices from column A and one from column B. It was Buddy's job as waiter to prevent this.

When it comes to the variable pay Chinese menu, you can pick from any column that fits your needs, mix and match variable pay solutions, and change them as needed—and your waiter won't try to stop you. Variable pay can "float like a butterfly, sting like a bee"; like Muhammad Ali, it's that flexible and dynamic. We've dedicated Principle 6 to rewarding results with variable pay. We were positive about variable pay in our book *The New Pay* and support it even more strongly now that it's grown whiskers a bit. Many companies also share this belief. Variable pay is the most popular performance pay solution, without challenge.

However, a few storm clouds are gathering over variable pay. We're at a point where course corrections may be necessary to reemphasize the business reasons for using variable pay in the first place. Don't panic; positive solutions are available. The growing pains of variable pay are over, and those who capitalize on what we've all learned can move forward briskly.

VARIABLE PAY AND ONGOING VALUE

Variable pay can reward business results promptly and in the long run. In Chapter 5, we discussed rewarding individual ongoing value by emphasizing skills, competencies, and consistent individual performance over time. But achieving business results is often a collaborative challenge that requires many people to share capabilities and resources and work together to accomplish the desired results.

Alone, individuals are often unable to generate the key results needed for companywide success. This doesn't diminish the importance of the individual, who remains the repository of the enterprises's ongoing value in terms of skills, competencies, and knowledge. The individual is the center of our belief in rewarding ongoing value, suggested in Principle 5. Given the importance of the individual, variable pay is the best collaborative performance pay solution and the one most likely to help generate the bottom-line results needed. Even so, it has to be integrated with other reward tools as suggested in Principle 4.

THREE TYPES OF VARIABLE PAY

Business results are the name of the game. Sharing them with the workforce is part of the better workforce deal. Companies and workforces can't thrive unless they meet financial goals.[2] Try explaining how "good" a pay change is to an executive, and see how long it takes before you hear "What are the business advantages?" or "Tell me again why we're doing this." Variable pay can address these questions.

Variable pay is a family of three related tools:

1. *Short-term variable pay.* Cash that rewards short-term business results. *Short-term* means time periods of one year or less. There are various possibilities: goalsharing, winsharing, gainsharing, profit sharing, team variable pay, individual variable pay, and combination plans.
2. *Long-term cash variable pay.* Cash intended to reward business results over a sustained period of time, more than a single year and generally two or more years. The results are from multiyear projects, key events, overlapping performance periods, and a family of performance-unit solutions. These approaches are popular for executives and are becoming increasingly common for others in the organization. They may include all, or part, of the workforce as participants.
3. *Long-term equity variable pay.* Stock options and other stock solutions. They're forms of variable pay because the value of options and stock depends on the performance of the company's common stock in the equity market. Options are a major element in executive compensation and are used broadly to recognize, reward, and communicate with some or all of the workforce.

Although *Pay People Right!* deals with the three types of variable pay separately, they're closely related and should be integrated in the total pay picture. Sometimes one is more useful than the others. Or a company might determine that two or three can be deployed to address specific business goals and objectives. We cover short-term variable pay in this chapter and long-term cash and equity variable pay in the next chapter.

WHY VARIABLE PAY?

Dynamic business requires variable pay. The simple reason variable pay makes sense is that it can deal with many business issues, challenges, and opportunities that no other pay tool can handle.[3] The reasons for variable pay are outlined in Chapter 3, on total pay. Variable pay is an essential element of the four reward components; it partners with individual ongoing value to link business-aligned goals with the performance feedback process.

Nimble Communication Tool

When all is said and done, variable pay is a communication tool with which leaders share what's important to the business. At a time when speed and adaptability count, the major attractiveness of variable pay is its agility and flexibility. It's fairly easy to show that variable pay awards are granted only if the business wins economically and if people meaningfully add value to the business.

Variable pay is also helping to manage total pay costs by keeping base pay inflation in check. Because it's not a "gift that keeps on giving" after results are achieved, it requires re-earning and attention to the goals for the next performance cycle. There's more room for experimentation with variable pay than with base pay and benefits. An enterprise can correct or improve variable pay in the next year because it gets its money back, so to speak, to start afresh; errors aren't plowed into fixed base pay or permanent benefit costs.

More Value Still to Come

We believe, though, that the potential positive value from variable pay is only partially being realized. Many companies use variable pay to communicate business-aligned goals, extend people's line of sight, reward results, and share success; they've created the win-win partnership of Principle 2. But some are struggling. This is why it's critical to remain positive on variable pay. Let the workforce know the enterprise is committed to variable pay as a tool to reward results, but remain flexible and experimental until a way becomes evident to design variable pay for your enterprise most effectively. New product development doesn't stop at the first barrier; neither should development of variable pay, or for that matter any total pay solution we propose.

PROBLEMS OR OPPORTUNITIES?

Sometimes there's trouble in variable pay paradise. Let's talk about how the reported problems can be turned into strong opportunities to communicate primary business directions and the better workforce deal.

Here are some common "noise opportunity" quotes that challenge variable pay:

- "Variable pay's an entitlement. Everyone receives the same award and gets it every year. People aren't paying attention to it. I thought the company was trying to get away from automatic payments. What difference does it make if we call entitlement 'lump-sum payment variable pay'? How are we better off than we were before we went to variable pay?"
- "What do we get from variable pay? Why did we implement it? How's our variable pay doing? We haven't heard anything about the variable pay plan for some time. Are we still making awards under variable pay? What were the goals we used, and where did they come from? Who's been receiving awards, and why?"
- "Why doesn't variable pay 'pay off'? Is this just a management trick to reduce our pay? The goals for variable pay are beyond our reach. We just don't understand what we need to do to achieve these goals and earn an award."

If variable pay is so good, why are some variable pay solutions receiving negative press? Why is variable pay in some cases becoming a source of negative messages rather than positive ones? Clearly, it's sometimes not accomplishing the objectives for which it was implemented in the first place.

MINOR SURGERY REQUIRED

We believe challenges and opportunities have arisen because some variable pay solutions don't take into account the reward principles we believe are essential to helping create a positive better workforce deal that makes solid business sense. What we hear from managers and workforce members are clear indications that our advocacy for the six reward principles is sound and on the right track. Now let's get back to the basics of why and how variable pay can add business value.

Organizations should evaluate and recalibrate variable pay periodically if they are to get to the Emerald City of effective variable pay that communicates and stimulates achievement of business goals. If the variable pay journey is the yellow brick road to Oz, then some enterprises may now be in the poppy fields, although solutions are available to get them back on their journey.

Many of these solutions are points you've heard before, but they're worth repeating.

Communications

Communicate, communicate, communicate! Variable pay is a vehicle for business communications, and some companies are implementing it without involving the workforce and educating people as to the reasons for variable pay and the measures and goals used. You can't just hang it onto a poorly designed existing pay solution and count on it as a golden fleece to overpower poorly designed total pay. Even though it's potentially mighty, it typically constitutes a smaller part of total pay than base pay does. So you need to align base pay to reward individual ongoing value, as suggested in Chapter 5.

Many of the questions concerning variable pay are communication issues. You can address them positively, creatively, and from a strong business perspective—changing a problem into an opportunity and staying consistent with Principle 1.

Communicating doesn't stop with the rollout of the plan. It produces ongoing messages about progress on variable pay goals and expands into education about the business and how people can affect variable pay goals, to stimulate everyone's involvement in the business.

Win-Win

Principle 2 is the win-win partnership. Variable pay must be a win-win if the company is to maintain it and if people are to commit to it. The enterprise must get added value from variable pay cost, and people must believe they have a reasonable win for the performance and the effort expended. People consider the win in terms of total cash if variable pay has funding from base pay at risk or potential pay at risk. They want the measures within their line of sight, although Principle 3 suggests that the horizon should be extended through education and involvement to create the potential for a greater win.

Goals need to be reasonable and achievable. Variable pay can't make an enterprise achieve excessive stretch goals; only a caped crusader can do that. This can make a win for people impossible. The company can't simply set unreasonable goals and then hope that variable pay single-handedly improves results. If people feel that goals and measures are out of reach and that the variable pay solution will never generate rewards, it's probably because the company assumes that, like some Archimedes or Atlas, if it has a lever long enough it can move the world. In fact, the lever is *not* long enough.

If goals are really high, it's critical that variable pay begin to grant awards at some reasonable level along the way. It makes no sense to have a company miss goals by a bit when they are extremely tough to achieve, only to find that there's no funding or awards under variable pay.

On the other hand, variable pay goals shouldn't be so easily attained that people don't have to do anything differently to earn awards, or else they'll start viewing variable pay as an entitlement. With continuous improvement, increasing customer expectations, and global competition, goals can go on having reasonable stretch. Variable pay can not only reward achieving goals but also provide larger awards for exceeding them, so that people stay in the game to attain the higher level of performance.

Agility and Flexibility

Our theme is adapting to business change in a positive fashion through the reward principles, which we suggest are essential. This is a period of rapid change. Speed counts, and goals and measures must adjust. Sometimes variable pay doesn't adjust as goals and objectives change. Variable pay mustn't become an entitlement or an uninvolved bystander in the business evolution process. When and if directions and messages change, the variable pay solution should reflect them.

Course corrections are a way of life for pay, and for organizations as well. Changing circumstances mean changing measures and goals, and maybe variable pay design. The best time to change variable pay is when the plan is periodically reviewed for the next performance cycle or period. As a side benefit, changing and refreshing variable pay to better align it with the business can renew interest in a plan in which people have lost interest.

Limiting Change During Performance Period

Variable pay needs a bold Teddy Roosevelt to lead the charge up San Juan Hill in making change stick. For the people to feel like a partner, they have to know when and why the rules change. The types of conditions and timing for making changes should be outlined in the plan document.

But sometimes variable pay fails because a company makes arbitrary changes that influence the variable pay measures and goals and doesn't communicate and involve the workforce to understand and help make the new directions a reality. Sometimes variable pay participants get an April Fool's surprise that creates distrust and dislocation. This doesn't mean goals and measures can never change; it means the workforce has become a stakeholder in measures and goals by virtue of a pay solution that's tied to these measures. So, if change they must, the company owes it to the stakeholders to involve them in the process and explain the logic of the change. It's just good business, and another outstanding opportunity to communicate about the business.

Championing

Total pay and other rewards are part of the strategic business process. This requires leadership championing and communicating. Variable pay is so common that it sometimes becomes a human resource project rather than a primary messenger of the leadership team. Sometimes the emphasis is on only the technical aspects of variable pay design rather than on the process, the business importance of variable pay, and business-aligned goals. Variable pay seldom fails for lack of technical expertise; it fails most often because the workforce doesn't believe company leadership is associating pay with the business and sharing the results. Think of the questions in the prior section about where goals come from and queries about how variable pay is working. These are fixable by involving leaders actively and creatively.

Involvement

In Chapter 16, we discuss the importance of involvement to make total pay work. Too often, enterprises skip this important opportunity for understanding because variable pay is so common that management believes they can just "put it in." People accept things they understand, and acceptance is critical. Involvement helps accomplish this and usually results in a better variable pay solution. A high-involvement pay design team can address all of the concerns about variable pay that we listed, in material that communicates answers to, say, "20 key questions about variable pay." Again, this amounts to turning a supposed problem into a creative business opportunity.

Involvement must go beyond variable pay design, communications, and implementation. Workforce involvement in the business and work processes is critical. The company must engage people by educating them on their influence on the business and allowing them to make a difference. Those who are involved solve problems to enhance performance and become actively committed to the business. This is when variable pay is most successful.

Celebration

People work for more than pay. Think about the better workforce deal we're suggesting. It's important for people to celebrate a success and then go on to the next one. Even if they don't accomplish what they thought they would, addressing what to do to get the ball rolling again can be a critical positive for total pay. Also, celebration can give variable pay some visibility if it's in a rut. Chapter 9 addresses the partnership between pay and recognition and celebration. The concerns about variable pay that we've listed suggest workforce dislocation from variable pay and a clear message that the people asking these questions probably aren't having much fun working in the company.

The New Pay

The six reward principles are founded on the positive role of total pay and other rewards in making and keeping a great company great. In *The New Pay,* we outlined a strategy and tactical route to successful variable pay design, implementation, alignment, communications, and workforce involvement. Although most of the great companies are getting the value they deserve from variable pay, some others are not. It's time to take positive steps to enjoy the promise of variable pay for both people and the company. Again, variable pay is here to stay; it just makes sense to do whatever is possible to make it a positive business tool.

SHORT-TERM VARIABLE PAY DESIGN ISSUES

Variable pay is the premier way to reward short-term business results.[4] Short-term variable pay can also link to variable pay that measures results over a longer time period to provide a sustained, consistent message. Measures and goals are at the heart of getting back on track with variable pay. The suggestions we made about business-aligned goals in Chapter 4, in the context of measuring and managing performance, apply to variable pay.

Organizational Level for Rewarding Performance

Exhibit 7.1 gives suggestions on where to measure performance for variable pay. We devote a chapter to team pay later (Chapter 10), but here we need to address the influence of company, business-unit, team, and individual measures and goals. Group or team variable pay, as we discuss them in the next few pages, typically involve higher-quality goal setting and measurement than individual variable pay or base pay because group or team goals are more closely aligned with the operating plan. They're one or more steps higher in the business-aligned goals process. Group and team goals are also under more scrutiny by a wider range of people and have less variation in consistency than individual goals that every manager and individual set.

To put a new spin on an old line, be careful what you pay for—you just might get it. If you emphasize only individual performance, don't be surprised if that's all you end up with. Individual variable pay works best in an individualistic work environment rather than a collaborative one. Small-team variable pay works well if teams are autonomous, but it can also create competition between interdependent teams if performance isn't optimized and rewarded at a broad organizational level. Site, business-unit, and companywide performance measurement have, in that order, increasingly longer lines of sight, so the communication and education effort must grow stronger.

You can use more than one organizational level for measuring and rewarding performance. How many you use depends in part on your

Exhibit 7.1. Determining Where Performance Is Measured for Variable Pay.

Element	Company or Business Unit	Team	Individual
Line of sight	Long	Medium	Close
Optimization	Both organization and people win at same time	May optimize team performance at expense of organization	May optimize individual performance at expense of team and organization
How to increase effectiveness	Bring line of sight closer to people—educate and engage people so they understand how individual and team results contribute to organization results	• Effective for autonomous teams • Measure interfaces between interdependent teams • Show how team results influence organization results	• Effective if individuals totally autonomous • Measure individual's contribution to team or group results • Have individual performance determine distribution, not funding • Show how individual results influence team and organization results

willingness to communicate and address line-of-sight challenges. For example, interdependent teams may have variable pay measures at both the team and broader organizational-unit levels to encourage integration and performance optimization at the higher level. Some solutions determine funding on a broad organizational level and distribute awards at a narrow organizational level—for example, they draw funds from business-unit performance and distribute them according to individual performance. Some approaches provide funding at multiple organizational levels.

It's best, though, to select the few organizational levels that send the clearest and strongest message about what's needed for business success. Too many levels spread variable dollars too thin. Also, remember that you can set, track, and recognize more goals than variable pay needs to include. These additional goals can serve as stepping stones to show how to achieve the variable pay goals.

Variable Pay Measures and Funding

In designing variable pay, you should emphasize the few reasonable and key business-aligned goals that drive the needed business results, are consistent with the operating plan, and can be influenced by the participants. Chapter 4 discussed the process of selecting measures and setting business-aligned goals. In Chapter 3, we discussed the amount of variable pay opportunity relative to competitive total cash and total cash mix. Measures and goals also influence variable pay opportunity; it grows larger the closer the goals are to the bottom-line results that the company can pass on to shareholders or invest in the business because the company knows that the money is there for variable pay.

THRESHOLDS. If goals have significant but achievable stretch, a threshold level of performance permits some award to acknowledge the difficulty in achieving the goal. It's important that people can achieve these business-justified thresholds. For example, the threshold is recent performance and the goal represents improvement.

Model the relationship between results and rewards by applying the funding formula to recent performance and to several possible future performance scenarios. Recent performance provides a perspective of how variable pay works, but hopefully performance will be better after implementation of variable pay since it focuses people on the needed results.

INDEPENDENT AND INTERDEPENDENT MEASURES. Consider whether measures are independent or interdependent in generating variable pay awards. A company wanting to optimize performance on several measures makes the measures interdependent. For example, performance on one measure magnifies or modifies the award for performance on another measure. Customer satisfaction scores may modify the award for cost performance by plus or minus a specified percentage to keep people's eyes on both balls simultaneously. Another alternative is a matrix in which participants must meet specified levels of performance on two measures before they can earn any award.

In another approach, one measure can serve as a gate for earning an award based on another measure. Where labor cost is a high percentage of total expense, a threshold level of bottom-line financial performance may be required before earning an award based on other goals such as quality, delivery, productivity, and customer satisfaction. This threshold level ensures that the company can afford the awards. These solutions work better if the gate isn't all or nothing, if possible, but instead sets a reduced level of awards for customer, operational, people, and future-focused goals should the financial threshold not be met.

Even goals that produce awards independently can be interdependent if award size increases exponentially rather than equally for each goal achieved. For example, achieving any one goal of three is worth $200; achieving two goals is worth $500; and achieving all three goals is worth $1,000.

Remember our elevator-speech suggestion? If you can't generally communicate the measures and goals (and how the variable pay solution works) to a potential participant during a 20-story elevator ride, the communications challenge is probably too daunting and the message may not get through.

Performance Period

It helps to grant awards as closely as possible to the time the performance is delivered so as to strengthen the link between pay and performance. But the length of the performance period also depends on a variety of factors: business tempo; variability in the measures; ability to measure results meaningfully; administrative capability; typical award size; type of workforce; and whether variable pay is add-on, base pay at risk, or potential pay at risk.

High-technology companies tend to have shorter performance periods than many other types because with the rapid developments in their industry a year seems like a lifetime. The more variability in the measure over time, the more likely the performance period will be longer, although smoothing mechanisms can be used to lessen this concern. These mechanisms include year-to-date cumulative payouts, deficit reserve, loss recovery, and rolling average payouts.[5]

The ability to determine meaningful results on a measure helps to decide the performance period. For example, monthly profit awards make little sense because of their variability and the ease of shifting dollars from one month to another. The closer the line of sight of the predominant funding measure, the shorter the performance period typically is. For example, piece rate approaches may pay out every two weeks, while gainsharing that pays out monthly usually has a smoothing mechanism. Some approaches pay out awards less frequently so that the award is more likely to be of meaningful size.

Typically, performance periods are shorter if the participants are lower-paid rather than higher-paid, reflecting in part the nature of goals that tend to be long-term if the participant is high in the organizational structure. If variable pay is add-on, the performance period may be longer, all other things being equal, than when base pay or potential pay is at risk.

Basis for Sharing Team or Group Variable Pay

The sharing basis is generally one of the most debated design issues for team or group variable pay because each method sends its own messages:

- Same percentage of base pay earnings: communicates that variable pay opportunity should generate similar motivation and relative value compared to base pay, meaning a larger dollar award for higher-paid people than lower-paid individuals
- Equal dollar amount for similar job or role levels: communicates that people in similar roles should have the same variable pay opportunity regardless of their base pay and that the higher the role or job level, the larger the dollar award, to provide similar motivation between levels
- Equal dollar amount for all participants: communicates we are all in this together and all contribute to team or group performance, while base pay reflects the person's role and individual ongoing value relative to the labor market
- Equal cents or dollars per hour worked: communicates that people need to be at work and contributing to earn an award
- Equal cents or dollars per hour paid: communicates individuals are not penalized for taking vacation or sick leave

If the mix of total cash is changing or if base pay or potential pay is at risk, then the first two methods afford relative value. If you have a similar level of roles or jobs in the variable pay plan, choose from any of the methods. Ensure that scarce talent doesn't feel negative impact from the method selected. Diagonal-slice pay design teams typically select an equal-dollar approach like the last three.

An organization must also comply with the Fair Labor Standards Act (FLSA) concerning the calculation of overtime for nonexempt workers with nondiscretionary, performance-based variable pay, incentives, and lump-sum payments (except for profit-sharing plans). By calculating awards as a percentage of base pay earnings including overtime, a company need not add variable pay into the overtime calculation. However, if awards are paid by any other method, then to comply with the FLSA the company must make a computer calculation that adds the variable pay award back into the base rate to recalculate overtime.

SHORT-TERM VARIABLE PAY SOLUTIONS

In some ways, saying a company has variable pay alternatives is like saying no two snowflakes are alike. The possible combinations and permutations are nearly unlimited. This sometimes makes it difficult to categorize a variable pay plan. Exhibit 7.2 summarizes the categories of short-term variable pay.

Goalsharing or Business Goal Plan

Many companies are willing to award short-term variable pay for meeting goals that are aligned with the operating plan. In this instance, short-term variable pay may not self-fund in the same sense that profit sharing and winsharing do. Goalsharing rewards achieving or exceeding goals.

FUNDING. Typically, the funding either is a pay expense or is determined by the value of goal achievement. If the funding is a pay expense, the goals prove their value to the business by being key drivers of success. Sometimes the value of goals can be determined. For example, improvements in quality can reduce rework and scrap and thus reduce cost. Also, in the retail industry, customer satisfaction has proven to correlate strongly with the number of times a shopper returns to an establishment. Goalsharing is useful when an enterprise wants to highlight goals in addition to cost and other financial measures and when gainsharing has driven out most of the costs that can possibly be reduced.

VARIETY OF MEASURES AND GOALS. Goalsharing is becoming increasingly popular. In large part, this is because goals that are important to the business can provide awards independently of cost or financial

Exhibit 7.2. Types of Short-Term Variable Pay.

Variable Pay Plan	Basic Design	Indicators	Requirements
Goalsharing or business goal plan	Award achievement of predetermined goals	• Several goals, including cost, are important • After gainsharing has squeezed out most cost • Introduce new directions	Must have value added from goal achievement to fund plan
Winsharing	Funding based on income performance and distributed for meeting predetermined goals	Key strategy is financial (self-funded) plus additional measures are important and provide focus	Must create understanding of financial measure and how people affect it
Gainsharing	Share gain from cost savings or productivity improvements	Key strategy is cost reduction (self-funded from cost savings)	Must have broad enough cost measure not to suboptimize overall cost performance
Combination plan	Combination of designs	Customize to align with business needs	Must clearly communicate priorities
Cash profit sharing	Funding based on income performance	Goal is financial; self-funded	Must create understanding of financial measure, of how people affect it, and of importance of other measures
Team variable pay	Team plays a key role; funding based on organization or team performance; award distribution based on team or individual performance	Organization is team-based	Must optimize performance at all organizational levels
Individual variable pay	Award achievement of predetermined individual goals	Individuals work autonomously	Must link individual goals to team, group, business unit, or company goals

results. Some goalsharing solutions are defined as such because only a small portion of the award opportunity is actually self-funding from group, business-unit, or company financial results. Other goalsharing measures involve customer goals (for example, customer satisfaction if it can be measured accurately), operational goals (say, delivery or quality of the product or service), people goals (implementation of process improvement), or strategic goals set for a specific performance period (bring a specified number of products to market that generate a specified level of revenue).

GOALSHARING AT WEYERHAEUSER. Weyerhaeuser, a Fortune 500 forest and paper products company, has goalsharing in its containerboard packaging and recycling plants to optimize performance and to use its asset base fully. The objective is to enlist the workforce in a major performance improvement initiative to achieve world-class performance. The approach focuses on incremental performance improvement in core measures such as safety, quality, waste, and controllable costs.

The emphasis is on key goals within the control of the workforce. The hourly workforce does not have a measure of operating earnings because the fluctuating cost of the commodity raw material and the cyclic nature of the industry greatly influence operating earnings. This is also because the company wants to optimize business across the plants, so that they don't necessarily control the price of the product they produce. Exempt workers have a few additional key strategic plant goals that focus and drive the plant to higher performance. Goalsharing at Weyerhaeuser supports the move to high-performance work systems.

Winsharing

The need for self-funding short-term variable pay is one reason for the existence of winsharing. Winsharing is closely associated with the enterprise's ability to pay and is often the choice in situations where labor cost is a large percentage of the organization's total cost and profit margins are small.

FINANCIAL EMPHASIS. Extending people's focus to the measures that ultimately influence overall company or business-unit financial results is the objective of winsharing, which builds funding in proportion to profit or income performance and pays out proportionally to achievement of other important goals. Financial results can be measured at the division, group, business-unit, or company level or some combination of these levels—wherever profit or income can be calculated.

The additional winsharing measures are customer, operational, people, or future-focused ones. Goals for these measures magnify, modify, or serve as a gate for the availability of variable pay dollars to the workforce. However, the key characteristic of winsharing is the relationship between the financial performance of the organizational unit in which winsharing exists and award payments. Unless financial goals are met, it's little solace that other results are generated.

Winsharing can emphasize optimizing performance at multiple organizational levels and highlight a few essential goals. For example, although a measure of business-unit financial contribution may determine funding, winsharing may use other measures as additional steps in connecting people with the business-unit financial results. Some may emphasize business-unit operational goals; others may focus on team goals that are closer in line of sight. This requires keeping the communications message strong and effective to ensure a focus at multiple levels and types of performance measures.

The dividing line between winsharing and goalsharing is arguably sometimes fuzzy. In our minds, however, the difference has to do with the dominant source of variable pay funds. If it's bottom-line financial outcomes, the approach is most likely winsharing. If goals that aren't bottom-line generate funding, it's probably goalsharing. Again, both are powerful and critical elements in effective pay design.

COMMUNICATING THROUGH WINSHARING. Workforce understanding of the business, company communication about business performance, and workforce involvement in performance improvement are critical to successful winsharing. Unlike profit sharing, which is also funded according to financial performance, winsharing offers additional measures to focus people on what generates the financial performance needed for funding. Winsharing tests the organization's ability to communicate the relationship between what the workforce can influence and the financial success of the organization. We believe this need makes winsharing attractive as a way to show people how they make a difference.

WINSHARING AT COVEY LEADERSHIP CENTER. Covey Leadership Center (now Franklin Covey Company) has been one of the most successful training and development enterprises in the world. Starting with Stephen R. Covey's *The 7 Habits of Highly Effective People,* and continuing with a wide range of products and services, the center grew quickly and successfully from dozens of consultants and advisors to hundreds. The new product development focus created new products consistent with Covey's theme for many years. His son, Stephen M. R. Covey, became chief executive and focused his efforts on improving alignment of the growing and youthful workforce with the seven habits. The pay solution had been a conglomeration of base pay, pay based on new product development and execution, sales commissions, and a wide range of individualized pay plans that gave mixed messages about roles and goals for everyone.

A new pay strategy extended Covey Leadership Center's goals in terms of financial performance and growth. The strategy defined not only what to do but also how to do it in terms of values and behaviors. The objectives were to live the seven habits and to achieve goals. It implemented—for all associates—variable pay with funding dependent on financial performance, but it required that they achieve measures of customer value and quality service before distributing the funding. Variable pay permitted alignment of the workforce on key measures of success as well as the route to results. Alignment of everyone and variable pay have been suggested as key changes that refocused the company and led to an attractive merger and formation of Franklin Covey Company.

Gainsharing

Gainsharing is a grandparent of variable pay. It works well in stable organizations with predictable goals and measures but is less flexible and useful in dynamic industries that require rapid business adjustment. It got its start in manufacturing in the 1930s and has a shorter history in service organizations. Its objective is to share a percentage of cost savings. If a company needs to communicate to the workforce about the importance of cost reduction, gainsharing can do it effectively and in short order. To the extent sharing savings comes from a cost measure sufficiently broad so as not to suboptimize overall cost, it's a win-win for both people and the enterprise.

CLOSER LINE OF SIGHT. Gainsharing has a closer line of sight than profit sharing and winsharing, encouraging people to seek ways to reduce costs within their control. Plans tend to generate most of their cost savings in the early years; effectiveness depends on whether people find ways to reduce cost after picking the low-hanging fruit. Because the dollars for sharing come from cost savings, gainsharing is challenged when the company needs other types of performance improvement from the workforce. Gainsharing designs may predicate qualification on a measure of quality; many only count good-quality products and services to ensure acceptable quality; and still others may have added additional measures and goals, such as safety and delivery, to send a balanced performance message.[6] This places a priority on other important drivers of success and encourages optimization of performance on all the essential measures, not just cost.

Gainsharing has been successful in unionized work environments because the cost measure is verifiable. Agile businesses (especially in manufacturing) often use it as their initial form of variable pay and then transition to solutions with other measures and goals in successive generations of design. Some argue that it may not add value to the longer-term goals of the business when it only rewards cost reduction because of the limited number of measures used. Gainsharing may migrate to goalsharing or winsharing, especially in the fortunate situation where cost has been reduced about as far as it reasonably can. Even so, many gainsharing solutions have a long history.

GAINSHARING AT OWENS CORNING. Owens Corning is implementing gainsharing in many of its union and nonunion plants. The objective is to improve cost performance and productivity to have acceptable margins and remain competitive in fiberglass production. In Chapter 2 you read about one plant's business case for changing rewards, involving more than just a gainsharing plan. It also includes role restructuring and market-based utilization pay, which is Owens Corning's form of paying for the skills used. All manufacturing workers are oriented on their plant's business case for change and the reason the plant needs to implement variable pay to sustain and enhance itself as a business.

Owens Corning's gainsharing approaches share a percentage of manufacturing cost reduction in terms of cents per pound. The majority of the funding accumulates automatically; the remainder pays out according to safety and other measures of importance to a plant. To facilitate implementation, there are communication and educational objectives for everyone to understand Owens Corning's business, markets, and competitive issues; the plant's vision for the future; the plant's key current and future goals and why change is necessary; high-performance organizations; and the variable pay plan in detail.

Mixing and Matching Variable Pay: Combination Plan

This is where we believe variable pay is going. Pay solutions are increasingly becoming less easy to pigeonhole. The reality is that a company should do what works, and a mix-and-match approach fits the situation. For example, all of the group and team short-term variable pay solutions—goalsharing, winsharing, gainsharing, profit sharing—can be combined with individual variable pay based on the specific situation on which pay is to be focused. Where a combination of shared and individual goals is important, one portion of variable pay can be based on shared goals and another on individual goals.

COMBINATION PLAN AT AN IT SOLUTIONS COMPANY. An example of a combination plan is from an IT company that offers a variety of enterprise applications to client businesses. Its objective is to attract and retain the scarce IT talent required to achieve its primary goal of profitable growth. Short-term variable pay is one element of a total pay strategy that also includes competency pay that quickly responds to the labor market, enhanced recognition and celebration, and long-term variable pay.

All IT professionals participate in short-term variable pay that emphasizes financial success and customer satisfaction. It has three separate components: company results, to create synergies among lines of business; line-of-business results; and either project team or customer team results, depending on the type of service the team provides. The weighting of the three components varies depending on the individual's ability to affect results. This is a winsharing design for the company and line-of-business components and a team variable pay design for the project and customer teams component. Individual performance distributes the funding from the three components. The approach constitutes the umbrella framework through which measures can be specified for the particular business situation.

MANY VARIATIONS. In mixing and matching variable pay, there are opportunities to "innovate into infinity." Starting with the business strategy and operating plan, the company chooses the messages that it wants to communicate. It selects measures and goals that drive the results needed. A close association is required between the business strategy and the message people receive concerning what's expected and how they're recognized and rewarded for their successes.

Cash Profit Sharing

We called gainsharing a grandparent of variable pay; then cash profit sharing is one of its great-grandparents. We focus here on profit sharing that provides annual, semiannual, or quarterly cash and shares a percentage of profits, generally after achieving a profitability level that represents a specified level of return on investment. Cash profit sharing is a way to communicate to people that a company's bottom-line performance counts. It can also communicate and reward business-unit, group, or division financial success. Like winsharing, it can work wherever bottom-line performance can be calculated. Profit sharing is clearly self-funded because it shares a portion of overall profit performance—no profit, no profit-sharing award. From the company's standpoint, profit sharing is a win because if profits are there, it pays off.

The challenges faced by profit sharing are that it has a long line of sight and is often only an annual event. In a large company with little ongoing communication about profit results or how the workforce can influence profits, annual profit sharing based on overall company profit performance becomes an entitlement. People often make little connection between their performance and what they get in terms of profit sharing; there's a belief that they can't see how they have any chance of influencing the company's overall profitability. Profit sharing is frequently viewed as a Christmas bonus: appreciated but not aligned with any message the company has to communicate about the role the workforce plays in organizational performance. Profit sharing can easily become an entitlement that's difficult to change.

In our experience, the dollars spent on companywide profit sharing could be better used for variable pay approaches of alternative design. Except in small companies, profit sharing based on overall performance is typically not a teacher of the workforce; some believe that although it does offer feedback on company performance, it communicates little about how people add value. In our view, other alternatives are more powerful communicators of business directions.

Team Variable Pay

A team can be broadly defined as a group of people who work collaboratively toward a common goal and have mutual accountability. Whether a loosely woven collaborative team or a tightly knit process team, teams are about shared goals. Because of the importance of team variable pay when the company's organizational design includes teams, we address team pay in some detail in Chapter 10.

COMMUNICATING THE BUSINESS ROLE OF TEAMS. Team variable pay communicates the role the team plays in adding value to the company results. The challenge is to focus on collaboration among teams such that they don't compete with one another or suboptimize performance at a higher organizational level when they optimize their own performance. For example, defining and rewarding shift teams so that one shift leaves all the difficult work for the next shift to do suboptimizes the plant's performance.

Team variable pay fosters communication with process teams and project teams about what is important. For example, team pay can emphasize the team over individual members, thus helping to break the grip of individual pay.

Short-term variable pay at the team level may encompass goalsharing, winsharing, or gainsharing. For example, team variable pay is funded at the company, business-unit, group, or site level from financial or other measures of performance and distributes awards, depending on how effectively each entire team achieves those of its measures that are important to attaining the longer line-of-sight measures and goals. When funding for team variable pay occurs at the team level rather than a broad organizational unit level, it's typically goalsharing.

DIFFERENCES IN TEAMS. Teams may differ a great deal. At Ford, for instance, the Taurus design team had more than 1,000 members with a wide range of skills, from manufacturing, marketing, and finance to heating and air conditioning engineering and interior design. When the time came to reward team members for a job well done, more than 1,000 workers were recognized. In contrast, at XEL Communications in Aurora, Colorado, the teams are much smaller and have full-time members with similar skill sets. Defining the team and membership has implications for designing team pay.

TEAM VARIABLE PAY AT UCLA MEDICAL CENTER. Chapter 10 includes illustrations of team pay, but we give one example here. UCLA Medical Center is a teaching and research tertiary-care medical center. With 4,800 full-time equivalent workers, organizationwide measures had too long a line of sight to drive understanding and performance on two critical objectives: quality and customer satisfaction. The center implemented team variable pay that rewards goal achievement at the team level on each of the two objectives and increases the funding according to the financial success of the center. The team is defined as a department, a subteam within a major department, or a line of service that includes both inpatient and outpatient. Teams develop goals with input from their internal customers on the appropriateness of the goals to ensure that team goals are aligned with broader organizational needs.

Individual Variable Pay

Another senior citizen of variable pay is individual variable pay, with its roots in the textile industry of the 1800s. You may ask why we'd consider a variable pay alternative for great companies that was developed so long ago. The reason is that businesses are finding that base pay alone can't fill the bill for rewarding results (as we described in Chapter 5) and are turning to individual variable pay, combination plans, and lump-sum payments when they want to reward individual performance outcomes.

MEASURING INDIVIDUAL RESULTS. Individual variable pay is most often developed around measures and goals that can be directly influenced by the individual participant. The most common plan of this type is the sales incentive, discussed in more detail in Chapter 12. Another individual variable pay approach is piece rate, which rewards individual productivity. Check processing, fruit picking, sewing garments, and medical transcribing provide examples of productivity-based approaches to paying individuals with variable pay. These are useful when work is very individualized and working collaboratively would not measurably improve business results.

Individual variable pay is suitable in situations where performance can be measured with individual goals whose achievement requires little interaction with other members of the workforce. However, individual variable pay is also clearly a better solution than individual base pay increases as recognition of individual performance. This is because it doesn't inflate base pay and permits re-earning performance recognition from one performance period to another.

When variable pay has a portion based on individual performance and the rest on the shared goals of some larger work group, the challenge is the messages the solution gives if there's a conflict between individual goals and shared goals. Also, if the individual goals and larger group goals are funded independently of one another, then the goal weighting must accomplish the appropriate balance between individual and group goals to communicate effectively. Because of line of sight, a smaller weighting on individual goals can give similar emphasis to a larger weighting on group goals.

INDIVIDUAL VARIABLE PAY AT A MEDICAL GROUP. Physicians in one medical group changed their pay by introducing individual incentives based on a combination of such measures as patient access and satisfaction, quality of care, and patient load. In addition, pay responds closely to competitive practice for medical specialties. This requires adjusting the total cash opportunity consistent with the labor market changes occurring in each medical specialty. The objective of this solution is to increase variable pay in the total cash mix, differentiate pay according to individual performance, and, overall, pay more consistently with the competitive labor market. Incentives focus on key measures of physician performance that add value to the organization.

INFLUENCING LONGER LINE-OF-SIGHT MEASURES

Look again at Exhibit 7.1. Much is said about measuring results achieved and selecting measures. Our case in *Pay People Right!* is strongly in favor of extending everyone's line of sight to business goals (Principle 3). This creates the need for the company and the workforce to talk about how the latter influences measures and can achieve results. It is critical to show people how their role adds value. For example, if a customer result is the goal and manufacturing workers ask how they influence exceeding customer expectations, the company has an excellent education opportunity. But communication with and involvement of the workforce are critical ingredients to making this work.

Hundreds of opportunities for education exist to make measures real to those involved. In some instances, the message is strongly needed. We once parked in the lot of the corporate office of a large retail company in the East. The "guest" parking and "customer" parking were filled with autos having "employee" stickers on them, so we parked elsewhere as best as we could and put a note on our windshield saying we were visiting a particular senior person. Our discussion with the executive focused on providing customer value, growing the chain's customer base, and measuring customer satisfaction. When we got out, we saw that security had pasted a large sticker on our car window. It practically covered the entire window and said, "Park Only in Customer or Guest Spaces." Our reaction was, what if we had been *customers* of this company, working on a major business deal?

RETURN TO EMERALD CITY

Variable pay is widely used. It will grow in use, so it's worthwhile expending the effort to make it work well. We hear people from important companies reporting negative outcomes. As we explore more closely, we learn that what's not working is something called "variable pay"—but clearly not variable pay as driven by the six reward principles we introduce as the foundation of this book.

The exciting part of implementing pay change is that great companies can and will make variable pay work positively. Those that don't follow some commonsense business practices end up with variable pay solutions that look like the hand-me-down rigid pay solutions under which people suffered before the mid-1980s.

In the future, pay for everyone will begin to look more like sales compensation. Variable pay continues to become a larger portion of the total pay mix. Measurement for determining variable pay awards is improving. It's been easier to measure sales performance than the performance of many other functions in the past. In the future, we believe it'll become easier to measure the economic value of a process or a body of work that's completed by a group of people or organizational unit. This is because measurement is becoming more sophisticated and we're learning to determine the value of a body of work as we outsource it. This drives thinking about the value of a body of work done by the workforce, not just contractors, and in turn helps determine variable pay opportunities.

Organizations may also begin to compare these measures among themselves just as they've been comparing sales compensation cost as a percentage of revenues. Thus integration of total pay moves in both directions: general workforce pay adopting elements from sales compensation, and sales compensation adopting elements from general workforce pay in terms of linkages through business-aligned goals with the rest of the workforce. We expand on these issues in our discussion of sales compensation (Chapter 12).

CONCLUSIONS

Variable pay is the most important positive total pay communication tool of all. It's useful to those specifically interested in communicating with the workforce and to those who mainly want to vary labor costs according to their ability to pay. It's a mature and effective tool, associated with some of the most critical performance initiatives in the world. It's a tool that can bring positive messages of win-win and sharing in company success. Variable pay provides flexibility to move from one set of measures and goals to another; it introduces the opportunity to emphasize a collaborative workplace and the importance of shared goals.

Variable pay can be increasingly effective if people understand the connection between what they do and company and business-unit goals. Communication works best in making the connection between individual contributions and the performance of the team and organizational unit.

The information is in on the value of variable pay. Workforces with variable pay that matches the reward principles we propose are more likely to understand performance expectations and business results than are those with a pay solution founded only on base pay increases and individual performance. Clear evidence exists to support the business value of variable pay. It facilitates collaboration and teamwork, and goal achievement is more likely if variable pay awards are a result.

CHAPTER 8

Rewarding Performance

Long-Term Variable Pay

Because winning enterprises aren't shrinking to greatness, few companies have become successful by getting smaller. This is especially true during times of business globalization and an increase in the number and scope of mergers and acquisitions. Sustained success requires a long-term view. Some people criticize excessive emphasis on short-term results. In large part, this is a product of the investment community's expectations.

The need for long-term focus argues for people in key roles adding value on a sustained basis. Also, individuals and teams of colleagues often have the responsibility for achieving business results that take longer than a year to accomplish. In these cases, long-term variable pay design can make it attractive for a workforce to concentrate on achieving some important goal in the future. In fact, as Peter Block says, "There is no question that economic ownership facilitates emotional ownership."[1]

Intensifying emphasis on the future of the business increasingly drives enterprises and total reward strategies toward more long-term variable pay, and deeper in the organization. This means extending the line of sight to business results that are now commonly viewed as beyond the purview of the general workforce. In turn, this requires that a company be smarter in how it communicates with and educates people on influencing longer-term results.

We believe that sustained results should be rewarded by means of long-term variable pay and that both a short-term and a long-term focus are worthwhile. Many times we hear arguments about how people have a chance to influence only goals that are close to their daily routine. Our view is that making some portion of pay dependent on measures with a longer line of sight requires that the company take the time to communicate the connection between what people do and why this is important to the business. It's part of the better workforce deal that helps people understand how they can grow to count even more in the future.[2]

LONG-TERM CASH VARIABLE PAY

Long-term variable pay includes both cash and equity. Exhibit 8.1 outlines long-term variable pay approaches, including cash and stock. We will discuss all but the last two because they're less often used for the general workforce and because of the greater interest in broad-based stock options.

Our interest in this section is on cash; the next section addresses stock options. Awards under long-term cash variable pay are most often cash (of course), although other forms, including common stock, may be substituted on a cash-equivalent basis.

Cash long-term variable pay is a primary tool where common stock isn't available and results are to be measured over a period longer than a year. Not-for-profit organizations such as those in health care use this approach for key individuals. Such a solution is also useful when publicly traded companies believe they have too much dilution to use additional stock options and when privately held companies want to offer long-term variable pay that simulates the changing value of the company. In some instances, cash solutions emulate equity designs; approaches such as stock appreciation rights often join options as parallel long-term variable pay.

Exhibit 8.1. Types of Long-Term Variable Pay.

Type of Plan	Basic Design	Indicators
Multiyear project (cash)	Reward successful project completion	• Project success is critical to company performance and is measurable
Performance unit (cash)	Grant units where people earn the appreciation in unit value based on performance on predetermined measure(s)	• Measures performance at or below company level—team, group, business unit, division • Use if dilution is a problem, but like all cash plans is a charge to earnings • Can be independent of or parallel stock
Event-related (cash)	Reward results at the end of an event or accomplishment	• Need outcomes by the end of an event
Overlapping performance periods (cash)	Reward results on each overlapping performance period	• Provides long-term focus that can parallel annual variable pay • Must be able to set realistic multiyear goals
Stock option	Grant right to purchase a specified amount of stock at a prescribed price over a specified time period	• Communicates the market value of company • Easy communications in a bull market; more challenging in a bear market
Restricted stock	Grant stock with future service restriction and (occasionally) performance requirements	• Retains people during mergers, acquisitions, business transitions, bankruptcies, or turnarounds • Provides stock in lieu of cash for incentive payment to retain talent and encourage ownership
Performance share	Grant stock that people earn if predetermined goals (typically company financial goals) are achieved	• Communicates both company goals and market value of company

Paying for Sustained Performance

Long-term cash variable pay plays a critical role in communicating and rewarding business results with these objectives:

- *Focus on needed longer-term results.* Many people play roles that enable them to influence performance over a period longer than one year. This applies to executives, managers, and key professionals in roles such as marketing, research and development, and product development. Often, teams and groups share responsibility for goal results over time. For example, a team of IT professionals working on a major client assignment for more than a year may be jointly responsible for a number of deliverables that are sensitive to time, cost, and quality.
- *Emphasize business results other than stock performance.* Common stock performance is essential for most for-profit businesses that have common stock, but additional kinds of results may also be important. In other situations, such as with a not-for-profit organization, long-run results measured in terms of operating income may be the organization's primary measure of success. In Principle 3, we indicate the importance of extending the line of sight of the workforce to include viable measures of business results. In some instances, measures may represent long-term team, business-unit, division, or group performance. In other instances, interim measures and goals point the way to shareholder value. This mostly involves quantitative goals that can be accurately measured over time, but some qualitative goals may be clear enough to use.
- *Reward multiple long-term measures and goals at the same time.* More than just one measure and goal are important to optimizing the business overall. Also, achievement of short-term results can serve as milestones for longer-term results. For example, annual revenue goals may be milestones for achieving a three-to-five-year objective of sustaining revenue growth at a specific level. At the same time, accompanying net income goals ensure that the result is profitable growth. In this case, variable pay can comprise annual variable pay (emphasizing annual revenue and profit performance) and long-term variable pay (for example, rewarding continued revenue and profit growth over some longer period). Here, annual results may be an element of long-term results.

- *Create an overlapping performance emphasis.* Both annual and longer-term goals and measures can change for a company in a dynamic business environment. For instance, one set of measures and goals may be critical for a specific work group for one three-year period, and a second set may be most important for another. Long-term cash variable pay permits one set of measures to be used for years one through three and the other set for years two through four. Thus, the performance periods overlap.

What about performance that's more observable than measurable? Variable pay, especially long-term variable pay, does a better job of communicating needed objective or measurable results than important performance that may be just observable. For this reason, a definition of performance that includes goals (such as dealing with customer service), behaviors (such as leadership and teamwork), and skill and competency improvement is best addressed through individual ongoing value and acknowledged through base pay or lump-sum payment designs.

Long-Term Cash Variable Pay Approaches

The business goals, required business results, and the specific situation of the enterprise serve as sources of ideas for developing long-term cash designs. The many regulations that apply to stock plans do not generally encumber these approaches, thus creating a significant chance to think outside of the box. Our examples serve as the start of matching and customizing the long-term cash variable pay to specific situations.

One possible use of variable pay is to reward major breakthroughs that change the business forever. For example, legend has it that a long time ago a major soft drink company was approached by an "inventor" who offered what he called a major new business breakthrough. The soft drink maker had seen many such pitches before; the executives listened with hesitation. The inventor said, "I'll tell you what it is. If you use it, you'll pay me a million dollars." The executives agreed. "Bottle it!" The rest is history. There are great opportunities to reward major breakthrough results that are long-term, whether expected or unexpected.

MULTIYEAR-PROJECT VARIABLE PAY. This approach sets goals for accomplishing a long-term project, such as product or service development, opening a new factory, or major IT software customization and installation. The company may grant smaller awards for meeting project milestones to keep people's attention on accomplishing the short-term steps that lead to long-term success. The largest award is at the end of the project because only then can the final result be evaluated, and because the company wants to retain people to the end.

An engineering company implemented project variable pay for its IT workforce. The objectives were to implement a major companywide software and hardware conversion while maintaining the existing system and retaining talent. Retention was paramount before the conversion, particularly since people knew that some of their current technical skills wouldn't be needed once the new system was operational.

Project variable pay for IT awarded "points" at key junctures according to a combination of meeting installation milestones and attaining existing system maintenance goals. Full completion, debugging, and on-time operation of the installation delivered the majority of the points. Also, these completion points increased or decreased depending on the date the new system was operational. To retain talent, the points converted to dollars only at project completion. In addition to this solution, the company provided retraining as part of the better workforce deal. We discuss multiyear project variable pay in more detail in Chapter 10, on rewarding teams.

PERFORMANCE-UNIT VARIABLE PAY. Performance-unit or share-unit plans take their design from the stock option. They may parallel stock options to give cash for the exercise of the option itself. Sometimes the value of the unit is the same as the option share price, so that the unit approach is a "phantom share" design. Other times the basis is a division or business unit's performance to provide closer line-of-sight focus. Other distinctions are possible, but for our purposes what's important is the concept of the unit and how it increases in value over time. In equity approaches such as stock options, the individual actually takes ownership of the stock, whether only momentarily in a cashless exercise or for a longer period. The unit in a performance-unit design is just a way to measure change in performance results over time. Nobody takes units home or "banks" them.

A unit variable pay design often starts with an arbitrary unit value, say, $1.00 per unit at the time the plan begins. The company then grants people a number of units for a variety of reasons: as a performance award, for a promotion, as an annual award for being a member of the workforce, as part of a hiring package, and for the same reasons outlined in guidelines for granting stock options.

The units can have vesting schedules similar to those of stock options. For example, an individual can be awarded 3,000 $1.00 units. A third of these vest at the end of three years, another third at the end of four years, and the final third at the end of five years. At the end of three years, the participant can cash in the first third of the units. Say the units are now worth $2.00; they've appreciated by $1.00. The individual gets 1,000 times the $1.00 per unit appreciation, or a cash payment of $1,000. A year later, the unit value may be $2.50; cashing in the next 1,000 units generates 1,000 times the gain of $1.50, or a cash payment of $1,500.

Although a unit value may start at $1.00, future grants are most commonly at the new unit value. In this example, units would be granted at $2.00 or $2.50. In other words, the appreciated unit value is the value at which new units are granted. Subsequent appreciation depends on the starting place of unit value. If the unit value doesn't appreciate, the individual doesn't receive any cash gain from the unit plan.

The change in the value of a performance unit depends on one or a few measures of business success. Indeed, the message from performance units is in the measures used to determine how the value of the units changes. Performance units can be based on measures at the level of the group, business unit, division, or other organizational unit, such as a product development team that sees unit value increase in proportion to the success of a new product. This shortens the line of sight for people to the organizational unit where they're responsible for adding value.

A host of measures and goals work in performance unit variable pay. With the current strong concern about global growth, measures that represent the company goals for growth often determine the value of performance units. Measures from the economic-value-added family (profit in excess of cost of capital) are possible, as are measures of financial return (for example, return on equity, capital employed, sales, or assets), income, and revenue growth. This approach is useful where stock is unavailable for not-for-profit organizations, and in some global applications where implementing stock options of a company headquartered in a different country poses difficulties. The requirement is for one or two primary measures that reflect how the business is doing.

A high-technology company wanted to use long-term variable pay for its communications product division to focus key people on the division's performance. It also had concerns about stock dilution. The division implemented a performance-unit plan that rewards division earnings growth. The long-term plan started soon after the division was formed from existing businesses. Everyone in the division received at least a few founder's "shares" to acknowledge past contributions, to celebrate the new organization, and to enable widespread continuing communication about "share" value. But the number of shares granted varied significantly with an individual's current and projected future contribution, to retain needed key talent. This long-term variable pay solution was instrumental in the success of the division.

EVENT-RELATED LONG-TERM VARIABLE PAY. This approach operates for a specific period of time greater than one year and rewards performance related to a meaningful event or accomplishment that's part of the ongoing business rather than a specific time-defined project. It has similarities to project team long-term variable pay but may apply to just one individual or a larger group of people. In an example of the former, an individual accepts a three-year assignment to build the business in another country. The company sets specific goals that relate to expected growth by the end of that period, and the individual's award depends on how successfully they position the business by the end of the assignment.

An example of a larger group of participants is in a company that provides health care services to the federal government on a five-year contract. Renewal of the company's contract at the end of the five-year period depends on both the government and the company's shareholders. During the third year of the contract, the executive team realized that they needed to do something to ensure stable staffing through the end of the contract, regardless of the renewal decision.

Instead of reacting with higher base pay, this company developed a long-term variable pay solution that awards the most if the company is successful and the contract is renewed, and less if the company is successful but the contract is not renewed. It pays out the least—but still something—if the company is less financially successful and the contract isn't renewed. Level of participation depends on how key the individual or individual's role is to the business. Rather than communicating this solution as a retention or stay bonus, its objective is a futures award: winning the contract with the company being financially successful, such that shareholders are willing to continue the investment.

OVERLAPPING LONG-TERM VARIABLE PAY. This approach uses overlapping performance periods, commonly two to three years in length. Figure 8.1 is an example of how three-year overlapping variable pay works. Goal setting for the first three-year performance period occurs prior to year one. At the end of the three years, the variable pay award is determined and paid. At the beginning of year two, another period starts that will pay off at the end of year four. This continues for as long as variable pay is in effect. The overlapping performance periods have retention power because stakeholders leave something on the table after a few performance periods of participation.

This variable pay solution allows flexibility because goals can change from one performance period to the next and eligibility can change for each subsequent one. Simplicity is important, and a few measures and goals get more attention than many, but goals can have different weights. Overlapping long-term approaches tend to be simple in design and similar to those of short-term variable pay. Indeed, a similar approach can pay off both annually and at the end of a three-year performance period. This approach meets our elevator-

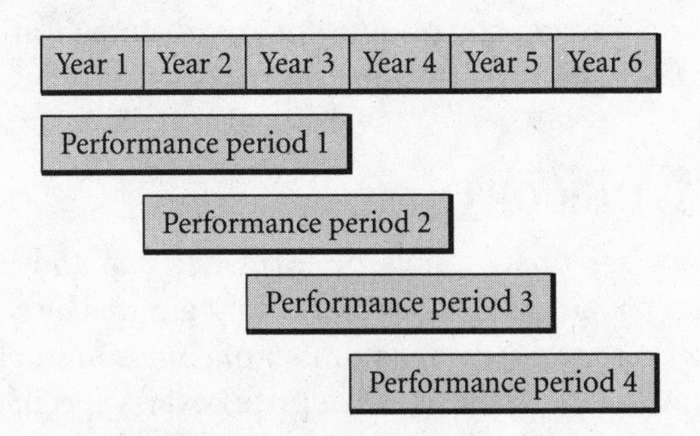

Figure 8.1. Example of Cash Long-Term Variable Pay with Overlapping Performance Periods.

speech standard of communication because it requires only brief orientation on how the solution works and what people can do to earn awards.

A not-for-profit health care organization uses this way to reward its key people for financial success. The measures relate to sustained financial performance. The variable pay opportunity is a percentage of base pay, to allay government concerns about not-for-profits sharing a portion of each dollar of income.

Tax and Accounting Consequences

It's beyond our objective here to address the tax and accounting consequences of different pay solutions, but differences do need mention.[3] At the time of this writing, cash long-term variable pay awards are taxed as ordinary income and are charged to earnings, as is other cash compensation. It's impossible to gain tax or accounting advantage from this form of award. These are tools of performance pay, not of tax avoidance. Stock options, common stock, and cash all have different tax and accounting consequences (as we write this book). Although cash payments, restricted stock, and performance shares are a charge to earnings, stock options are not.

Many hours of work have been dedicated to determining the tax efficiency of long-term variable pay alternatives. So we suggest that whenever you develop these solutions, you need to consider tax and accounting principles in place at the time, including local country requirements if the solution is global. We believe, though, that pay solutions offering the best tax advantages may not necessarily be best suited to communicating what's required in terms of business results. Performance and company results, not tax advantage, are the goal of everything we're sharing with you.

STOCK OPTIONS

Stock options are one possible performance pay and equity long-term variable pay solution. They're the right granted by a company to purchase or exercise a specified number of common stock shares at a prescribed price (the grant or strike price) over a specified period of time (exercise period). Typically, the individual must meet a prescribed period of time (vesting period) before exercising stock options. Options are an alternative to or a supplement for cash variable pay. They do some things that cash variable pay does, but options and cash variable pay are clearly not an either-or trade-off.

Objective of Options

Options potentially pass real equity in the enterprise to those awarded options and result in a workforce of owner-workers. Avis, United Airlines, and Southwest Airlines make note of this in their advertisements by implying that customers are better cared for by owners than by nonowners. Options can be a reward for performance. They can also be a benefit, retirement supplement, form of recognition, and a way to make a company attractive to people who are in essential roles or who have talent that's scarce in the marketplace. Stock options are a multipurpose tool in the total pay tool kit.

Stock options are an increasingly common reward for major segments of a company's workforce—even for the entire workforce. Perhaps only 30 percent of the largest publicly traded U.S. companies provide stock options deep in the organization, but we expect this practice to increase (in fits and starts) over the next decade. Stock options are very popular; unless a major sustained market correction breaks the option bubble, they'll increasingly become part of total pay.

The objective of stock options is stakeholdership: making those granted options owners in the company. The riddle is that many options don't result in long-term stock ownership. Instead, options are exercised and "cashed in" as soon as options vest. The vesting period is really the time when stock options retain people and create stakeholdership rather than after the stock option vests, unless the company has made sustained stock ownership a "heritage" in their company—something to be proud of. Chapter 11, on scarce talent, describes ways 22 IT companies in our survey use options to stimulate real ownership.

Broad Option Participation

Chase Manhattan, Du Pont, General Mills, Procter & Gamble, PepsiCo, Merck, Eli Lilly, Kimberly-Clark, Starbucks, Microsoft, Amazon.com, and many other household names provide the workforce broad opportunities for stock option participation. Options are a tool of involvement and stakeholdership. People like options, enterprises like options, and boards of directors like options. It's reasonable to expect stock options to play an important role in total reward strategies, not just for executive compensation but for communicating and sharing the results of performance with the general workforce (or specific elements of it).

Some believe stock options are a gift to the workforce, but we suggest that how they are deployed can affect workforce involvement in making the business a success. They're powerful when used in mergers and acquisitions, transitions, or turnarounds and a viable alternative to other variable pay approaches. They're also part of the future of total pay design for the general workforce and support the total reward component of a compelling future.

Now that we've admitted we favor using stock options as a reward for the general workforce, we must explain the "yes, but—" in the logic of our support. Broad-based options enable a specific portion or all of the workforce (in addition to executives) to potentially receive stock options. They place requirements on company leadership that are unparalleled in challenge and importance. Offering options seems simple at first blush, but considerable work is necessary to get the most from broad-based stock options. To be a success, they need to address five important criteria: understandability, demonstrated value, business justification, flexibility, and patience.

UNDERSTANDABILITY. People must understand stock options. Although executives close to company performance and experienced in personal investment in securities may understand options, this isn't always the case for the general workforce. Remember that our reward principles propose what constitutes useful pay design. The foundation here is that the workforce must understand options and common stock.

For example, it's difficult enough to explain how a company makes profit, satisfies customers, and grows market share, and how people add value to achieving these goals. Strong arguments can be made about how people meet intermediate goals that influence company performance measures such as cost management, sales targets, and meeting delivery schedules. If stock price goes south despite positive movement in these shorter line-of-sight results, it's hard to explain. We heard a story of an administrative assistant at a major biotechnology company who failed to exercise her vested stock options because she didn't understand how they worked. The cost to her was supposedly more than half a million dollars!

DEMONSTRATED VALUE. Stock options must prove to have value. What good is a variable pay solution that doesn't pay off over a period of time? Even if everyone gets a clear message when results are missed and variable pay doesn't pay off, getting something is better than not. This is especially true if the company does a viable job of communications and education that suggests options have potential value. During long bull markets, this may not be a perceived problem. But many current option solutions have been initiated during the (current) long bull market. When the tide turns, people will not have had experience in the downside, no matter how effective the communications may have been.

A number of factors determine the price of stock and thus the value of options. One is the performance of the company; others are the performance of the equity market in general and that of the specific industry group. The line of sight between the value of the options and how the workforce adds value is generally less direct than the line of sight to other possible company success measures, including a measure or combination of measures of financial and strategic or tactical performance.

As long as common stock and underlying options increase in value, people generally accept that options are valuable. But it may be difficult to convince people that the enterprise granted them something of value once it's worth less than it was when they received it.

BUSINESS JUSTIFICATION. Stock options must match the variable pay objectives of the total reward strategy to reward needed business results better than alternative variable pay solutions. Options can work in a variety of ways, but it's important to make sure they fit the business plan. If the goal of pay is to align people with the performance of a specific division or global organizational unit, options based on overall company performance may not be a viable carrier of the key alignment message.

Stock options have vesting periods that cover a number of performance periods. Most commonly, once options are granted time is the only thing that must transpire from when the options are granted until they can be exercised. However, performance goals may change from year to year. To align stock options with strategic measures, the number of options granted should vary as a result of differences in performance. The company can also provide for acceleration or extension of the vesting schedule as a result of performance.

FLEXIBILITY. Stock options must be agile and adaptable to match changes in business directions. Because options are time-sensitive and depend on the common stock for their value, a company may hesitate to change designs even when necessary. For example, it seems obvious that in addition to time requirements for vesting, options need performance requirements; but this change is sluggish because of the hesitation to adapt stock option designs to changing situations.

Options must compare favorably to other possible alternatives. Short-term and long-term cash variable pay can adapt to a host of measures, time periods, and situations, but stock options often don't do this quite so well. There can be many reasons for granting options, and the number of options granted to an individual can vary, but the primary measure of the success of the option is limited to the performance of the company's common stock price.

PATIENCE. The company must have patience to make options work. As a change to pay design, they require communication and education. They're not a quick fix, and sometimes leaders must respond fast to changing business needs and priorities. Any pay transition, including stock options, tests patience.

People must view options as something other than a crap shoot. Some individuals (especially those with scarce talent) are likely to move from company to company and gamble on the next parcel of options from their new firm. Nothing we've said so far suggests that such a "talent gypsy" mentality should properly generate a major financial hit. Moving from company to company for still another option windfall isn't part of the better workforce deal. This is not the stuff that value is made of over the long run.

These issues are part of pay design in general. In a way, stock options compete with alternative selections in the smorgasbord of pay tools. In addition, though, going global with stock options entails challenges and complexities. A company must address numerous local legal, tax, accounting, and worker-expectation issues to make global equity participation a reality.

Stock Option Approaches

There are several uses for stock options, and a company must determine which objective or objectives in the next discussion they serve.[4] Exhibit 8.2 outlines six approaches.

Exhibit 8.2. Stock Option Approaches.

Characteristic	Executive	Key Talent	Performance-Oriented Workforce	Special Achievement	Organization-wide	Hiring Award
Business case	Build ownership; serve as leadership role model; be competitive with labor market	Reward sustained performance or recognize potential; retain key talent	Reward performance as part of regular review for integrated total pay	Celebrate and recognize outstanding individual or team contribution	Create shared destiny; communicate status of business; support teamwork	Recruit talent; encourage commitment from start
Message	Shareholder alignment—keep it up!	You're important to the future of the business!	Reward value added—you did it!	Congratulations!	Everyone counts! We're all in this together!	You're part of the team! Make a difference!
Eligibility	All executives	Worker group(s) or all workforce	Worker group(s) or all workforce	Worker group(s) or all workforce	All workforce	Worker group(s) or all workforce
Number of eligible receiving grants	All	Few to some	Some to many	Generally few	All	Generally all
Emphasis on retention	Yes	Strong yes	Yes	Yes or no	Yes	Yes
Number of options per person	Largest	Large	Variable	Variable	Small	Variable
Grant frequency	Annual or biennial	As needed	Annual	When contribution happens	Periodic	At hire

EXECUTIVE STOCK OPTIONS. Stock options are accepted long-term variable pay for members of the executive team. The message to the workforce from this use of stock options is that executives share in the success of the company with the shareholders. Clearly, options can attract the executives the company needs to succeed. Executive stock options provide the largest number of option grants per participant of any type of stock option usage.

The message to the workforce is also that managing people and assets makes one a stakeholder. Our view is that other things in addition to becoming an executive or manager bring important value to a company. For example, the true core competency of the company may rest in people not in the management ranks. In this case, everyone counts, but people with key skills and competencies count more.

In Chapter 13, we address executive compensation in general and use of stock options in particular. Our guidance concerning executive compensation is related to what sort of role model executives play in setting an example, as far as how they are paid. If executives have stock options or own stock, we believe the workforce in general should have options (if at all possible from a dilution standpoint) or own stock. This isn't necessarily only for the potential economic gain and chance to share in the company's success, but to make it necessary for everyone to understand how businesses in general, and theirs in particular, work to be successful and provide attractive employment. Options create a common focus for both the workforce and executives.

KEY-TALENT STOCK OPTIONS. In terms of core competencies, some people are better positioned than others to provide the critical capabilities needed by the business. Key-talent stock options generate significant upside financial opportunities to people the company believes are central to its future success. The objective is to place a premium on these people so that a competitor interested in such talent has to offer a stock option opportunity at least as attractive. This tells essential people they count and are important; it answers the question, "What's in it for me?" The message to the workforce in general is that certain skills and competencies are critical and must be emphasized, and that the company is betting that people with certain capabilities will generate the business results that make stock options grow in value. If these people fail to add value, their options won't generate expected financial gain.

The tendency is to offer highly valuable people large option grants that vest over an extended period of time. If the company uses only this stock option approach for the workforce in general, it's hard to communicate who is "critical" and who isn't, unless clear guidelines are announced. Does the company keep secret who is key? If so, what message does this deliver? In Chapter 11, on scarce talent, we suggest that although options help in the battle for key talent, it's important to offer more than options. The best people want what we call the better workforce deal—and this requires much more than liberal stock options.

In our experience, options for essential individuals may have significant upside value. Although gains in the millions of dollars are unusual and legendary, it is not uncommon that key individuals find option values growing to the hundreds of thousands over a successful career with a successful company. Time and again, we see second careers financed from options granted to key individuals.

PERFORMANCE-ORIENTED WORKFORCE STOCK OPTIONS. To us, performance orientation marks the real broad-based stock option solutions offered to large portions of the general workforce. Stock options can be part of total workforce pay—in other words, they're as much a part of total pay as base pay and other forms of variable pay. Either everyone or major categories of people (for example, all professional workers) are *eligible* to earn some options as part of the pay package.

Typically, an established company offers performance-oriented stock options in addition to competitive total cash. A start-up or pre-IPO may offer them instead of some base pay and short-term variable pay to save fixed pay costs and conserve cash. The objective in either case is to share company success with the people who contribute to it. Individuals must do something to earn options because stock options are part of the emphasis on paying for performance at either the individual or the team level.

This use of options usually has wider eligibility than actual participation, meaning that just being able to receive an option grant doesn't make it automatic. Individual performance determines the size of the grant, and there may be significant variation in size according to the performance of individuals in a given role. Because of the complexity involved, the more people the company includes as eligible for these options, the more that what needs to be done to earn options must be clear and easy to understand. Options may be granted more as a bet on people's future contributions than on what they've accomplished in the past because options reach their value in the future rather than as a result of the past. Option grants of 5–20 percent of total cash are not uncommon as part of a pay solution that includes them.

SPECIAL ACHIEVEMENT STOCK OPTIONS. "Your outstanding contribution made a difference to the company! Here are 100 stock options!" Options are clearly a part of recognition and celebration for doing something that benefits the enterprise. They reward exceptional one-time contributions by individuals or teams, such as a research team reaching a major technology breakthrough or another team succeeding in getting quick FDA approval for a potentially profitable product. Options are powerful and are appreciated as a visible and publicized award for doing something significant. The value of options isn't limited to the people who get them; their value is the message to everyone else who can make major breakthroughs that add to the business.

Options as a way to recognize people complement the material we discuss in Chapter 9, on recognition. They tell people who've made a difference that it's worth making them owners of the company. The message to the workforce is that stakeholdership requires both investment from shareholders and outstanding business contributions from the workforce. This type of stock option may have a shorter vesting schedule to heighten its impact and because it acknowledges a contribution that has already occurred rather than positioning for the future.

A major electronics company uses stock options principally as a special achievement award. In management's view, using them for other purposes as well diminishes their value as a significant reward for a breakthrough business idea. The president tells a story about two people who meet in the hall and are happy to have received stock options. One says, "Wow, I just got options for that new engineering design the company adopted. What a great deal!" The other says, "Wow, I just got stock options for being around another year! What a deal!" The president argues that options for the second person's "Wow!" make the first "Wow!" less valuable. Think about what message stock options should give in your company.

ORGANIZATIONWIDE STOCK OPTIONS. An enterprise may want to get "everyone in the stock option pool" to make them feel as though they're part of the team. Doing so says we're all in this together, and everyone counts in making the company a success. Individual grants are usually small because of the number of participants involved. These options can be a source of pride and participation. We've seen people frame even the one or two shares they have and hang them in their work area. Some firms give options to every individual at the time of hire and annually thereafter. Others give them after a service period, and still others when something significant happens—perhaps after a good year or when the company engages in a major product introduction or business repositioning.

If individual performance counts for participation, it's a gate that serves to exclude those who don't meet performance expectations. Either everyone gets the same number of options or they're distributed according to base pay level, organizational level, service to the company, workforce group, or some other fairly easy-to-determine difference. A more egalitarian view of rewards favors giving the same number to everyone. The objective is tying the workforce to the company. The way to do this differs with the company.

HIRING AWARD. A company may want to make people stakeholders from the start. Sometimes the objective is to replace stock options left behind. The goal is to close the hiring deal and make the individual an owner in the business future of the enterprise.

Multiple Reasons That Options Work

Options can be used for all of the reasons we've described. Perhaps your company can think of more. In our view, the challenge is to communicate meaningfully why options are granted. Those who earn them for performance as part of total pay and those who receive them for a recognizable outstanding contribution need to understand the reason for the option grant. After the grant, the company and individual share accountability for doing what they can to make the options valuable by increasing the market value of the underlying common stock. But it's most important to impart the logic of why they were granted the options.

We like the use of options as part of a team or individual reward for specific results. A selling team brings in a major client. An engineering team solves a critical engineering-business riddle. A business unit has an excellent year. This pins definition of what's being rewarded first on why the options were granted, and then on stock price improvement once the options are in the hands of the workforce.

Economic Cost of Stock Options and Dilution

Options are not free. This is why it's important that a company get something for the expenditure on options in terms of results, association, retention, or identification with the company. It's true that at the time of this writing, stock options have cash flow advantages compared to other total cash tools and don't involve a charge to earnings for compensation expense on the income statement. However, dilution, which reduces the value of shares owned by existing shareholders, is one cost of options. To prevent dilution, the company may buy back shares in the market when people exercise options. This avoids reducing the ownership stake of existing shareholders. Many businesses elect to keep the number of outstanding shares constant and buy shares in the market with cash. But this cash can't then be used in other ways (such as investment in research and development).

If you believe the results of the stock option valuation tools used to evaluate the market cost of options, you see that options have a cost.[5] For example, if a company grants options on $15 million of its stock, the cost can range from 25 to 80 percent of this amount depending on the volatility of the stock. We also discuss the opportunity cost of stock options in Chapter 13 (executive compensation).

Dilution and buyback costs occur only if the workforce exercises the options. This means stock price has risen beyond the option price. Some argue that dilution is a fair trade-off for workforce stock options. A strong argument exists in support of increasing acceptable levels of dilution in exchange for more options for the general workforce. This seems a reasonable argument, assuming the general workforce shares in a large portion of the options created by that dilution.

Given the competition for scarce talent, we believe in being ready to change the age-old "rules" of dilution. Even so, if we were on a board of directors and were asked about dilution, we'd ask management about its total reward and total pay solutions. Are stock options the only good thing about total rewards? In addition to more stock options, should they do more in terms of the better workforce deal? How about thinking outside of the box regarding scarce talent? See what people really want, and try to change the switching-companies-for-more-options game that's been prominent.

To us, the argument that options are free is folly. So what? What good is giving something to the workforce that the company believes is free? Instead, acknowledge the economic cost of options, and make sure the company gets added business value from those to whom options are granted. Nobody wants to hear that in exchange for adding value to business results they get something that costs the company nothing.

Repricing Stock Options

When the current market price of shares is below the price at which the individual can exercise options, repricing cancels old options and regrants them at a lower price. A company with these so-called underwater options should consider option repricing only if the reality is that if it doesn't, critical talent will leave and reprice their options themselves.

Let's add quickly that we hope an attractive total reward and total pay program, and commitment to a better workforce deal, diminish the focus on "options or bust" that exists, especially in technology-based companies. If the only attractive thing about your company is its stock option gambles, it's nearly impossible to stabilize a talented workforce over time. Thus, repricing must be "linked at the hip" with the messages of *Pay People Right!*

We don't believe that any option repricing should apply to the executive team. After all, if anyone can significantly influence the price of stock, they can. Ineligibility for repricing is what executives exchange for a substantial upside opportunity if they make the company a success.

Along with repricing of broad-based stock options, there must be some concession to the shareholder. This can vary, but we like reducing the number of repriced options granted by value-for-value repricing, adding performance requirements to vesting of repriced options, getting board approval, or changing the vesting schedule so it extends beyond the vesting of the underwater stock options. Or just granting more options may be the answer, which avoids repricing altogether. Accelerating future option grants gives new options a lower grant price while the underwater options continue to serve as a long-term incentive. Shareholders have less concern with accelerating future options because the total number of options stays the same. Another alternative when cash flow is tight is stock grants with cliff vesting, or pledging to give stock to an individual on a certain date in the future; this serves as a retention tool.[6]

Communications

"What's a stock option?"
"How do options work?"
"How do I exercise the options?"
"What is vesting in options?"
"What have I given up to get options?"
"How much are options worth to my family and me?"

People must understand the answers to these questions before value is realized. What they don't understand may not influence behavior in the desired fashion. This is why the stock option communication process tests the communication ability and patience of the company. Communication is essential to getting people to perform as well as possible to increase the value of stock.

The allocation of options is a critical communications message. If only a small portion of the workforce other than executives are eligible, the requirements for eligibility must be clear and challenging to the workforce. If options are distributed according to a pool, by managers or by a formula, the logic of this process must be communicated effectively. If enterprises use options instead of other pay elements, this needs care in communication to ensure understanding and acceptance.

Picture three IT professionals, who work for a major software development company, at a cocktail party. One says, "I got options for meeting our customer requirements on the team project I worked on over the last few years." The second says, "I just got an annual allocation of options because some of my existing options were about to expire." The third says, "I was pleased to get some options for my promotion to project manager." All three scenarios can easily be part of the options story in the same company—and even for people with the same career skills. The messages can range from *perform* to *stay*, and everywhere in between. Indeed, options can impart any or all of these messages, depending on the company's situation.

CONCLUSIONS

Experience suggests that a few primary measures and goals deliver the most powerful message about what an enterprise needs from its workforce to be successful. How the measures and goals are put together clearly matters, and some combination of funding (that makes sense to the company) and a message (that makes sense to people) produces the proper balance and direction. Long-term variable pay enables people to share in the future. Stock options, for example, communicate stakeholdership and ownership in a way that cash variable pay or other forms of rewards cannot. Individuals can keep abreast of the value of their potential ownership in the company in most cases simply by looking in a local daily newspaper or using their computer.

CHAPTER 9

Recognition and Celebration

On the wall of an actuary's office was a framed picture of an eagle soaring. It was part of a recognition program to acknowledge what the company called "over and above" behavior and deeds.

In one global company, the process improvement teams whose successful projects had resulted in measurable process improvements met in Singapore to make presentations that relived their accomplishments, share ideas, and celebrate.

A worker at an IT company took her spouse out for a candlelight dinner after her manager thanked her with a dinner-for-two award for successfully completing an important rush project that delighted the customer.

A scientist who acquired a major patent was highlighted in the company newsletter and received a check for $5,000.

All of these are forms of recognition and celebration. They all have a place in a chapter on recognition and celebration (although some people might suggest that no *serious* book on pay would have a chapter on this topic). Clearly, we don't believe a company can recognize and celebrate as an *alternative* to a base pay and variable pay solution designed around the reward principles we advocate in this book. However, we do feel that a solid pay approach and strong supporting recognition and celebration are inseparable partners in making rewards communicate effectively. Recognition and celebration don't replace pay; they're in addition to pay. Communicating key messages comes from a variety of sources, and businesses associate recognition and celebration with the pay process as well as address them separately.

Recognition and celebration help create the positive, natural reward experience of Principle 1. To be effective for the long haul, they must align with business goals (Principle 2). Recognition and celebration support initiatives such as customer excellence, as an example. Recognition relates to Principle 3 because in most cases it's no longer limited to individuals; it also acknowledges teams and groups for outstanding contributions. Finally, recognition goes hand in hand with Principle 6 (rewarding results with variable pay) because—although it's retrospective, with variable pay being prospective—the reward may be a lump-sum cash or equity award.

TWO SIDES OF THE SAME COIN

Recognition is celebration, and celebration is recognition. They differ only as far as when they're likely to occur. Celebration and verbal recognition should be continuous as people and their enterprise progress toward meeting and exceeding goals and people make significant contributions to the business; they can occur without other forms of recognition (financial, tangible, work-related, and symbolic). Recognition is just what the word says; it can be formal or informal, involve a reward of monetary or nonmonetary value, and acknowledge individual or team performance. Recognition is given for something the company wants to frame positively and celebrate. What is critical is that each recognition makes people feel special for something good that's happened or is happening. It's like getting a star on your shirt in grade school for doing something well.

More Than T-Shirts

Celebration and recognition can be formal or a bit corny, depending on what works with your company, or even in a given situation. If you look at some of the idea books on recognition and celebration, you see examples of what has worked for the organizations reporting on their experience.[1] Whether you should give out T-shirts or movie tickets is actually less important than the fact that you recognize and celebrate visibly. We've seen all sorts of recognition and celebration solutions go well, and seen some go badly; success has little to do with what the actual award is. Rather, the dialogue, sincerity, involvement, and personalization as well as the relevance of the contribution to the business are the sources of success or lack of it.

Available to All Companies

When Picabo Street won her first Olympic medal, it was a big deal and established her for life as a star American skier. Her childhood home was near the Sun Valley Ski Resort. The resort named a ski run after her, "Picabo's Street" no less, and gave her a major celebration and one of the few lifetime passes to ski at Sun Valley. Major recognition? It's probably worth so much because it was given by the place where she grew up skiing. No money could make up for recognition such as this. Any company can do this sort of thing as well, and we believe they should.

ANOTHER OPPORTUNITY FOR ALIGNMENT WITH THE BUSINESS

Done properly, recognition and celebration are opportunities to communicate the role that people should play in making the enterprise a success. Just like pay, they're primarily *tools* of potentially effective communication. This means the same logic that applies to pay should apply to recognition and celebration—in fact, they're all part of total pay.

But recognition and celebration are cold change items compared to other elements of total pay. Thus they're adders, not replacements for pay. Recognition and celebration don't serve as lead change elements as base pay and variable pay do. For example, it's difficult for a CEO to get many followers for major change with only T-shirts and lunches leading the way. They're important but not something that can do the heavy lifting of change. They're easy to do, but ease shouldn't be the reason they're chosen as part of total rewards.

Specifying the objectives of the recognition program and what it intends to commend focuses and enables recognition to become a vehicle for communicating what's important to the company. It also keeps the program tight so that it maintains meaning and doesn't become a giveaway.

Pay that's not designed to create continuous excitement and attention is the ideal subject for partnering with attractive recognition approaches. For example, where traditional pay solutions fail to acknowledge issues of business opportunities, organization design, and competency, recognition can address them. A business unit of one large firm labored under the burden of traditional pay based on internal job value, automatic pay increases disguised as merit, and retrospective unaligned bonus solutions that were centrally controlled by corporate staff. To try to change this paradigm at least partially, the business unit implemented an exciting recognition and celebration program. This solution didn't fully counter a regressive pay message, but it helped.

Communications Tool

Recognize what you want to communicate to the workforce. If competencies such as innovation are valued when demonstrated, make this clear. Give visibility to accomplishment achieved through collaboration between organizational units that should work together better. Use recognition to reinforce desired changes in culture. As company or business-unit goals are incrementally achieved during a performance period, make this an achievement of note.

If fortunes are not as they should be, visibly call attention to what's required to redirect the organization toward a successful performance period. Don't wait until the end of the period. Celebrate and recognize incremental progress, and rally everyone to emphasize areas that need improvement. A plant with an unsatisfactory safety record celebrated simply its commitment to change behavior and practice during the performance period so people didn't give up for the year on performance improvement. Thus, recognition and celebration highlight what must be accomplished in the context of the business.

Recognition Success Factors

Exhibit 9.1 shows the success factors for recognition. The first, alignment with the business, is most important; we touch on the others in the rest of the chapter. Making recognition and celebration a success involves doing more than buying a bunch of stuff and giving it out. It

Exhibit 9.1. Successful Recognition.

- Recognizes what is important to the business
- Communicates recognition criteria
- Specifies the reason for recognition
- Matches recognition to the achievement
- Personalizes recognition to the individual or team
- Is timely
- Is sincere
- Is fun
- Publicizes recognition in most cases
- Is frequent—especially verbal and written recognition
- Is creative, customized, and varied
- Recognizes the recognizers
- Involves workforce in developing and implementing recognition
- Is refreshed periodically to keep interest high

means making celebration and recognition a natural extension of everything else the enterprise does to show people how they count.

Some management styles and cultures support more recognition and fun than others do. Disney, Ben & Jerry's, Microsoft, Hewlett-Packard, Motorola, Nordstrom, and Wal-Mart are good at recognition. Consider Southwest Airlines, whose recognition and celebration are lauded even by senior management and workers with other airlines. This doesn't mean the other airlines would not benefit from recognition. They just have a longer way to go to make it a natural, positive experience. We believe that every business should raise its recognition and celebration one notch, and then continue increasing it periodically.

TYPES OF RECOGNITION

Because recognition is a style issue, it needs to be natural to the company using it. Not recognizing people for doing good things, however, is not an acceptable style.

There are several types of recognition.

Verbal and Written Recognition

Examples of verbal and written recognition are an expression of praise ("Great job!"), a personal thank-you note specifying what was worthy of recognition, and appropriate credit given when passing an individual's idea on to others. Everyone can always do more of this; it makes people feel good, and it costs nothing. Give verbal and written recognition, and specify the reason for it as soon as possible after observing the behavior or achievement.

Work-Related Recognition

Involvement in a process improvement team, a special project assignment, lateral and vertical career opportunities, special office and work equipment, education and training opportunities, and earned time off are examples of work-related recognition. However, the problem with time off is that it reinforces not being at work, and the company may not get its work done while people are off.

Social Recognition

Examples of social celebration of team or organizational-unit success are pizza parties and barbecues where senior management serves the food. Examples of social celebration of individual or team success are recognition dinners and articles in newsletters.

Financial Recognition

Because financial recognition—cash, stock options, stock grants—often acknowledges more significant accomplishments, it may justify greater cost and a higher level of approval for awards.

Symbolic Recognition

Examples of symbolic recognition are T-shirts and coffee mugs with the name or logo of a performance initiative, jackets and sculptures with the company logo, and plaques celebrating a recognition-worthy contribution. These are visible signs for the individual and others to see; the value is more in what the item symbolizes than in monetary worth.

Tangible Recognition

Tangible items with monetary value are tickets to entertainment events, gift certificates, trips, meal tickets, earned-value credit cards, and merchandise. Some of these items, such as credit cards and merchandise, may be part of a formal program in which points accumulate toward purchase of merchandise, trips, or other things that the individual values.

Choosing Recognition Tools

Which type of recognition to use depends on the company's style and what's being recognized. The size of the award should match the achievement. Make clear what you want to recognize. One health care organization's recognition program had as its objective customer excellence, where the customers are the patients, patients' families, physicians, health insurance providers, and other workers. Anyone can suggest a person for an award as long as the nominator documents the reason for it. Points are awarded, which can be traded in for a variety of items.

RECOGNITION AT AN IT COMPANY. A custom software provider has two recognition programs. Their objectives are to enable recognition, give everyone a chance to be recognized, and support managers in improving an important leadership accountability: recognition and celebration. One is a spot award program for managers to acknowledge and celebrate individuals or teams immediately for going the extra mile in areas such as outstanding customer service, innovation, extraordinary efforts, process improvements, and achievements beyond the normal scope of the job. The second one, a special-achievement award program, grants significant cash awards and allows vice presidents to recognize major contributions to the enterprise or departments, such as significantly exceeding performance expectations or project goals, breakthrough innovation resulting in business improvement, and unplanned major contributions to the business.

Human resources provides tools to facilitate managers' recognition efforts (for example, certificates for dinners, names and telephone numbers of providers of recognition items such as florists), but it's up to the managers to be creative in personalizing recognition. Some of them are already very good at recognition; others are improving. The company trains managers for this purpose, as in exchanging and brainstorming ideas for recognition.

INVOLVEMENT AS RECOGNITION. Don't forget about work-related recognition, especially involvement. Experience suggests that making people part of what's going on is a major recognition tool. Give people being recognized the chance to participate in an important work session or on a critical high-involvement work team.

Both the company and the workforce gain from involvement. People gain by working with others who are seeking to add value and share knowledge and experience to achieve a business objective. The company gains by keeping the people who've added value in the quest for new opportunities to continue doing so. Involvement as recognition can get enterprises out of the rut of selecting the same people repeatedly to be involved in addressing issues; it can breed new ideas and be a catalyst for new collaboration on issues and solutions.

LENGTH OF SERVICE. Should length of service be part of the recognition solution? One company was registering only about 25 percent attendance at anniversary recognition dinners. People didn't want to go because they viewed it as a chore more than a celebration. Awards, pins, and rings just weren't very important—certainly not as much as the increased vacation benefit that often comes from years of service.

Look at service as more than the traditional marking of 5, 10, 15, and 20 years of service. The enterprise should determine *when* it loses people, and customize the service awards to counter this situation. One enterprise that tended to lose people in the third year added vacation time at that point and geared the vesting of its cash long-term variable pay to retain people at the critical time.

HOW RECOGNITION ENHANCES OTHER TOTAL PAY ELEMENTS

If pay is the accelerator pedal to speed the business process and success, then recognition and celebration are the overdrive. They magnify the influence of pay and thereby add value to the acceleration process. Though they add value to pay solutions, they don't replace pay since people can't buy groceries with theater tickets and a logo hat. Serious companies would not, for example, partner recognition and celebration with something like banding to lead alignment of rewards with the business—unless, of course, they wanted to select things that had minimal change implications and make it look as if they were adding something.

Recognition Advantage

Whether cash or noncash, recognition has an advantage over base pay and variable pay because it can immediately reward something of importance that the company wants to reinforce; it doesn't have to wait until the end of the performance period. Recognition can respond quickly to acknowledge things that weren't planned—the unexpected outstanding achievements that were not part of the individual's or team's goals.

Noncash recognition has an advantage over a cash reward because it can be customized or personalized to be particularly meaningful to the recipient. If someone being recognized loves chocolate ice cream, have chocolate ice cream during the celebration. If an individual is a fan of a sports team or a lover of ballet, surprise them with tickets to whatever event means the most. Customization takes some thought, but the best recognition is personalized. Because there are a wide range of possible noncash recognition awards, the opportunity is great to match awards effectively with individual preference.

Hopefully, the individual feels proud of the recognition, which gives it communicative value not only at work but also at home and with friends. If noncash recognition is done well, a small expense may go a long way relative to a base pay increase, variable pay award, or cash recognition, because of the trophy value of recognition. It's also easier to change from a noncash recognition program to a cash program than to go the other way.

Pay Advantage

Pay, however, does have advantages over recognition. Cash has universal meaning. People can use the award in any way they choose. Also, recognition is mostly retrospective, and though guidelines are available for what's worthy, recognition doesn't communicate prospective goals as well as variable pay does.

Eventually people want to share in the success they create. If they reduce waste and improve productivity and quality, they eventually ask, "What's in it for me?" and want to share in organizational success. It's easier to share in success through cash variable pay, which clearly describes the relationship between performance and reward. It's easier to vary the award meaningfully according to levels of performance with variable pay—for example, the more outstanding the performance, the larger the variable pay award. In a culture where people view some forms of recognition as trash and trinkets and say "Show me the money," cash variable pay can literally show them.

Together Is Best

Thus, both cash variable pay and noncash and cash recognition have value. We would argue that they are a both-and formula, not an either-or decision. Celebration and verbal recognition complement and support pay programs, both variable pay and base pay. Kash n' Karry is a good example of pairing group variable pay and individual recognition. This regional Florida grocer offers monthly variable pay dependent on store sales and customer satisfaction. Each month, the store holds a brief meeting to celebrate results; the store manager hands out checks individually and verbally recognizes what each individual contributed that month to help the store be successful. This recognition is powerful because the manager not only knows what individuals are doing but also recognizes them publicly.

ENHANCING RECOGNITION AND CELEBRATION

Here are ways to get maximum value from recognition and celebration.

Recognize the Recognizers

"But our boss never recognizes or celebrates anything!"

This complaint is sometimes heard even when the company has a recognition and celebration policy that enables—or requires—recognition. Although such programs offer guidance for using a wide range of solutions and tools to acknowledge positive accomplishments, some don't recognize even with a formal plan. In contrast, some recognize without a formal program, often with managers paying from their own pockets for the items used in the process. Merely providing money and guidance doesn't lead to usage.

One important action is to acknowledge those who actually recognize. Recognize the leaders whose celebration of success takes the form of organizing and granting recognition to members of the workforce. In other words, make the actual recognition and celebration something to recognize and celebrate. Make it more than OK to recognize people who are doing the right things—to make them feel special and want to keep on doing so.

Also, don't rely only on managers to recognize people. In high-involvement organizations, people can do much of the recognizing themselves. Anyone can either nominate or recognize someone else, provided the recognizer documents how the contribution being acknowledged adds value to the business.

Pay Is Boring; Make Recognition Fun

Take a look at the materials that describe pay at your company. Does what the printed matter says excite anyone? Most pay plan descriptions look like fugitives from legal depositions, or worse. They're driven by protection of the company, negative messages, and prohibitions; they seldom say anything about the business and its objectives. (Hopefully, this will change as a result of some of the guidance in this book.) Fortunately, recognition and celebration have escaped the legalese method of communication.

But to keep the fun from getting boring, change the tools of recognition and celebration often. Combine formal and informal recognition, and maintain variety. Be open to experimenting with everything from traditional gifts and parties to approaches that are different and unique and press the limits of your company's style. If one thing doesn't work, try something else. Make the process as much fun as the company can tolerate.

Publicize

In most instances, sharing the reasons for recognition and celebration is the real benefit the company gets from the process. Clothing and athletic shoe advertisements say "Be just like Mike," suggesting that the audience should buy what Michael Jordan wears to emulate him. You'll find that publicizing the reasons for recognition and celebration makes the idea of doing something worthy of recognition catching.

Publicity does another important thing for the company. It helps build a "book of lore" about recognition and celebration. There's no reason a company can't develop its own "100 Ways to Recognize and Celebrate in XYZ Company." Publicizing the ideas makes it acceptable to acknowledge positive activities in the company.

There may be a reason not to publicize recognition in certain situations. Perhaps the individual's ethnic culture might make them uncomfortable with being singled out for recognition. However, lack of public acknowledgment often means something's wrong with the program. Either the objective isn't clear (or shared by the people who determine awards) or the reasons people receive awards don't hold up under examination. Publicizing recognition keeps the program on its toes in terms of quality and consistency and avoids making it subject to favoritism. The amount of a financial recognition award doesn't need to be publicized, just the recipient and—always—the reason for the award.

Recognize Both Individuals and Teams

Most recognition is more effective if there's flexibility in recognizing both individuals and teams, not just one or the other. For example, under an initiative to recognize customer excellence both individuals and teams may deserve recognition. Team-based organizations may let teams determine who receives individual recognition; in this case, individual recognition complements team variable pay. Team recognition is often the best way to reward the results produced by parallel teams (which we describe in Chapter 10 on rewarding teams).

Recognition and celebration that suggest internal competition may create more problems than they address. Recognition should give everyone a chance to win. Contests are more effective if everyone can become a winner, rather than only a specified top percentage of people. Everyone has an opportunity if an absolute criterion is set so that all who exceed it win. The goal in a sales contest might be that everyone (not just the top 10 percent of the salespeople) who sells at least a predetermined level of product or revenue earns an award. A set number of winners creates competition; exceeding a performance level facilitates everyone being in the game and helping each other win.

Evaluate and Refresh Regularly

Although recognition and celebration need to be spontaneous and flexible to keep attention, the process needs a sponsor and champion —not to control and manage but to ensure alignment and excitement. Make what's important to the company important to everyone through the reward-and-recognition process.

Evaluate recognition approaches periodically to assess their business relevance and vitality. Subject them to a periodic review process, just like other total pay elements. For example, lunch with the CEO is a common source of recognition and communication. Whether people see this as a reward depends on the specific company and CEO. Even though it may make CEOs feel good because they're sponsoring recognition, members of the workforce might attend because they believe it's the prudent thing to do (while wishing they could receive other forms of recognition).

It's essential to refresh and rethink these ideas. Many companies have used the Employee of the Month or Year to death, rotating people through the award because the monthly time period, not an outstanding event, drives the award. Even the most outlandish recognition can become mundane. A computer hardware company had a "dunk the president" recognition for anyone making a major difference. After a while, not only did the boss get tired of being dunked, but the people got tired of dunking the fellow. So they updated recognition to add variety and vitality.

Try something spontaneous, like giving a group of managers or workers some money and letting them decide what to recognize in terms of how people help the company prosper.

CONCLUSIONS

Celebrating and recognizing are important. The total reward strategy should enable them, whether the company gets its inspiration from an idea book (such as those we refer to in the endnotes) or develops its own solutions. These programs don't replace pay, obviously. But they bring an added dimension and should be included where they yield value.

Recognition and celebration should be an integral part of total rewards. This means recognition and celebration are not an afterthought or added on. High-involvement pay design teams are naturals for developing unique and exciting recognition and celebration solutions that match the company well. What's more, members of the workforce can work wonders in keeping these on target, agile, and in the limelight of what makes an enterprise special. Take a look at the literature that describes the "most wonderful places to work on the globe." None is credited with becoming so wonderful because it avoided visibly recognizing and celebrating important events, contributions, or milestones in making the company successful.

PART III

Addressing Critical Business Opportunities with Rewards

The Six Reward Principles

1. Create a positive and natural reward experience.
2. Align rewards with business goals to create a win-win partnership.
3. Extend people's line of sight.
4. Integrate rewards.
5. Reward individual ongoing value with base pay.
6. Reward results with variable pay.

The Four Components of Total Rewards

- Individual growth
- Compelling future
- Total pay
- Positive workplace

CHAPTER 10

Rewarding Teams

Peter Drucker says: "The modern organization cannot be an organization of boss and subordinate. It must be organized as a team." He continues: "This means people cannot report to both their old boss and to the new coach, or team leader. And their rewards, their compensation, their appraisals, and their promotions must be totally dependent on their performance in their new roles on their new teams."[1] This is a pretty strong statement about the coming of teams, their importance, and the implications for total pay.

Whether teams are inevitable as a feature of organization design is up for debate. But it's beyond question that if a company decides that teams are important to effective business operation, then teams have potentially dramatic implications for reward design. If pay change is noisy in general, it's cacophony to implement team pay. This doesn't mean that a company shouldn't or can't do it with a positive flair; it's just a really hot change experience. In one situation, an individual said, "I've been here for over 20 years and have never had my performance judged for pay purposes before. It's not going to start now, nor will I be judged on what something called a 'team' does in terms of performance. I am an individual and insist on being treated as such."

This shows the noise and lack of acceptance of team membership that businesses face as they change organization design, culture, and pay.

TEAMS AND REWARD PRINCIPLES

Our task here isn't to argue the advantages and disadvantages of teams. They're clearly right in some situations and not in others. But the six reward principles directly apply to team rewards. Team pay doesn't come naturally to the rugged individualism of American culture, a fact that makes Principle 1 important. It's a challenge to make team pay a positive element of work life. Principle 3 places importance on extending the team member's line of sight from focusing only on what one individual can do to how the individual makes the team a success. Perhaps most important is Principle 2, identifying the individual with the team goals for sharing success. The famous battle cry of the Three Musketeers, "All for one and one for all!" applies to team pay. This is very hard to do where pay has historically been an individual issue.

In Principle 5, the words *individual ongoing value* suggest the importance of paying for a combination of the skills and competencies relevant to the team, consistent contributions to the team over time, and market value so variable pay can reward team performance. Variable pay (Principle 6) makes members of teams stakeholders in the results the teams were formed to generate. If you think of a small team as a "little company," team pay is how the stakeholders who work in it share economic success. In this chapter, we discuss team rewards for small teams that generally range in size from 3 to 50 members, with the median being around 10–12.

WHY TEAMS

Many things that businesses need to do to be successful are done better collaboratively, by organizing a team and having the team members share accountability for getting the job done. This creates a close, synergistic business environment that facilitates pyramiding what all team members know and can do; it enables the team to do what each individual alone cannot. When the focus is on work processes, teams make a complementary organization design.

During times of business-related change, small teams are often capable of dealing with organizational "carcinogens" by addressing challenges and taking advantage of opportunities that can't be as effectively exploited by other means. Teams have proven to be resilient, adaptable, and flexible. They rely for their power on the fact that as business becomes increasingly complex, the skills and competencies needed to perform well are vested in more than one person. No matter how multiskilled an individual may become, given the need for continuous professional growth to add value, it's often better to sum the talents of a team to generate needed results.

Ed Lawler says, "Teams have emerged as a widely used vehicle for facilitating the movement of power, information, and knowledge to lower levels of an organization. . . . Traditional pay that emphasizes individual jobs and performance is not adequate to the team task."[2] Thus, ready or not, it seems that teams are here to stay. The issue is having effective reward solutions fit the team organization design.

WHY TEAM PAY

Teams communicate that "we're in it together," and this has implications for pay. *Pay solution* is an oxymoron if, under a team organization design, the solution emphasizes only the individual and ignores the team. By considering only the individual, pay may erode team cohesiveness and encourage competition among team members. Research and experience suggest that small teams where members have some portion of total pay based on team results are more likely to achieve team goals than are small teams with only individual pay.[3] Because team members focus on shared goals, it makes practical sense to tie pay to achieving these goals.

Because pay is such a strong communicator, the message it delivers makes the company attractive to the type of people with the talent it wants. Team pay attracts people who can, and want to, work effectively on teams. Also, because pay gets everyone's attention, pay based on team results is particularly likely to get the attention of people who are reticent to accept team membership. If people are hesitant to help make a team successful, it makes little sense to pay the individual rather than the team because doing so creates a this-too-will-pass state of mind. It simply makes sense to pay for the outcomes the enterprise wants. If that's just individual performance, the company should pay for only individual results. If the business wants team results, a decision to implement team pay makes practical business sense.

REWARDING TYPES OF TEAMS

Many types of small teams exist.[4] The distinction becomes increasingly fuzzy when addressing the diverse and changing realities of the work to be done. Our emphasis is principally on project teams, process teams, and networked teams; in our mind, they have the strongest implications for total pay. Parallel and coordinating or management teams have some special implications for total pay, though hardly anything that we haven't already developed so far in this book. The important things to keep in mind in designing effective team pay are the expected results and the organization of the teams to accomplish the required outcomes.

Project Teams

Project teams are sometimes also called customer teams because they're commonly chartered to address a critical challenge focused on fulfilling customer requirements or expectations. For example, a product development team is such a team; it comprises a wide range of members representing the skills and technologies required to design a product and bring it to production and eventually to market. Knowledge workers typically make up project teams: scientists, engineers, marketing managers, salespeople, production experts, information technologists, and financial analysts. Other examples of project teams are IT project teams and facility startup teams.

EXAMPLE OF CUSTOMER PROJECT TEAMS. A division of Litton Industries offered commercial companies such IT services as system integration, applications implementation, outsourcing, and e-commerce solutions. The division had teams of IT professionals working on customer projects. The team members had a multitude of IT skills. They were project managers, programmers and systems analysts, and applications experts. Each brought a specific technology, or knowledge of a work process, to the customer application. Project managers and team members earned base pay according to competitive practice for their skills and competencies.

Successful project completion resulted in project team variable pay awards. The teams had specific customer goals. For example, one variable pay measure of completing a project with customer satisfaction was whether the customer is "referencable," meaning that the customer gives a positive recommendation to potential customers. In addition, team variable pay used measures such as delivery on budget and on time so the customer project is completed to both the customer's and the division's satisfaction. Team members who made major contributions to project success earned larger awards than other members did.

This Litton division is an example of project teams that are a regular element of organization design. Although customer assignments vary and team members change in person and in role, project teams are the way the organization conducts its business. Other project teams (such as factory start-up teams) may not be a permanent feature of organization design; they're a temporary but potentially long-term assignment. Membership on a project team may be part-time or full-time, depending on the scope of the project and the team member's involvement. Projects have specific objectives, are knowledge-based and complex, and typically require innovation.

EXAMPLE OF PRODUCT DEVELOPMENT TEAMS. The product development teams of a computer component manufacturer are instrumental in achieving the company's objective of coming out first with new products. Capturing the market for a limited time generates significant revenues and profit during the period when competitors can't yet release a competitive product. It's critical that the product ramp up quickly to produce a large volume in a very short time, immediately after product release, to capture the market.

The product development teams are cross-functional, with members representing engineering, operations, marketing, quality, and sales. The life of a product development team varies but is usually around one year. Being on a product development team may be a full-time job for engineers but generally part-time for other functions. The team requires incremental work above and beyond the member's regular role. It can be a somewhat risky role in terms of career potential for the full-time members, depending on the success of the product.

Product development teams participate in team variable pay because they're critical to the objective of being first to market. Funding for team variable pay is contingent upon meeting the mass production date. Finishing at an earlier date than target results in a larger variable pay pool, and a later date results in a smaller pool. Once funding is determined, three factors affect distribution: the team's performance on measures such as product quality and cost or profitability, the team leader's and the sponsor's evaluations of the individual's technical or functional contribution to the team, and the individual's performance based on peer review. This is a fairly complex plan, but it rewards a combination of team performance and individual performance.

Process Teams

Process teams are part of the permanent design of the organization structure. In this way, they differ from project, parallel, and networked teams. These latter teams may come and go, but ongoing process teams with stable membership are the organizational basis for how the company does business. Solectron and Motorola are notable team-based companies of this sort; there are many more.

EXAMPLES OF PROCESS TEAMS. Process teams are self-contained and identifiable work units that produce defined work products or services and control the work processes in which they operate. Some examples are production teams, assembly teams, administrative support teams, insurance processing teams, sales teams, and service teams. The Veteran's Administration in New York City has process teams for a full range of services (application, adjudication of a wide variety of claims, and customer service) to a specified group of veterans. Teams that have considerable control over *how* the work is done (for example, scheduling and work assignments), not *what* work is to be done, are sometimes called self-managing teams, self-directed work teams, or high-performance teams.

TEAMS AT SOLECTRON. Solectron offers customized manufacturing services to original equipment manufacturers of electronics. The company has grown significantly, even though it faces ever-increasing customer expectations and new market entrants. To create a business advantage, Solectron has evolved its teams in the supply end of the business to customer-focused teams that include external supplier, internal inventory, engineering, scheduling, production control, operations, quality, and customer satisfaction reporting. Each team is directly involved with the customer and runs its own business. Teams are made up of both exempt and nonexempt workers.

The performance of the site or hub (a unit within a large site) on such key measures as profit before taxes, revenue, ROA, and customer service determines variable pay funding. Team goals that determine the funding earned as awards tie variable pay to the customer. These team goals are based on customer expectations and include such primary measures as customer satisfaction, productivity, and quality. Total cash compensation aligns people with the business, reinforces running a successful business, and shares the wealth. Although Solectron positions base pay below the competitive labor market, it sets variable pay and thus total cash above the competitive labor market for meeting or exceeding target.

Networked Teams

Networked teams frequently cross distance, time, and organizational boundaries, with members rotating on and off the team as their expertise is needed. Membership is fluid and diffuse. In fact, members may not know all the others on the networked team because they're from other work teams, organizational units, or companies. The core of the team taps into a network of resources to accomplish the team's goal.[5] On a continuum of membership fluidity, process teams are the most self-contained; cross-functional project teams are in the middle, and networked teams are the most fluid.

An example is a technology development team that doesn't have all the answers itself and uses other internal resources or external partners to solve a problem. One consideration for rewarding networked teams with cross-company membership is that pay solutions are specific to companies while goals are shared.

Parallel Teams

Parallel teams are often problem-solving teams. They supplement and are separate from the regular organizational structure and have as their objective to recommend business improvements within clear boundaries. Two examples are quality improvement teams and worker-participation teams assembled to deal with some specific problem or opportunity that's best addressed collaboratively. The teams are part-time and generally temporary, although their work can continue for a year or more. Team members continue to perform their regular roles while participating on the parallel team.

To accommodate parallel teams, we see no reason to change base pay or variable pay from what the organization already has. Celebration and recognition can effectively acknowledge progress milestones and successful completion. These teams do need recognition and the acknowledgment that their progress and recommendation are important. However, the proof of the pudding is whether organizational performance improves as a result of implementing their recommendation, and this is rewarded through existing variable pay solutions that acknowledge results at the site, group, or business-unit level.

Coordinating or Management Teams

Leadership teams are sometimes formed to provide oversight, allocate resources, and ensure progress toward achieving important business goals that require integration and cooperation among organizational units. The work is ongoing and typically highly interdependent. In our experience, these teams are usually part of the management process of the company where they're used. We see no special need for a change in what we're suggesting for executives and other key professionals, in terms of total pay.

WHAT TO REWARD

Exhibit 10.1 shows the factors that affect reward design for teams. To start, the form of reward varies by type of team.

Project Teams

At a minimum, project teams should have team performance management. This focuses the members on accomplishing the objective that is the reason for creating the team, and it keeps things on track by monitoring milestones toward accomplishing the end result. Customer feedback helps ensure that the customer's objectives are being met.

Exhibit 10.1. Factors Affecting Team Rewards.

- Type of team
- Team autonomy
- Interdependence of teams
- Diversity of technical expertise within a team
- Level of supervision or self-management
- Work flow
- Scope of team's work
- Importance of team to company's business strategy and operating plan
- Size of team and number of core and extended members
- Fluidity of membership within and among teams
- Ability and ease of measuring results
- Time frame of team
- Diversity or variety among teams
- Maturity of team organization approach

If the projects are large, project teams may have team variable pay at the end of a significant project or at milestones. If there are many short-term projects that, in administrative terms, are difficult to manage for team variable pay, project teams might receive recognition (cash spot awards or noncash recognition) for their accomplishments, and variable pay can reward performance at a broader organizational level (business unit or department). An example of this is an IT organization with many small concurrent projects.

Process Teams

Like project teams, process teams have team performance management. They may also do peer performance review, particularly if team members are interchangeable in the roles they perform for the team, since they're knowledgeable about the role requirements and technical skills.

Variable pay may take a variety of forms for process teams:

- Team variable pay that rewards only team performance (for example, team variable pay with specific goals for each autonomous team)

- Team variable pay that combines the performance of the team and a broader organizational unit (the Solectron approach described earlier, which is funded in proportion to site or hub performance and allocates awards depending on team performance)
- Group variable pay, for example, site gainsharing or business-unit profit sharing

The type of variable pay depends on the degree of interdependence among process teams, or among process teams and staff groups, and the team's degree of autonomy or the amount of support it needs to operate. The less interdependence and more autonomy, the more that variable pay emphasizes the performance of the team, not the larger group. If process teams are interdependent, the enterprise may still use team variable pay if it involves the internal or external customer in setting goals and reviewing performance or if it measures interfaces between teams. The type of team variable pay also depends on the degree of integration desired or needed for the organization to operate effectively. The more integration, the more emphasis on the larger group for variable pay; however, the line of sight also increases.

Networked Teams

Companies should handle networked teams similarly to project teams: team performance management at a minimum and variable pay to reward achieving the significant goal that is the team's purpose. Networked team variable pay works best when core members can easily be identified. The buck stops with these members achieving the common goal. Larger-group variable pay or individual contributions to team results may be rewarded in addition to team recognition if the tasks of the networked teams aren't major in size, the time frames are short, membership is very fluid, and there are many networked teams operating.

It's generally difficult to reward the extended members who work for a short time on many networked teams or spend most of their time on other assignments because of administrative difficulties or because they're external to the company. Here recognition may be most appropriate.

Additional Factors Influencing Rewards

A number of other factors influence how to reward teams.

WORK FLOW. Typically, the work in teams flows in one of two ways: sequentially, as in a continuous-process manufacturing operation, or interactively, where team members work collaboratively to produce an outcome, as with a research-and-development team. In the sequential process, the team is no stronger than its weakest link, so it's imperative that team members help each other be successful. In the interactive process, the successful team makes a whole that is greater than the sum of its parts. In either case, team variable pay is appropriate to reward outcomes.

A third type of work flow involves individuals with equivalent roles and individual performance summed to determine team performance. For example, a group of people do piecework assembly of products where each individual assembles the entire product and individuals are responsible for their own output. Pay based on individual performance is appropriate, and team pay may not help. Still, it might make sense to include a component of team variable pay in situations where people perform the work independently but the company wants them first to help each other in terms of sharing knowledge or dealing with difficult customers and second to focus on achieving an overall team goal. For example, a telephone service center that answers customer problems may want to reinforce teamwork to accomplish a body of work for a specific group of customers. In this case, team variable pay rewards accomplishing a volume of work if quality is acceptable and customers express satisfaction.

DIVERSITY OF TECHNICAL EXPERTISE. Some teams, particularly project teams and networked teams, are cross-functional, with members representing various areas of technical expertise. Others, such as manufacturing process teams, have basically a single area. Most teams with one area of expertise are moving beyond narrowly defined jobs because for the team to function most effectively it needs multiskilled members who can perform a variety of roles within that area.

Regardless of the diversity of technical expertise, a team organization design results in job definitions that are less narrow and clearly delineated, so teams move more toward paying for the individual—that is, the ongoing value that the member provides—and less for the job. We've found that team members accept differences in base pay based on the technical skills the team member uses and on how the labor market values various skills.

Cross-functional teams present a peer-review challenge. It's difficult for members to assess the technical expertise of others from different technical functions. But they can give feedback on behavioral competencies. This often results in cross-functional teams focusing team variable pay more strongly on team results than on distributing awards based on peer review. Alternatively, a technical expert or technical manager may review the team member's technical contribution to provide input to the award process. Cross-functional teams support not only in-depth technical skills but also competency in understanding the business and cross-functional knowledge because of the need to integrate the contributions of team members.

For teams incorporating basically a single area of technical expertise, team members are better able to offer performance feedback on technical skills to fellow members. Emphasizing the skill-and-competency dimension for determining an individual's ongoing value rewards multiskilling, which creates the flexibility teams need for their members to be successful. It can also reward development of in-depth skills in an area of technical expertise required by a team.

LEVEL OF SUPERVISION OR SELF-MANAGEMENT. The level of supervision, or self-management as is the case, has an influence on the performance management process. The more the team is self-managing, generally the more involvement the team has in goal setting and the more likely it is to use peer review, recognize members, and play a role in determining individual pay.

WHY NOT MORE TEAM PAY?

So, why isn't there more movement to team pay in organizations with teams? On the "go" side of team pay is the business case and the practical reality that a pay solution emphasizing only individuals (while the company expects people to make a small team successful) is more likely to harm team cohesiveness than support it. Research shows that simply rewarding the behavioral competency of teamwork may facilitate cooperation, but it doesn't improve team results. Teamwork rewards how team members perform but doesn't focus on what the team is chartered to accomplish. Emphasis on developing team goals, monitoring progress, and rewarding achievement of team goals is necessary to produce team results.[6]

In fact, some companies believe the benefit of team pay may be less in the actual awards than in the discipline of setting the sound goals that team pay requires and generating the corresponding workforce involvement and empowerment. Thus, it's fairly easy to justify small-team pay from a business perspective. Companies do much more aggressive and risky things to grow profitability than merely implement team pay, so why not do it and get on with something else?

We believe the reasons more companies don't use team pay have to do with a number of questions they must answer, some relatively easy and others a struggle. Exhibit 10.2 shows the key design questions. The difficult questions may keep the team pay transition off balance and cause the transformation to hesitate. Because people are so accustomed to being paid only as individuals and naturally resist the unknown, the time it takes to answer the difficult questions is enough to immobilize the company and shift the balance away from team pay. Here are the tough questions we've identified and how certain companies answer them.

Addressing Complexity

How can an organization address the complexity of team variable pay for project teams and networked teams? In our view, these teams pose an interesting opportunity for total pay design.[7] This is because of the variety in such areas as design opportunities, goals, relationships between the team and people, and length of performance periods. The alternatives for process teams are clearer and the solutions more permanent.

COMPLEXITY CHALLENGES. Among the issues that create some of the challenges for project and networked team design:

- Projects don't begin and end with the accounting cycle of quarters and fiscal years. Measurement of process teams is compatible with accounting cycles.
- Project and networked teams may differ in the level of participant involvement: some may be part-time, others full-time. The work is full-time for process teams.

Exhibit 10.2. Key Design Issues for Team Rewards.

General

1. What is the objective of team rewards? What is the business case for changing rewards to include team performance?
2. What are the criteria for determining if a team is eligible for team rewards? If a member is eligible for team rewards?
3. What are the measures and goals that determine team success?
4. Who sets and approves measures and goals to ensure consistency and fairness across teams?
5. What role should base pay, short-term variable pay, recognition, performance units, and stock options play in rewarding team performance? Individual performance?
6. What differences are acceptable between rewarding teams and rewarding people in the rest of the organization?

Variable Pay

1. What is the basis for variable pay funding?
2. What portion of the variable pay is based on team performance? Individual performance? Larger group performance?
3. What is the win-win? What is the results-reward relationship? How high is the upside opportunity and for what level of results?
4. What is the methodology for allocating awards to team members?
5. How is variable pay opportunity determined when people participate in multiple teams concurrently?
6. What happens to the awards of people who join or leave ongoing teams?
7. What is the definition of equity among teams? How is divisiveness prevented?

Base Pay

1. What is the objective of base pay in teams?
2. What determines base pay adjustments in a team environment?
3. Who provides input on individual performance management?
4. What is the review process?
5. What portion of total cash comes from base pay and what portion from variable pay?
6. What is the transition as the total cash mix changes because of a shift in focus from individual to team performance?

- For project and networked teams, there may be a variety of teams of diverse nature on different cycles, while process teams often have less variety and variation.
- For project and networked teams, people may participate concurrently in more than one team while being members of only one process team.
- The success of the output of project and networked teams may not be known until sometime after completing the project or achieving the team objective. This certainly applies to research-and-development teams. The success of process teams' output can be assessed regularly.

FLEXIBILITY IN ACCOMMODATING DIFFERENCES. To address complexity, project and networked team variable pay design needs to be more flexible in accommodating variation. For example, project team variable pay is most effective when awarded as soon as is practical after project completion or achievement of milestones, rather than waiting for a fiscal quarter.

If the company wants to offer project team variable pay and people participate on more than one team, then it may allocate opportunities for team variable pay in one of these ways:

- Create an annual level of target variable pay opportunity that's allocated to projects based on time spent on a project. For example, if the annual target opportunity is either 10 percent of base pay or $7,000, allocate half of the amount to a six-month project.
- Determine variable pay opportunity according to the criticality of the project and the impact it has on the business. For example, opportunity for opening a factory at a global location may be $20,000 for each full-time team member because of the importance of getting production up and running by a certain date.
- Establish categories of target variable pay opportunity based on the size of a project. For example, set target variable pay opportunity for small projects at $1,000 for full-time members, $3,000 for medium-sized projects, and $5,000 for large projects. This approach simplifies the calculation process for teams made up of full-time members.

TIMING OF R&D AWARDS. One important issue for rewarding R&D teams is the timing of awards. The true result of these teams is evident only in the long run, once the product demonstrates success in the market. However, this must be balanced with the need for ongoing focus by recognizing or rewarding people frequently for achievement of milestones along the way (though the largest award targets product introduction because being on time is critical).

Still, one company decided not to pay for milestones because product development teams might appear to be on track at the milestones but not end up on track at product commercialization. Few companies reward team members for longer-term results after product commercialization, when product reviews and sales are known because they are onto a new product. But this misses a chance to make team members stakeholders in the product they create.

Identifying and Rewarding Excellent Members

How does a company identify and reward excellent-performing team members? The definition of *outstanding individual performance* often changes in a team environment. The performance focus shifts from individual goals (either specifically related to a job or role description or related to a larger organizational unit's goals through the business-aligned goal-setting process) toward the team's goals and how the individual contributes to them. Setting individual goals in a team setting is easier if members are less interdependent. If individual goals are set, they should clearly emphasize the individual's part in making the team successful.

Even if specific individual goals aren't set, the team discusses what role each person must play to make the team successful. Such skills and competencies as communications, teamwork, conflict resolution, joint problem solving, participative decision making, coaching, giving feedback, and accepting diversity help the team function smoothly so it can accomplish its goals. These skills and competencies are often part of team training because they weren't part of the skill set of the organization before the advent of teams.

FEEDBACK. Giving performance feedback also changes in moving to a team environment. Typically the manager, coach, or team leader plays a central role initially. As the team matures; shows an advanced stage of team building; and becomes more self-managing in such functions as choosing work methods, setting goals, monitoring results, training, coaching, giving performance feedback, handling selection and termination, and dealing with customers and suppliers, team members play an increasingly significant role in giving feedback.

Members typically know each other's performance better than a manager does because they see each other's work regularly. They can use peer pressure to improve performance. However, it takes significant training for team members to be skilled in giving feedback, coaching, conducting performance reviews, and receiving and processing feedback.

EXAMPLES OF FEEDBACK. In one medical-technology company, the team begins the feedback process with a group discussion of total team performance and then moves on to how each individual is contributing. Team goals constitute the anchor for discussing individual contribution so that the team stays focused. The product development teams of the computer component manufacturer described earlier use peer review as a factor in determining team variable pay awards. There are two reviews. A preliminary review halfway through the product development cycle provides feedback to the individual, not to leadership, and does not determine awards. Leadership and the individual receive the final peer review feedback that's part of the criteria used in determining awards.

REWARDING TEAM STARS. In a team environment, rewarding the stars requires looking at all the pay components—base pay, team variable pay, other variable pay, and recognition—to determine the most appropriate vehicle(s) for rewarding individual performance. Individual ongoing value that rewards *consistent* outstanding performance is one way; individual recognition is another; stock option grants are still another. Individual variable pay or lump-sum payments are alternatives, to the extent they don't erode team cohesion. However, depending on the interdependence of team members, it may be difficult to relate specific results to an individual in a team situation. An exception is the situation we discussed (in the section on work flow) where the team is made up of a group of parallel individuals whose performance is summed rather than interdependent members.

DIFFERENTIATING AWARDS FOR INDIVIDUAL PERFORMANCE. Most team variable pay grants equal awards to members of the same team—whether in the form of equal dollar amount, equal percentage of base pay earnings, or equal dollars-and-cents amount per hour worked or paid—because the objective is to reward team performance. Although distributing team variable pay awards according to individual performance gives the funding to those who are most deserving, this also adds complexity and lessens the strength of the message that team performance is what counts.

During the performance period, the distribution methodology of individual performance also dilutes ongoing communications about the size of the award that members will earn if performance remains consistent until the end of the period. Assume, for example, a 10-member team is on track to share $10,000 if it sustains the current level of results throughout the performance period. Under an equal-award approach, there's a clear message that each member has the chance to earn $1,000 if they keep team outcomes at current levels. It's less clear what an individual's award will be if individual performance determines actual award shares at the end of the period.

Success in differentiating awards according to individual performance depends on the level of comfort and trust the people have with the feedback approach and the methodology for determining variations in awards. Differences, if drawn, must be highly credible to team members or else erosion of collaborative focus is likely to result. It's often easier if the team starts with identifying the outliers—the outstanding and unacceptable performers—and doesn't concern itself with small differences in acceptable performance when determining awards.

Funding Source

What's the funding source for team variable pay? The source reflects the team's importance to the company, autonomy and interdependence of the teams, affordability, and the organizational level at which the company wants to optimize performance. Funding at the team level optimizes results at the team level. Funding at some level above the team, such as the site, group, business unit, or company, optimizes performance at the levels where results are measured and enables synergies among teams. The latter funding situation may result in communication challenges because of the longer line of sight. Even so, we view this as an opportunity to demonstrate how the team fits into the overall business strategy, and to extend members' line of sight.

TEAM AUTONOMY. Performance measurement for pay can be at the small-team level for autonomous teams since there's no fear of interteam competition. But if the objective is strategic—say, to optimize performance at the organizational level above the team—measures should come from a combination of the team and one level higher in the organization.

As an example, for a process team, the plant may be the next higher organizational level. A division management team may have measures of company direction. These measures mean extending the line of sight above the team such that the team not only sees the immediate results it needs to achieve but is also educated on how the measures that are under the direct control of the team add value one organizational level higher.

IMPORTANCE OF TEAM. The team's importance also plays a role in the funding. Team variable pay for the product development teams of the computer component manufacturer we've discussed focuses only on team performance because the teams are fairly autonomous. Team variable pay is extra pay over and above the company's normal competitive total pay position. The logic is that the teams are strategically critical to the success of the business, represent somewhat of a high-risk assignment, and require significant extra effort to produce the required outcomes. For its part, the company reasons that getting the product to market on time or early generates considerable revenue, which makes the awards affordable.

PERFORMANCE OPTIMIZATION AND AFFORDABILITY. Funding for team variable pay can come from other existing variable pay opportunity, awarded according to a broader level of organizational performance than the team—for example, the site, group, business unit, or company. People generally accept this shift of funding because the line of sight moves closer.

The issue for the company is the affordability of paying out team awards even though the broader organizational unit may not achieve its goals. A company in a low-margin industry and with labor cost as a large portion of total cost may not be able to move funding to the team level as easily as higher-margin businesses where labor cost is a smaller percentage of total cost. However, some are willing to reward team performance regardless of the broader organizational unit's performance because they believe successful teams bring up the performance of the entire unit more than otherwise.

The opposite funding methodology, using individual variable pay opportunity to fund team variable pay, may be more difficult for people to accept because the line of sight increases. Like other pay changes, it must be business-justified. For example, a fruit packing plant that grades and packages oranges and lemons had packers on piece rate. The company wanted to have multiskilled people who could rotate assignments between packing and grading to respond to work flow changes efficiently, have everyone spot incorrect grading at all stages of the process, simplify scheduling, and permit variety given the physical or visual intensity of each role.

A combination of skill pay and facility variable pay replaced base rates for all the people as well as piece rate for packers. The company modeled the financial impact to determine the effect on both individuals and the plant. It realized that packer productivity would most likely decline initially (like the typical conversion off piece rate) but believed the change was important enough for long-term plant success to justify the change.

Other approaches to converting from piece rate to team pay may involve a buyout, a guarantee for a period of time, or an increase to base pay.

Still other companies use some of the future potential base pay increase budget for team variable pay funding, plus offering additional upside variable pay opportunity (see Chapter 3 for an in-depth discussion of this). Another variation is at XEL Communications, where a combination of individual skill-based pay and team merit increases exists. XEL funds the merit budget for a team according to its achievement of outcomes. Teams that exceed their goals enjoy a larger merit increase than those merely meeting goals, and in turn the latter teams receive a larger merit budget than teams not meeting their goals. The majority of the team members receive close to the average of their team's merit increase; only the highest and lowest performers earn a variation further from the average. XEL uses peer review to help determine this. It makes a powerful statement because base pay increases are contingent on team performance.

For XEL's funding methodology to work, teams must be fairly autonomous since they compete for a set budget and funding is determined at the team level. To counterbalance this, XEL also has profit sharing to focus on broader organizational performance. Profit sharing complements the team merit increase because its distribution is not zero-sum, so helping another team helps the funding pool grow for everyone; one team's strong performance doesn't reduce another's portion of funding.[8]

Rewarding Extended Team Members

How does a company reward members of an extended team? It's usually relatively easy to figure out who is a core member of a process, project, or networked team. But teams are seldom autonomous entities and are dependent for their success on other people. One of the central questions is whether team variable pay should include or exclude a variety of extended members upon which the team depends for success.

EXAMPLES OF EXTENDED MEMBERS. In addition to core team members, teams may have extended members who generally spend less time on one team, may serve on multiple teams, and bring expertise to a particular area of the team's accountability. For example, a vehicle design team has core members whose full-time assignment is to work on designing one vehicle, while a windshield wiper engineer works on multiple vehicle teams for a short time.

Other extended members are support people for line process teams or project teams. Customer teams (described in Chapter 12, on sales compensation) include direct selling professionals plus other core and extended members from such areas as marketing, customer service, technical support, and finance.

A VARIETY OF APPROACHES. The approach to team pay is often different for extended members, depending on how many members there are, how much time they spend on the team, and what administrative complexities apply. Approaches include:

- Counting extended members in team pay but reducing their variable pay opportunity per team. Core and extended members work together to achieve the same team goals, but this approach may be cumbersome if there are many extended members and many teams.
- Using brief input on the extended member's contributions from each team to determine an award based on an individual's overall contribution to the group of teams served. At an engineering and construction company, project managers submit to each extended member's line manager a brief review of no more than one-half page on the member's performance, and the manager in turn determines the variable pay award. This lessens the impact teams or team leaders

have on the member's award; but if there's collaboration between the team leaders and the line manager, the team messages get through.

• Using the same funding measures of a team's core members to generate a fund for awards to extended members. The team leader or core members distribute awards by determining the value of the contributions made by extended members. Similar to the first approach, this defines core and extended members as co-stakeholders in terms of team variable pay funding. Depending on the team's degree of self-management, either the team or the leader determines the award distribution to extended members. The product development teams of the computer component manufacturer have criteria to reward extended members out of such a fund.

• Recognizing extended members. Recognition and celebration are useful when individual goal setting is difficult, the company is in the early stages of moving to a team organization design, or there are networked teams.

• Using individual goals for determining variable pay awards for extended members. Individual goals must be closely connected to supporting the teams. In some companies that use this approach, teams participate in developing the extended member's goals.

• Having extended members participate in a broad-based variable pay plan that measures the sum of the team contributions or the performance of the larger organizational unit in which the small teams reside. This is an easy solution but has longer line of sight for extended members than the other approaches.

• Allowing extended members to receive the average award of core members. To strengthen focus on their internal customers, support teams at an electronic systems company earn the same average payout percentage as project teams, provided they meet a goal such as a collective support budget target.

Thus the questions that some companies have struggled with regarding team pay have answers that vary with the specific situation. These questions need not hold a company back from team pay when it's appropriate; instead, they can stimulate discussion about the role of teams in the business.

CONCLUSIONS

Our main message is that questions about team pay should not defer moving forward if it makes business sense, because they can be answered. Our experience is that much of the opposition to team pay comes from those who have no experience with teams and team pay. Those experienced with teams and team pay tend to be positively disposed to the practicality of this approach to both organization design and total pay. Teams and team pay are attractive to individuals who can accept a collaborative, win-together workplace. People who insist on working as individuals and are unwilling to move to a shared-destiny workplace only delay the migration to teams if the move makes business sense. If a company moves to a team organization design, it's logical to have a supporting pay approach. Teams without team pay work, but it's uphill sledding.

CHAPTER 11

Rewarding Scarce Talent

A scarce-talent situation exists when the demand for talent significantly exceeds the supply. The stakes become higher when the talent in demand reflects the company's core competency or is essential to its performance. A chronic lack of quality people can affect any company's ability to grow. Instances of being less able to meet workforce supply objectives than competitors magnify this problem. We argue that this is where the better workforce deal and a total reward approach pay real bottom-line dividends.

Many recruitment and retention efforts focus on people who bring a critical technology-based core competency, such as IT, engineering, or scientific capability, to the company. However, talent shortages are not limited to knowledge workers. As we write this book, shortages challenge the fast-food industry to keep stores open in retail facilities as strategically important as the Mall of America in Minnesota. Scarce-talent situations are clearly not unique to a specific industry; the likes of McDonald's and Burger King as well as Microsoft and Intel share it. As long as enterprises strive for continuous profitable growth, people shortages remain a challenge.

Turnover is costly; measures of the cost include the recruitment and training process, the reduced productivity of the new hire, and the work left undone because of staffing gaps. It's also quantifiable as lost business opportunities and the disruption caused by the need to reestablish fractured working relationships. Perhaps more important, where people deal with customers, turnover creates unsettling customer interaction by changing the composition of the workgroup. It's difficult to create a collaborative work environment and a positive working atmosphere in the absence of stable staffing.

An executive asked, "Why do we all focus on people only when they become scarce and expensive in the labor market? Why don't we worry about all of our people all of the time?" This is the point of *Pay People Right!* If the only time a company worries about hiring and retaining the people it needs is when the wolf is at the door, then it's too late. The basis of our push for the better workforce deal and a total reward approach is the belief that all people count, and great companies realize this. A business is a team sport. Organizations don't become great because of only a few key people; everyone must count, all the time.

WOE IS ME? OR POSITIVE STEPS?

Most discussions of scarce talent and what to do about it are noticeably negative. Enterprises often get into a woeful mentality, obsess about the expense implications of a talent shortage, and try to put it behind them as rapidly as possible. But a scarce-talent situation is instead an opportunity, a positive sign of growth and success. Already, instances of talent shortage have resulted in positive total pay changes. For example, changes in the market value of scarce talent have created the much-needed opportunity to move from internally focused pay solutions to those based on the realities of the external market. This has stimulated a focus on total rewards, moved variable pay into the mainstream, and facilitated customization of recognition to personal preference. Now, it's supporting the advance to individual ongoing value, business-aligned goals, and development and performance feedback.

Scarce-talent situations unfreeze reward practices that just can't keep up. This is an excellent chance to make significant positive changes in total rewards, changes that add value beyond merely filling immediate talent needs. Our emphasis is on building lasting value as well as addressing short-term staffing needs.

TRANSITIONING TO THE BETTER WORKFORCE DEAL

In Chapter 2, we described the better workforce deal. Scarce-talent situations support our case. Wise companies must now make themselves attractive to gain ground in a continuing talent race. Refresh your memory on the four components of total rewards that make up the better workforce deal by looking again at Exhibit 1.2 (or any of the four part-opening pages). Those challenged in the race for scarce talent have been emphasizing mostly the total pay component, but the other three—individual growth, positive workplace, and a compelling future—are proving to be the package that can help make a company a great place to work.

We don't recommend the commodity view of dealing with scarce talent. But at least two other, positive approaches exist for addressing scarce-talent challenges. One is directed toward getting past the talent-shortage crisis; the other helps the company migrate toward a total reward strategy.[1] Let's look at these three broad scarce-talent approaches (also summarized in Exhibit 11.1).

- *Approach 1: commodity solution involving increasing pay levels.* "Keep the current total pay solution," the advice goes, "and increase the levels of base pay, any short-term variable pay, and any long-term variable pay." This is a common—but in our view unacceptable—remedy to scarce talent. It ratchets up total pay cost and may only afford temporary relief from scarce-talent challenges. It uses old ways to address new problems. Companies developed most such solutions well before recognizing the value of people to be as critical as it now is.
- *Approach 2: total pay solution.* Change the design of total pay, while responding to competitive practice. Adapt total pay such that the response to the scarce-talent situation is an integrated pay solution, not a mere increase in pay levels. This approach principally emphasizes resolving the total pay issues surrounding scarce talent. Such solutions often include elements of total reward changes, but in this second approach pay is the "lever" most readily used to try to control talent shortages. In some instances, this approach is a final solution,

Exhibit 11.1. The Evolving Scarce-Talent Reward Strategies.

Characteristic	Commodity Pay	Total Pay	Total Rewards
Emphasis	Pay to buy specific scarce talent	Integrated total pay solution to address strategic talent needs	Integrated total rewards to grow the business
Deal	Let's make a deal	Moving to the better workforce deal	The better workforce deal
Business case	Urgent need to fill jobs and retain talent	Total pay provides differential advantage and is flexible, agile, adaptive	Total rewards as instrument of strategic and tactical business plan
Action	Keep current pay design; ratchet up pay levels	Adapt all total pay elements to capitalize on what works best	Develop total rewards in balanced fashion—compelling future, individual growth, positive workplace, and total pay
Target	People identified as scarce talent	Scarce talent broadening to total workforce	Entire workforce with adaptability to address scarce talent
Time frame	Short-term fix through firefighting	Short-term to longer-term strategy	Middle-term to long-term renewal of workplace
Implications	Increase cost; wait for next emergency	Optimize balance of base pay, variable pay (cash and equity), recognition and celebration, benefits	More than just total pay ties workforce to company best

particularly if the enterprise views the scarce-talent situation as temporary and not long-term. In other cases, it's a milestone move toward a total reward solution.

• *Approach 3: total reward solution.* Meet the scarce-talent challenge with total reward design. Use this opportunity to transition to a total reward strategy that exemplifies the better workforce deal. Pay may lead the change, but the strategy is to recognize the critical role of people in the company. This process often addresses all four total reward components. Even if emphasis is on only one or two other components, the focus is on improving more than total pay. We believe this is the preferred solution.

APPROACH 1: THE COMMODITY SOLUTION

Corn, beans, and pork bellies are commodities that are bought and sold at a stated price. A pork belly from Nebraska is pretty much like one from Iowa. To buy commodities, you call a broker and pay the price for what you need. Sometimes the price is high, when commodities are scarce because of weather or other problems. At other times the price is low, as with excess supply over demand.

Some companies take a commodity view of talent, even when they realize the value of people to their business. Commodity solutions to competitive talent markets follow a predictable pattern: a company conducts or participates in market surveys, analyzes the data in comparison to existing total pay levels, and adjusts pay elements as necessary. If the initial response is insufficient, just crank up the pay levels and hope for the best.

We often see enterprises adopting the commodity approach when the scarce talent isn't part of the core competency of the company—for example, scarce IT, HR, and finance talent in a consumer products or vehicle components manufacturer. The scarce talent is not the primary driver of the business and doesn't represent a significant percentage of the workforce.

Prevailing Practice

A popular response to scarce talent is to pay hiring or sign-on awards, retention awards, and referral awards; another is to make counteroffers to people who are ready to walk out the door. Stock options, the champion of scarce-talent tools, are either the offensive tool of the IPO enterprise or the defensive tool of the growing or established publicly traded company. As we discussed in Chapter 8, stock options seldom make permanent shareholders of the workforce. Often, stock acquired from options is immediately sold.

Unfortunately, there's no evidence that differential advantage results from these commodity pay practices. Given the propensity to mimic each other, it would be startling to learn of any company actually gaining advantage over another by merely copying what competitors do. Focusing only on outbidding competitors for people in the free-agent market seldom integrates the talent into the business process and culture.

Not a Lasting Solution

A commodity view of pay is seldom a lasting solution. To their chagrin, managers of an engineering company called its commodity pay solution the "people reloader." As the frustrated vice president of technology put it, "Our pay plan continues to reload our most important job classifications. That's because we can't keep the people we have. We hire the people we need from other companies and start over and over again. There must be a better way to do this."

Another company conducted extensive focus groups with scarce-talent professionals to identify the reasons for high turnover and recruiting difficulties. The conclusion was that development, training, the work itself, leadership, and colleagues were all factors that counted in choosing a company. The common sentiment was something like this: "If we're worth it to some other company, why not this one? Our company's only interested in us because we have skills they need. When they don't need us, we're out the door."

A chief executive said, "We're the highest scarce-talent payer in our industry and have granted all our stock options. I guess it must be how we do everything else." The head of technology of a software developer was concerned about their having to reprice underwater stock options: "The company is not well served by changing the price of options for the workforce. However, if we don't reprice the options, people will go elsewhere and 'reprice' their options themselves." These comments indicate willingness to spend the money to grow their businesses profitably; it's just that the realities of the workforce have passed them by.

APPROACH 2: TOTAL PAY SOLUTION

Considering scarce talent as a commodity doesn't fulfill the *Pay People Right!* objective to make total pay changes positive and acceptable (Principle 1). Nothing in doing so extends the line of sight of scarce-talent people, shows them that they add value to the business, or tells them why they're important (Principles 2 and 3). This approach says nothing about the need to focus on the customer, and it completely misses the developmental role of total pay. It doesn't even come close to fulfilling the opportunities we propose in integrating total rewards (Principle 4). All of the tools used to compete for talent—base pay, variable pay including stock options, recognition, and benefits—are potentially critical to effective total pay, yet it's not *whether* but *how* they're used that counts.

Emphasis If Other Reward Components Are Weak

In some instances, a total pay approach is useful when the company can't compete on one or more of the other three components of total rewards. For example, many enterprises can't offer leading-edge work and attractive development and career growth opportunities because the scarce talent isn't part of the core business. In this case, the best available solution is total pay, although the enterprise can still work on the components of creating a positive workplace and a compelling future. Adopting this approach of using pay as a vehicle of communication strengthens the link between the company and the scarce talent and acknowledges the value that the scarce talent brings.

Base Pay

Chapters 5, 7, and 8 on base pay and variable pay discussed how to form a foundation to address scarce-talent situations and also add value to the business continuously. The underpinning for determining base pay—individual ongoing value—has three dimensions that acknowledge paying for scarce skills that add value. The foundation of individual ongoing value (paying for the individual's value relative to the labor market) makes it essential to pay according to how the external market pays for people's skills and competencies. It recognizes that various skills and competencies have different market value. Individual ongoing value also pays for needed skills and competencies that the individual applies to achieve results. The requisite skills may change rapidly, so it's important for people to stay current. The third dimension, consistent performance over time, rewards staying with the company and adding value over an extended period.

EXAMPLES FROM IT STUDY. Our research on reward practices of major IT companies suggests some examples that have broad implications.[2] One conducts quarterly formal developmental and pay reviews of all people having key skills or occupying positions with scarce skills. The review explores whether people have acquired one or more of a series of selected skills or competencies, whether they were using them on a current assignment, and what the results of the assignment were in terms of both customer and financial outcomes. Relying on this review, the manager takes action on increases to base pay and/or lump-sum payments to ensure that pay and the value of the individual correlate highly.

In another company, the reviews are not automatic, but one essential competency of project and program managers responsible for key talent is *core staff retention.* Managers' ability to keep talent in the organization over time plays a part in determining their own pay. People retention magnifies not only manager base pay adjustments but also variable pay awards. Managers receive a budget for base pay increases and lump-sum payments for key people. One of the manager's accountabilities is to adjust the base pay of people as they become more valuable.

One software development company designed a series of career ladders, describing a continuum of talent-growth definitions with corresponding base pay. Managers keep the ladders current by continuously refreshing the skills, competencies, and results that typify a specific level and communicating this to people. The individual and the manager are responsible for using performance measurement and management to assess how the individual is growing and contributing, as well as what constitutes an appropriate pay level. The belief is that the transparency of the career and pay information creates important dialogue about the correspondence among skill and competency growth, results, and pay.

Another company studied the possibility of implementing a formal competency pay system for key talent. The specific challenge was to get and keep people with fresh skills and competencies for customer applications. It determined that a formal competency pay solution would be too sluggish and instead expanded existing salary ranges into bands.

At another enterprise, an executive told us, "Bureaucratic competency pay in a dynamic talent industry like this is like watching paint dry." In a second breath, he went on to say: "Some people came in here and showed us some sort of iceberg competency model. I told them the name of this company is not *Titanic.*" (The complex model that he refers to includes deep, hidden traits and motives "below the waterline," not just observable behaviors and technical skills.) As a quicker solution, the organization loosely defined the "jobs" in terms of needed skills and competencies and uses this information to help make pay decisions. Consequently, managers have broad guidance for base-pay administration. It also lets them use a more familiar solution and avoid the move to a basis of pay that they viewed as excessively vague and subjective.

SCARCE TALENT AND ONGOING VALUE. The skill-and-competency dimension of ongoing value plays a significant role in determining base pay in our IT research. These enterprises don't raise base pay across the board for scarce talent, as does the commodity approach. Instead, they use a variety of nimble approaches to address it. In any case, base pay adjustments are frequent. Some are ad hoc, others are scheduled. These companies aren't passively waiting for people to think about leaving, or leave; they're actively responding to labor market realities.

Cash Variable Pay

Short-term and long-term variable pay is important for all the general reasons the company should use variable pay as the primary performance pay solution. People with important capabilities want a piece of the action, and a combination of short-term and long-term cash variable pay and stock options can accomplish this. Variable pay can make it a win-win proposition, not just for the period during which talent may be scarce but for an entire career with the firm.

WHAT'S SCARCE CHANGES. Variable pay is preferable in scarce-talent situations because what may be scarce talent today may not be so tomorrow. Consider aerospace engineers, whose talents were scarce in the 1960s, and petroleum engineers and geologists in the 1970s; none are scarce today. Computer software and hardware are areas changing so quickly that what were scarce skills at one time are no longer scarce. If an individual is already paid well for skills and knowledge that were once scarce but are not now, use variable pay in the form of lump-sum payments to reward learning and using new needed skills that may not increase the individual's current value. This gives a reward but doesn't inflate base pay over the individual's ongoing value.

EXAMPLES FROM IT STUDY. Our research shows strong preference for using customer project variable pay for professionals assigned to such projects. One company develops a variable pay solution for each customer assignment, and everyone assigned to the project participates. In this case, it bases awards on a combination of the individual's length of stay on the project, peer ratings, and project results. The primary project measure is delivery on time and on budget because the company believes this ensures maximum project profit. Another firm funds variable pay at the division level and allocates funding at the customer project level according to project profitability. Subsequently, the project manager allocates individual awards based on contribution to the success of the project. The performance management process helps the manager accomplish the award distribution.

SPECIAL AWARDS. A number of companies use not only project variable pay but also retention awards. Some pay cash to key people who stay for the term of a customer project. In one instance, an executive said, "It's worth it to pay as much as it would take to recruit and replace at least a third of the project team in the form of project bonuses if they make the project a success." Some professionals receive a "stay award" of as much as 10 percent of their base pay if they remain to the end of a customer project. One company pays retention awards annually. For each year that a key professional remains with the company, the cash retention award increases. The company believes this makes it more challenging for a competitor to take a key individual away.

To bring the most value to the company, retention awards should compensate a combination of outcomes and tenure, not just tenure, because the latter doesn't communicate to people how they can add value. Even if goals can't be set for the entire performance period, design the award so that the individual must meet measurable performance requirements, expectations, or goals that are set and reviewed periodically throughout the performance period.

In our research, participants use referral awards as a "bounty" to recruit people whom they need. In most instances, they pay the referring individual something just for a qualifying referral, and more if they actually hire the individual. One company uses stock options as an inducement for people first to refer candidates and then to stay involved to make sure the candidate actually joins the company. Another organization has a combination of referral bonuses and referral "parties," where it invites candidates to a hosted gathering with potential colleagues who represent different functional areas across the company so that celebration and recruitment happen at the same time.

Stock Options

The design of stock options extended to people with scarce skills needs to encourage a lasting association rather than a gamble or get-rich-quick relationship. Options must show value to shareholders by demonstrating that people with options do stay with the company and add value. This requires designs with longer vesting periods, effective sequencing of grants, and variation in the size and value of the grants, related to measures of individual, team, group, or business-unit performance. The objective is to design stock options that end the exercise-and-run mentality that often makes granting options to scarce-talent knowledge workers a detriment to longer-term career employment.

ENCOURAGE RETENTION AND PERFORMANCE. Our IT study adds value here as well. A combined problem noticed in the findings is people reloading their own options by changing companies, and exercising their options as quickly as possible and leaving unless they have more unvested options to look forward to in the future. A company exacerbates this problem if it grants people the most options they will usually get at the time at hire. The only way people can take control of their stock option situation is to go to another company.

People have to be rewarded with options for staying, by granting them more options that are within the individual's control—for example, some options and some variable pay for successful project completion. Alternatively, an enterprise must acknowledge significant growth in skills and competencies that add value to the company with a combination of base pay increases or lump-sum payments and stock options. An individual must find it at least as attractive to stay as to leave for a new-hire option grant at another company.

There are a wide range of practices that emphasize granting options with some longer vesting requirements, say, from five to seven years. This extends the period before the individual can take the money and run. Another popular approach is to offer options more frequently so people continue to think twice about leaving some unvested options on the table. Another alternative is to seek board approval to amend antidilution provisions and permit reloading of options for nonmanagement people with key skills and talents. This strategy involves extending an increasing number of options to the workforce as an inducement first to join and then to stay and grow with the company.

HOLDING STOCK AFTER EXERCISING OPTIONS. Several companies in our research provide "holding bonuses" in the form of more options, direct stock awards, and cash if members of the general workforce show evidence of keeping stock obtained from options. One enterprise makes a special option award for each year individuals hold stock acquired through options. Another grants more options to those who become long-term owners when new grants are made. Those firms with low turnover of scarce talent and a long history of broad-based options said they don't need to use rewards to encourage holding stock once people recognize that stock ownership means stakeholdership and "that's how it's done here."

OPTIONS TO MORE PEOPLE. The trend is to provide more options below the management level. In fact, many companies are emphasizing essential talent below management for options. This is because they believe the shortage is often most intense for key technical contributors, not managers, since these contributors may be more up-to-date on scarce technical skills and knowledge that the business requires. The priority is to get ownership in the hands of people on customer projects or with the needed skills and competencies.

Another objective is to make people owners in the company as early in their careers as possible. Some offer options to recruits from colleges and universities as well as to experienced talent. Also, a number of enterprises have replaced cash variable pay awards with stock options. Rather than basing awards on dollars, the objective is to grant variable pay awards in terms of number of options.

SAIC EXAMPLE. Science Applications International Corporation (SAIC), a diverse Fortune 500 high-technology research and engineering company, uses stock as a key component of its total reward package. The perspective of the founder and CEO, Bob Beyster, on what it takes to make a company attractive to scarce talent includes integrating effective use of total pay with the compelling-future component. Beyster said, "Those who contribute to the company should own it, and ownership should be commensurate to a person's contribution and performance as much as feasible."[3] In response, SAIC uses stock bonuses, stock options, and direct employee stock purchases as the glue for holding on to critical talent.

One objective is to get people committed to SAIC during the first three years, the period in which turnover has been the highest. Once it has this buy-in, turnover drops substantially. The focus is on the total work experience. Although incentives and stock options don't keep unhappy people in a company, these pay elements encourage them to look internally for another job first before they consider alternative employment. What makes SAIC attractive in the long run is the kind of workplace it is.

Recognition

The IT companies in our research shine on recognition and celebration. They're well-established enterprises with excellent track records, but they still use a host of awards and symbols of recognition, ranging from parking places to plaques. Though none of them dunk their CEOs, they do have visible recognition of people below the management level who have strong talent that the company needs. Teams have rotating or "traveling cups" that are awarded to members, teams, and even to entire profit centers for making goals. The most popular solution is to supply recognition and celebration funds to managers so they can develop their own recognition approaches and make them part of the culture of their own organizations. Flexibility is the rule, as opposed to structured programmatic solutions.

Benefits

A combination of scarce talent and difficulty in hiring and retaining people in general has been the impetus for flexible hours or work schedules and feel-good benefits such as casual dress, longer vacations, health club memberships, and in-house fitness facilities.

The IT companies in our research said that because of the age of their workforce, a 401(k) plan and medical protection are the only two benefits highly valued. The most popular approach to a 401(k) plan is to offer company stock as an investment alternative. Few attempt to keep scarce talent by means of qualified pension plans or deferred compensation. Medical protection tends to be liberal and void of any restrictive provisions about preexisting conditions or waiting periods. Flexible or cafeteria benefit designs offer a range of benefit choices.

The important point about a total pay solution is that we're not talking about different pay tools or techniques; we're talking about designing the pay solutions so that they ensure delivering a workforce that's there when the company needs it. This is not a commodity pay-to-buy focus on pay. Rather, it's a pay-to-keep mentality.

APPROACH 3: TOTAL REWARD SOLUTION

There are numerous positive examples of success and alignment in adopting a total reward solution. Enterprises have decided that they can be great companies by doing something different. One company identified the "big six" practices it expects from its managers to make the company exciting and positive for people:

1. Honest, frequent, two-way communication
2. Challenging and exciting work
3. Continuous opportunities to grow and learn
4. Recognition and reward for performance
5. Some degree of control over job/life
6. People knowing their work makes a difference

The company realized that things other than paying-to-buy are needed to keep itself staffed. This company is fairly small and competes effectively with giant businesses for some of the scarcest talent anywhere. It has limited stock options but makes up for this by promoting communication, offering interesting work for people to do, celebrating success visibly, and instilling a feeling among the workforce members that they're the best people in the business.

Another company instituted major changes in how it views people by announcing and putting into effect "five commitments":

1. Projects: get "hot projects" people want to work on.
2. Environment: provide access to management; no disrespect; a pleasing and physically comfortable space; and amenities such as a fully stocked kitchen, physical trainer, and workout facility.
3. Mentoring: hire talented individuals people can learn from.
4. Training: maintain a formalized training program.
5. Pay: offer competitive benefits and wages.

The tone of these two vignettes is important. Both highlight a total-reward, talent-retention solution; they're clearly not just paying people more and more. Their solutions integrate the four total reward components. They're examples of what we call the better workforce deal.

Great companies aren't in the business of buying talent at any price. Those that have proven themselves over the years focus on strategies that retain key people who add value. The solution is total rewards—more than simply how much people are paid or how many stock options they have. Exhibit 11.2 summarizes the most successful solutions of the companies in our research.

Exhibit 11.2. Scarce-Talent Rewards.

- Integrate total rewards in a positive fashion
- Customize total rewards to be unique compared to other companies
- Capitalize on any differential advantage
- Try to retain all contributors, but take special care to retain top 10–20% of key talent
- Be flexible
- Update individual base pay as frequently as needed to reflect growth and usage of skill and competency
- Use variable pay to provide link to business and reward results
- Grant stock options in ways that facilitate retention
- Customize and celebrate with recognition
- Enhance reward components of individual growth, positive workplace, and compelling future

Individual Growth

Many of the IT companies use fairly sophisticated mentoring programs that match new scarce-talent hires with a "career partner" during their first year with the company. They allot time for the partners to be together, pay for lunches, and create other opportunities for them to work together. The goal is to develop a career plan and to figure out, with the help of company resources, how to make it a reality.

Most have formal training and development programs, generally under the auspices of an internal university. The emphasis is on developing leading-edge technical skills and competencies and also on providing development in behavioral areas such as working in small or large teams, dealing effectively with customers, coaching, and leadership.

Nearly all of the companies include aggressive career planning and development support as a major leadership accountability. Some have active assessment centers to promote balanced learning and the opportunity to manage skill and competency growth by permitting individuals to test their own progress as they spend time learning new skills.

Although most organizations still have tuition reimbursement programs, they also stress a program of internal training and development with emphasis on coaching during projects so that people learn the most current technical skills. Projects are assigned not only according to who's next in the queue or who has free time but also from a skill development standpoint. A human resource executive told us, "The most valuable development is what we do with our own critical talent every day."

The development process closely links with the pay solution to effectively synchronize individual growth and pay. Performance management processes range from highly unstructured to fairly structured. Coaching is considerable. Some use a multisource feedback solution for performance management, and most rely on managers supplemented by colleague input interpreted by the manager and shared with the individual.

Positive Workplace

All IT companies in our research report that they have a specific "culture" that makes them attractive to their workforce. There's variation in these cultures; some have very informal work environments and others are more formal. They all say their culture influences the type of people they attract and retain. The participants listed some of what they do to make themselves attractive: management training, regular information on how the company is doing, the opportunity to meet and question the chief executive, and people-friendly work/life benefits.

SOCIAL INTERACTION. The tone of the workplace is clearly "We're all in this together"; the message is to "help everyone no matter where they are in the company." The priority is on communicating these messages directly rather than only posting them in the cafeteria or on bulletin boards. For example, one company provides coffee and soft drinks all day and a lunch for everyone who happens to be in the workplace on that day. Customers are included when they're "on campus," as are potential recruits and others interested in the organization. An executive said: "Providing free food and drink and an occasional party encourages people to talk with each other and exchange information. We can't get this done better in any other way, and it makes us special."

Another firm had recently ended a period in which a chief executive hired from outside had discontinued the "Friday beer bust," a company tradition from its inception; the departing CEO said, "Beer busts are not very businesslike." They were reinstated because the weekly event is a time for people from all parts of the company to talk about their new projects, ideas, and goals and share important information that helps everyone integrate around what the company is all about. Still another enterprise has Friday evening parties for new talent, calling them get-acquainted mixers.

QUALITY TALENT WORTH THE EFFORT. One of the IT companies indicated that its policy is "slow to hire and fast to fire." This sounds negative, but to the company it's quite the opposite. It wants positive people who fit the open and egalitarian culture. These people are hard to find and keep. However, should the firm accidentally hire someone who's negative and not enjoyable to work with, it ends the relationship as fast as possible. An executive reported: "We believe that a bad apple can spoil the entire barrel. We spend a lot of time and money on development, training, and growth of the workforce. Negative attitudes are not something we can easily undo."

Another company has a chief executive who "manages by walking around," spending one day a week in one location or another meeting people, exchanging ideas, and answering questions. He says, "I'd rather spend an enjoyable day each week with people who count, talking and thinking about things that help our business, than I would interviewing new people we must hire to replace the best ones who leave to [go to a job where they can then] meet weekly with a competitor's CEO."

Another respondent in our research has a "customer day" every two or three weeks, depending on availability. It invites customers to the company to exchange ideas and get better acquainted. As an executive said: "Getting feedback on how we're doing makes working in our company exciting because everyone has the chance to see how what they're doing is going over with customers. It makes it easier to talk to customers and to consider what customers may think when they're making a decision about our products or services. It's sort of an 'open customer book' way of doing things that the customers say they like too."

LEADERSHIP ACCOUNTABLE. One organization views a positive workplace as a leadership responsibility. It found that the people it wants need help on coaching, career counseling, development, training, and the like. The company made this a requirement for the "new leaders." These new leaders aren't traditional managers; many come from other than supervisory roles.

Most companies in our research believe that having excellent people helps immeasurably in making a better workplace. They stress selling business that people like to do. Most say it's doing "a little extra" that makes the workplace a good environment to come to in the morning. They emphasize some things that cost money, but also things that are simply nice to do and are convenience benefits: umbrellas in the employee lobby on rainy days, on-site masseuse, pets at work, buying discounts (for example, car washes, attorneys, veterinarians, tire centers), on-site cleaners, services to prepare income taxes, car pools, immunizations on site for the entire family, use of company travel services for vacation travel, and pickup and delivery for children before or after school in the event the individual needs to come to work early or go home late.

Compelling Future

Most of the IT companies in our research say they keep growing to provide excellent career opportunities. Management's responsibility is to position the company to obtain profitable and interesting business, to grow the business, to have excellent customers, and to ensure excellent leadership. Excellent leaders have a sense of destiny, communicate and create excitement about the vision and business strategy, gather input from the workforce on where the company is going, and encourage extensive workforce involvement in every part of the business.

One executive said, "It's up to the leadership group to show the key people we hired that they've bet on the right horse. We need to have work that not only generates profit but is also what people want to do. Sometimes we need to take work that doesn't have great profit margins to give our people the chance to do leading-edge work, or to work with a customer they can learn from."

R&D INVESTMENT. A major issue for the study respondents is how much to spend on research and development. Most said they spend a major portion of earnings on new product and process development because they must invest and build a compelling future even at the expense of dividends to their shareholders. As one executive reported, "We spend no less than 10 percent of our gross revenue each year on R&D, and we do this so we have a future. In our field, business isn't easy to get. But our company depends on what's coming next. Our best people want to work here because we can show them where we're going and what this means to them."

SURVIVING BUSINESS PARTNER. Another enterprise said it must acquire, merge, and grow. It must be the primary and surviving partner to ensure that people stay and are not insecure. The organization wants to impart a secure future so it won't need to rebound repeatedly with its workforce. Another company that had lost workforce trust from a layoff from which it took five years to recover wants to grow its workforce in parallel with revenue growth. It wants to be selective in hiring so that if individuals want to stay the company is willing to have them for a full career. Managers avoid hiring for the short haul and make sure everyone is a person they themselves would like to work with.

WHAT TO DO IN THE BEST OF CIRCUMSTANCES

Even if your company uses a total reward approach, it's difficult to retain all of your scarce talent because external opportunities are so easily available, from phone calls by search organizations to employment opportunities posted on the Internet. Smart companies identify the top 10–20 percent of the people whom they really need to retain and take special care to keep them. Some use information from the career-planning process to help make this decision. Sometimes these key scarce-talent people are high-potential individuals; other times they're critical to completing a major project or have essential skills. This takes the strategic-valuing concept that's applied to jobs or roles in Chapter 6 and extends it to people themselves. It is truly paying for the person.

APPLYING IT LEARNINGS TO OTHER SCARCE-TALENT SITUATIONS

The basic learnings in our IT survey apply to other industries, but you must customize them to the workforce, business situation, business strategy, and culture. Use the points in Exhibit 11.1 to start building integrated total rewards for scarce talent, though you may emphasize certain reward elements more than others. For example, in the fast food industry recognition is often essential. Enterprises may extend tangible recognition, such as accumulating points toward merchandise or trips, because doing so retains people while they're accumulating points. Starbucks is an example of integrated rewards, including stock options.

Attracting scarce talent is similar to selling a product. Just as the company must be clear in communicating the benefits, differential advantage, and value of its products before making a sale and must also follow through in delivering the products to retain customers, so too as an employer it must communicate the benefits, differential advantage, and value of its total rewards before hiring a person and also follow through in delivering the total rewards to retain scarce talent.

CONCLUSIONS

Consider unfreezing a reward practice that no longer adds value, changing the process, and then refreezing on a solution that best fits. A scarce-talent situation is an excellent time to do something beyond paying more money without adding lasting value. It's a superb opportunity to make lasting total reward changes that get complete leadership attention.

Scarce-talent realities are a major chance to align rewards effectively with business goals. Companies can innovate with total rewards and offer meaningful reward solutions to combat excessive turnover of key talent. Also, total rewards can be useful in making the company more attractive to the people essential for its growth. The solutions we've suggested for base pay, variable pay, and recognition for a company that wants to be great in terms of how its people perform also apply to scarce-talent situations. The only difference is the level of urgency. This is a time to make positive change in reward design. It's an opportunity comparable to that of globalization, a merger or acquisition, or a major change process such as migration to teams.

CHAPTER 12

Rewarding the Salesforce

What are your company's BHAGs (big, hairy, audacious goals)?[1] What is it that makes yours a great company with a visionary future? We wager it has something to do with becoming preeminent, growing according to your own stringent goals, becoming a market leader, and surprising customers by exceeding their expectations. We also bet that a new foundation for sales and marketing, one that's integrated into your total business strategy, is part of this vision.

SELLING IN TRANSITION

The pressures on selling are constant and dynamic. Somebody once said, "Things change and will change again tomorrow." Failing to anticipate the need to adapt and communicate it to the members of the salesforce can be a huge competitive disadvantage.

Some of the most admired enterprises have yet to tie sales compensation to the realities of their business. Designing sales rewards is a major opportunity to gain advantage by communicating accurately with the salesforce. But the power of follow-the-leader is strong and tempting; it justifies what your company is doing and lets you avoid doing the homework that leads to a business-aligned sales compensation solution. We believe the great companies, as well as those hoping to join the ranks, must take the high ground regarding sales compensation design. This means considering business challenges and opportunities rather than only prevailing practice.

Though Willie Loman is dead, the isolation of the salesforce from the rest of the enterprise often remains in full bloom. Siloing the salesforce gives a company's competitors a chance to gain advantage through better workforce alignment. In most companies, the salesforce has a pay solution unique from the approach deployed in the rest of the company. This may contribute to isolating the sales effort from the rest of the business because it makes it more difficult for the same messages about business direction or interdependency of workforce activities to get through. So designing sales compensation requires extra effort to ensure rewards based on business-aligned goals and synchronization of the interdependent efforts of people across functions to serve the customer.

CHANGING SALES REWARDS

Sales professionals expect pay to be designed in a specific fashion. When a company suggests changing the rules in a way that generates new messages and requires different actions, it often heightens the challenge and consequences.[2]

Strategic Alignment

It's critical to include the part of the workforce that has the most customer contact in the company's overall total reward strategy to align rewards with business goals (our second reward principle). Think of the business-aligned goals we discussed in Chapter 4. The salesforce should be part of overall workforce alignment with the business so their goals are a direct extension of company goals.

This means change because sometimes the salesperson is like the buffalo hunter of the last century. The buffalo hunter runs into the field to capture and kill buffalo. Once killed, the buffalo is dragged back into camp and dumped on those responsible for skinning the carcass, curing the skin, and preparing the meat. Meanwhile, the buffalo hunter runs back into the field for another buffalo. Whether or not the curing and dressing is done properly isn't the responsibility of the buffalo hunter.

Today, the entire process of "hunting, skinning, curing, and preparing"—acquiring and doing business to generate a great company—involves many people and functions. Goal alignment of total pay is critical. Selling is becoming increasingly complex and interdependent. Everyone is becoming a stakeholder in delivering what the sales organization has promised.

The reward principles suggest a way to address these opportunities. Principle 3 supports extending the line of sight of the salesforce so they know how what they sell affects the business. Variable pay for results, Principle 6, has customarily been an element of most sales rewards. Its effectiveness increases if a few key measures in addition to sales volume focus salespeople on growing sales in the direction that best fits the company's operating plan. Leveraging rewards can be customized to fit the performance challenge. Unless salespeople receive only commission, an individual's ongoing value (from Principle 5) is paramount in setting base pay; consistent performance, sales skills and competencies, and competitive total cash are core design opportunities.

The Customer's First Contact

Salespeople are the company's first connection to the customer. Therefore, it's important for them to translate customer needs accurately back to the company. As customers set increasing expectations and the selling situation becomes more complex, enterprises are calling on sales teams and customer teams to help the individual salesperson close the sale and satisfy potential customers.

In addition, the salesforce must know the implications of what and how it sells. The salesperson must identify with team, business-unit, and company success. Extending salespeople's line of sight involves having the salesforce think beyond sales volume to other measures such as the profitability of the business they sell. This also involves measures that define the strategy and tactics the company has regarding the kind of customer it wants, how it treats the customer, priorities concerning most important products or services, and other company strategies. This is tantamount to helping others in the company skin, cure, prepare, and deliver the buffalo to the customer.

REWARDING THE SALESFORCE STRATEGICALLY

Supporting the business process means thinking creatively about the customer.

Example of Xerox

Xerox is one of the icons of global business. The company invented an industry and greatly changed how business is conducted from a communications standpoint. In the 1980s, Xerox lost market share to Japanese copier companies, and its customer relations grew strained. The CEO at the time faced the choice of breaking up the company (since the parts were more valuable than the whole) or trying to regain alignment with customers.

The Xerox workforce having the most customer contact was the sales and service organization, traditionally separated strategically from the rest of the company. It was an elite corps of talent, proud of their long heritage of making Xerox what it was. A look at sales compensation showed that how many supplies and copier upgrades the salesforce sold principally determined their pay. Customers, on the other hand, reported an understandable interest in service and keeping their existing copiers running effectively. Thus, when a sales team came to see a customer, there were no goals shared between them.

Xerox changed sales compensation so customer satisfaction reports in large part determined incentive awards. This change aligned the salesforce (numbering more than 35,000 at the time) with the customer and made the sales process a primary factor in reinventing Xerox and regaining vital market share and customer credibility. From its past of being interested only in new business rather than sustaining customer relationships, the salesforce now became an important source of advantage for Xerox. The company has changed sales compensation many times since the 1980s, but it remains customer-aligned.[3]

Example of dj Orthopedics

Smith & Nephew DonJoy (now dj Orthopedics) in San Diego is a major supplier of braces and orthopedic supplies. They sell through a wide distributor network that's benefited them for many years. Traditionally, the company allocated a portion of revenues to fund distributor incentives. It worked with a team of distributors to develop a distributor pay solution aligned with its business strategy. The sales compensation approach not only involves commissions that emphasize the strategy concerning specific products but also includes a performance management system that recognizes application of needed skills and competencies and accomplishment of objectives.

These examples suggest that change is possible for companies that believe in alignment of the workforce and take steps to include the salesforce as well. What do we learn from stories such as these? We learn that businesses are changing and the salesforce is joining in. Imagine how powerful a company can become by aligning the entire workforce, local and global, including the salesforce and the leadership team, to the strategies and goals of the business.

Selling Goals and Business Strategy

Sales organizations are full of goals and objectives. It's a way of life. There are goals for territories and products or services. Quotas are set for new customers and new markets. Objectives exist for individuals and groups of individuals, and sales managers have goals for their organizations.

Unfortunately, some selling goals are out of tune as a result of goal development that focuses on the close line of sight of the salesforce and not on linkage with the business strategy. The salesforce goal of "making the numbers" in terms of quarterly company gross sales performance often dislodges the salesforce from the longer-term business strategy. The objective is often for the salesforce to overpower all obstacles to achieve the company's revenue goal. Whether making the revenue number is enough depends on what the company is willing to accept in terms of the sales role.

Companies now want more. They expect sales success that generates targeted profit performance, establishment of a continuing and mutually beneficial relationship with important customers, and the ability to point the selling effort in a strategic direction. They want a salesforce that is connected to the rest of the company and integrated into the overall business process. They expect a dedicated salesforce, not one they view as out of control, behaving more like a bevy of independent representatives and sometimes promising things the company can't deliver.

More Critical Selling Accountability

Increasingly, sales goals communicate that those who have the most contact with the customers have to work differently. Exhibits 12.1 and 12.2 summarize the changes in sales roles and sales rewards. Ever more integrated into the overall business strategy, salespeople are sharing accountability not only for the top-line performance of the company but also for the bottom line.

Again, positioning pay is one way to communicate what the role of the salesforce should be, but this requires much more than putting everyone on a sales commission. Getting the company's products and

Exhibit 12.1. Changing Sales Roles.

Characteristic	From	To
Business case	Salesforce separate from rest of company	Salesforce integrated with all who influence customers and products or services
Responsibility of salesperson	Sell, sell, sell only	Support overall company business process
Role of salesperson	Overpower customer resistance and sell what we have	Facilitator, listener, information gatherer, educator, relationship manager and builder, value-adder to customer's business, and communicator of customer feedback
Selling objective	"One size fits all"; "a sale is a sale"; products or services competing internally for sales emphasis	Mix and match; flexible and agile; change as business situation evolves; strategy is solid; tactics are adaptable
Selling opportunity	All selling opportunities—penetration, retention, conversion, and new markets	Focus roles and salespeople on what they do best
Role design	Only one sales job	More than one sales role or job to increase overall sales effectiveness
Interrelationships	Sell independently	May work in sales teams or customer teams
Time frame	Month to month; quarter to quarter	Longer-term focus on adding customer value

Exhibit 12.2. Business-Aligned Practice for Sales Rewards.

Characteristic	From	To
Reward design	Undifferentiated commission based on "top line" sales	Differentiated rewards based on strategies concerning customers and products or services
Measures	Volume measure only	Few key measures in addition to volume that focus salesforce
Linkage of measures with others	No link between salesforce and rest of workforce	Goals of salesforce and workforce linked
Results-reward relationship	Little differentiation in variable pay based on performance	Greater variation in variable pay based on performance
Emphasis on sales growth	Volume representing growth not worth more, or much more, than earlier volume	Larger reward for improving sales over target
Focus	Variable pay	Total pay and total rewards
Customer for sales compensation	Only salespeople; keeping them satisfied is critical	Many customers, including external customers

services to customers involves more than just the salesforce, more even than the sales and marketing organization. This is where the opportunity for sharing business-aligned goals comes in.

SALES MEASURES

Great sales reward designs mirror the business strategy of the company. For example, top-performing sales organizations often have pay solutions that emphasize not only overall selling performance but also a few additional select measures of customer retention and penetration and products or services that are either strategic to the business or most profitable in terms of the bottom line. The company closely links its business strategy and the selling process and uses pay to connect strategy and action.

Selling Opportunities Drive Volume Measures

The priority for business growth leads directly to the sales compensation measure of sales volume in units, revenue dollars, or gross margin dollars. But the salesforce needs more direction than just volume. Assessing sales opportunities shows where a company's strengths and weaknesses are and what should be shored up, either by directing the salesforce with sales compensation measures or by developing new sales roles to take advantage of selling opportunities. Selling opportunities include:

- *Penetration:* increasing business with existing customers
- *Retention:* keeping existing customers
- *Conversion:* acquiring new customers who've purchased from a competitor
- *New markets:* either creating new applications or attracting new types of customers other than those who've purchased the company's (or a direct competitor's) products or services[4]

PENETRATION. Customer penetration is typically easier and more profitable than conversion or new markets because there are costs associated with acquiring new customers and signing them onto the company's systems. At some point, though, customer penetration can't be milked any further to get the needed growth in revenue, and the salesforce must find new customers or new markets. Examples of measures of customer penetration are overall volume of existing accounts, share of existing-account business, and number of product types sold to existing accounts.

RETENTION. Retention of existing customers is especially important in a new company or with new products and services that need sales growth. Eventually this priority turns to retaining profitable customers, not necessarily all customers. To keep lower-margin customers profitable, the company may have to find alternative ways to sell, such as telesales. Examples of measures of customer retention are the insurance industry's percentage of customers retained or a reduction in "churn."

CONVERSION. Conversion of new customers takes time and requires a differential advantage in products or services, or else in the salesperson's ability to sell. Conversion measures include number of new customers and sales volume from these customers.

NEW MARKETS. Selling to new markets is probably the most difficult selling opportunity because it requires different knowledge and skills about product application, understanding and addressing the needs of an unfamiliar type of customer, and building relationships with a new group of customers. Examples of measures are growth in revenue from new markets, sales volume from new markets, and number of new customers from new markets.

More Than Top-Line Sales

Measures in addition to sales volume direct the salesforce.

MEASURES TO IMPROVE PROFITABILITY. Not all revenue dollars have the same value. A company concerned about profitability uses sales compensation measures that focus on and improve profitability, such as product mix, customer mix, price realization (a comparison of actual price to list price), and percent of gross margin. A measure of profit growth emphasizes several areas: profitable products, valued customer retention, sales to specific customers with high-profit buying patterns, and unloading unprofitable customers.

The incentive for a pharmaceutical company's salesforce that works with payors or health insurers on formulary approvals includes a profitability measure. It has a sales volume measure along with a matrix of price realization and market share. This two-dimensional matrix requires a threshold level of performance on both market share and profitability before earning any award for these two measures.

STRATEGIC MEASURES. Strategic measures are useful where the sale requires significant planning and the sales cycle is long. A maker of vehicle components for automotive manufacturers rewards the salesperson when it's named as a vendor during the vehicle design and preproduction phase, before the actual sale and supply of product during the automaker's production phase, because the selling cycle is multiyear. Or a major account executive who has a few key accounts may have as specific customer targets not only penetration but also customer profitability and product mix, geared toward improving business for both the customer and the enterprise.

Another example involves successful product introduction. Although the salesforce usually welcomes new products, the business may use a new product revenue measure if there's some resistance on the part of the salesforce to selling the new product instead of the existing product.

CORRELATE MEASURES. Variable pay measures may also correlate with but not actually direct measures of selling success. K-Mart uses customer satisfaction, measured by reports from "secret shoppers," as an element in its store sales incentive for Super-K associates. This focuses variable pay not only on sales success but also on how associates treat the customer on the way to selling success.

Limited Number of Measures

A company's sales and marketing strategy drives the measures for sales compensation. As with any variable pay solution, limit the number of measures to three to five to keep the focus and ensure that each measure has enough weight to be meaningful. Sales managers understand identifying just a handful of critical selling goals increases likely achievement, and that trying to reach many goals diffuses salesforce efforts. Too many goals result in salespeople focusing on those they are most likely to achieve, not on those that may be most important.

DESIGN OF THE SALES ROLE

Successful selling depends on how well the sales role is designed. Sometimes the sales role has more responsibilities than are within the capability of a single professional. For example, salespeople have responsibility for engaging the customer and closing the deal; but they're also credit checkers, bill collectors, inventory control analysts, delivery schedulers, expediters, product installers, testers, trainers, customer service analysts, and accountants as well. They may also share these business-aligned goals with other workforce members outside the sales organization. The best solution is to have a clear role and accountabilities accompanied by a limited list of responsibilities that take optimal advantage of the skill and competency of the direct-selling force.

Sales Teams

Sales teams made up of more than one salesperson are becoming common. Businesses are finding that people in various sales roles can work together more efficiently to achieve the overall sales goals of the company than can people in only one sales role.

EXAMPLE OF INVESTMENT SERVICES FIRM. An investment services business that offers mutual funds and oversees mutual fund assets serves as an example. Its salesforce was only external wholesalers, who influence brokers to sell funds to investors such as you and me. These wholesalers concentrate on the brokers who form a large percentage of the company's business, rather than on increasing their business with smaller customers or converting brokers to their products. The company added an internal wholesaler role that focuses on telephone sales to potential broker customers and on penetration of small broker accounts. The person in this role also facilitates sales to the larger accounts by having technical modeling questions answered by other functional departments, setting up wholesaler presentations to brokers, and being available to brokers regardless of the availability of the external wholesaler.

The internal wholesalers participate in an incentive plan that's similar to the external wholesaler plan but has much smaller incentive opportunity. This accomplished sharing of business-aligned goals. In addition, the incentive rewards results on a performance scorecard completed by their manager as well as the two external wholesalers they team with; it covers their sales presentation skills, development and implementation of a marketing plan, and service levels.

EXAMPLE OF HEALTH INSURERS. Some companies organize sales teams by starting with the customer. We surveyed the salesforce pay practices of insurance companies that sell group health insurance to employers. Most of these major carriers had independently conducted customer surveys to gather input on improving the customer effectiveness of their sales organization. The insurers had a similar major finding: lack of coordination or integrated effort in dealing with the customer. Account executives tended to keep customer information to themselves, so if these people weren't available, customers found it difficult to have their issues addressed. There was also a gap in the transition from the account executive to the sales service representative once the account was sold.

The insurance companies independently came up with a similar incentive design solution based on customer input. They developed sales team variable pay that rewards performance of sales teams (comprising one or two account executives and two or three sales service representatives). Again, members of the team share accountability for business-aligned goals. The primary performance measure is sales volume. Incentive opportunity for team members depends on their impact on the sale, so the account executive has greater incentive opportunity than the sales service representative. Additional secondary goals were specific to the role of the team member. This example shows how listening to the customer can result in linking the performance pay of a team of people who must work together to give the most customer satisfaction.

Customer Teams

Customer teams are multifunctional. Along with sales professionals, the other roles may include marketing, design, manufacturing, and finance. These teams are becoming more common in complex and customized selling situations. The resources of a variety of people are needed to customize a product or service for the customer. Sales professionals on customer teams directly share goals with others outside the salesforce.

EXAMPLE OF SOFTWARE PROVIDER. A provider of large customized software solutions to other companies found that its salesforce was selling projects that the company couldn't deliver profitably. It formed customer teams, led by the sales professional and including participation of both the line organization responsible for completing the project and the finance group.

Both the salesforce and the consultants who deliver the solution are aligned in terms of the project results. Not only sales revenue but also project profitability are measures of salesforce performance. For each sale, awards start with the initial sale and continue sequentially through the course of the project. This accomplished sharing of business-aligned goals of sales volume and profitable sales.

EXAMPLE OF MANUFACTURERS. In the manufacturing sector, people from engineering and customer service may be members of the customer team and share measures and goals with the sales professionals. The selling effort that addresses the customer may be individual or team-based at the point of sale; a strong supporting organization of engineering, marketing, service, customer support, and even manufacturing and logistics is often essential to the individual sales professional. This suggests that the goals of other people on the team should be consistent with those of the sales professional. This is the point we make about the importance of breaking down selling silos by sharing the goals used for rewards with others in the company.

DESIGNING SALES REWARDS

Business strategy, marketing strategy, sales strategy, sales goals, and the definition of the sales role all influence sales compensation design. Sales compensation is also an extension of the total reward strategy, which articulates the principles and foundation for rewards to communicate what's necessary to accomplish the company's business.

Salesperson Prominence and Mix of Target Total Cash

Sales prominence refers to the role the salesperson plays in making the sale.[5]

UNDIFFERENTIATED PRODUCT OR SERVICE. When the product or service is undifferentiated or a commodity, the sales professional is most critical in making the sale and thus has high prominence. If the product or service isn't unique then the sales professional must be.

Every life insurance company's product has features and provisions similar to all the others. Even costs are similar in many instances. Most often the salesperson makes the sale of life insurance rather than the product selling itself. How the salesperson performs and presents the company, products, services, advantages, and disadvantages generally makes the difference as to whether the customer purchases one life insurance product or another. Although life insurance companies have tried to give their products brand names, most customers are unable to differentiate the products themselves and rely on the sales experience to make a decision.

In some cases, the product or service itself is part of the differentiation for the customer, and the sales professional makes up the rest. In large part, the automobile business is such an opportunity. Customers may make the decision as to whether they want a Ford or Chevrolet depending on features and past experience with that brand of automobile. When they go from dealer to dealer, though, the sales professional makes the difference.

DIFFERENTIATED PRODUCT OR SERVICE. In instances where the product or service is unique, it makes the difference itself; the sales professional plays a different role in the selling process. Although some may identify the role as less important, it's probably just *differently* important. The salesforce often has significant product or service expertise, and the selling process is more consultative than transactional.

Gillette works to differentiate its shaving systems from others in the market in terms of design, features, outcomes, and overall attractiveness. Gillette often renders one of its own shaving products obsolete by introducing another to sustain advantage. Microsoft and Intel do this as well and focus on brand quality and exciting products. Here, the product isn't differentiated at the point of sale by the salesperson. Advertising, product features and benefits, and other ways to communicate with the customer are most important and actually make the major difference.

We recall working with Lawry's Foods, in the Los Angeles area (when they were an independent company), to develop sales compensation for the salesforce delivering products to stores. The Lawry's spice brand was extremely powerful and well differentiated from competitors. Advertising and reputation sold the product, but the actual role of the sales representative was to convince the retailer to reserve enough shelf space for the product so the advertising and packaging could sell it to customers.

MIX OF TARGET TOTAL CASH. The more the product sells itself with the help of pricing, advertising, and company reputation, the lower the prominence of the salesperson. The more the salesforce constitutes the differentiation that creates the value that makes the customer want to buy, the higher the prominence. The greater the importance of the salesforce in the marketing mix and the purchasing decision, the more pay is contingent upon successfully making the sale. This commonly means greater emphasis on variable pay in the target total cash mix.

The selling cycle also affects mix, with a long selling cycle implying a low percentage of variable pay, other things being equal. High prominence is a mix with 50 percent or more of variable pay; low prominence is a mix of, say, 90 percent base and 10 percent variable pay.

Variable Pay

The two types of variable pay approaches for the sales measures in sales compensation are (1) commission, a percentage of revenue or gross margin or a dollar amount per unit sold, used when the focus is on volume; and (2) incentive, based on performance compared to a goal, target, or quota, focused on achievement of predefined goals, and calculated as a percentage of base pay earnings or target dollar amounts.

Commission rates either are fixed or vary as performance increases or hits a specified level. A commission is effective if salespeople have high prominence in the sale, forecasting is difficult, the marketplace is new or the market potential for the product or service is unknown, the company can afford the cost because margins are sufficient, and territories have similar potential.

An incentive that varies based on level of goal achievement is effective if salespeople have less prominence in the sale, forecasting is accurate and based on knowledge of the marketplace and market potential, sales costs must take into account the competitive labor market and the company's ability to pay, and territories have significant variation in size but the company wants to create equal opportunity for members of the salesforce.

UPSIDE OPPORTUNITY. Upside opportunity (variable pay opportunity above target) depends in part on the market opportunity, the profitability of additional sales, and the total cash mix compared to competitive practice. The tougher it is to make sales above target, the more profitable additional sales are, and the greater the portion of variable pay in the total cash mix relative to competitive practice, then the higher the upside opportunity. Upside opportunity above target is typically one to three times the target opportunity.

PERFORMANCE DIFFERENTIATION. Some sales compensation approaches have little differentiation in pay between the star performer and someone at the threshold level of performance, not just considering total cash or total pay but also looking at variable pay. Still other sales compensation solutions pay very little extra for incremental sales over the previous year (the more difficult sales). Companies are changing variable pay to tie pay to performance strongly, so the best performers make more money and the low performers make less money; thus salespeople make relatively more for the incremental increase in revenue beyond the same level of sales as the prior year.

This means not paying commission on the first dollar of sales, increasing the commission rate after achieving a specified sales level, and paying more for specific new sales volume (for example, volume to new customers). For goal incentives, it means increasing the threshold performance level or reducing the award at threshold and increasing the award or the slope of the incentive line above goal. The objective is to make performance worthwhile.

GOAL SETTING. Goal setting starts with the company's overall revenue goal from the operating plan. This takes into account market opportunity, new products, services and technology, and the required return to shareholders. Market potential and market share of the territory, and salespeople's selling potential and prior performance, help determine the division of the overall revenue goal among salespeople. Sales management is typically more thoughtful in assigning quotas than applying a constant percentage across the board; they assess selling opportunity to develop reasonable goals.

COMPETITIVE PRACTICE OR SELLING COST. To determine how much to pay the salesforce, an enterprise considers sales compensation as a selling cost, a compensation expense, or a combination of the two. The selling-cost view allocates a percentage of revenue to sales compensation and often uses a commission approach for variable pay.

The compensation-expense view uses the labor market to determine competitive total cash and often relies on a goal or quota incentive plan for variable pay. Levels of performance match competitive levels of total cash; for example, meeting goals corresponds to the 50th percentile or median total cash. To ensure that sales compensation has sufficient leverage, the company provides sufficient spread in total cash such that the 90th percentile performer makes at least the 90th percentile of total cash and the 10th percentile performer makes no more than the 10th percentile of total cash. The company backs into base pay after determining the mix of base pay and variable pay.

CAPS. Although competitive practice counts, "capping" upside earnings opportunities is less viable and reasonable. We haven't seen a salesforce that liked having limits placed on the upside earnings potential. A biotechnology firm developed sales incentives for a new pharmaceutical product to avoid the upside limit. A careful financial model of the selling process related a salesperson's earnings opportunity to the value added to the company from sales, while ensuring reasonable pay from a competitive perspective.

Experience suggests that setting upside earnings limits is an excuse for not doing effective incentive design homework. If the salesforce earns "too much" (in the perception of some in the company), ineffective sales incentive design or goal setting is more likely than any other factor to be the cause for this perception. An alternative is to limit earnings for a short period of time, such as a quarter, but allow unlimited upside earnings for overall performance over a longer period, such as the entire year.

Base Pay

Individual ongoing value, Principle 5, should be the foundation of base pay for sales professionals. The three dimensions of individual ongoing value apply to the salesforce:

1. Skills and competencies
   - Customer relationship building and management
   - Selling process skills, including prospecting, preapproach, sales presentation, handling objections, closing the sale, and after-sales services
   - Understanding of customers' industry and business
   - Serving as a consultant to the customer's business—assessing, solving their problems, and enhancing their business
   - Product or service knowledge, including input on improvements to products and services

- Understanding of the business of the salesperson's company and industry trends
- Teamwork and collaboration with company resources (customer service, marketing, manufacturing, engineering, etc.)
- Innovation and creativity in gaining customer access and solving customer problems
- Communications (listening, presentation, oral and written communications skills)
- Knowledge of competitors
- Organization skills (such as time management)

2. Consistent performance over time
   - Meeting sales targets consistently
   - Successfully taking on larger targets relative to the potential of the territory
3. Market value (market value for base pay factored in after determining target total cash and the mix of base and variable pay)

BASE PAY RATES. If variable pay for sales results is a large portion of total cash, the company may use one or a few distinct base pay rates for salespeople. Individual ongoing value as represented by consistent performance in combination with skills and competencies determines an individual salesperson's base pay rate. Alternatively, a narrow base pay range may be useful if variable pay is prominent in the total cash mix.

LUMP SUMS FOR DEVELOPMENT. In conjunction with base pay rates, the business may also use lump-sum payments or variable pay to reward accomplishments and development relative to skills and competencies, provided the salesperson completes the basic requirements (supplying competitor intelligence, territory analysis, and a sales plan). The salesperson sets goals related to the skills and competencies that best enhance selling success. For example, an individual whose objective is to develop a higher level of customer relationship building and management skills may reflect this growth by setting a goal to develop and implement a sales approach that makes the company the sole supplier to a customer. Or an individual who wants to improve closing skills may set a goal of improving the percentage of closes, as well as demonstrating enhanced closing skills in the field with the sales manager.

THE SELLING PARTNERS

Who are the partners in the selling process? The importance of business-aligned goals throughout the enterprise signals the value of extending everyone's line of sight to the customer and selling success. Even though pay solutions may differ across the company in terms of design, we suggest that common goals should be the link across the workforce.

This means the sales reward design may share measures and goals with others in the workforce. For example, the salesforce may share goals of new product introduction with marketing, customer retention with customer service, delivery with manufacturing, and profitability with other elements of the workforce. This is part of aligning business goals. It includes customer alignment by emphasizing whatever is necessary to establish a close relationship with customers. Xerox did this by rewarding customer satisfaction, K-Mart by using secret shoppers, and dj Orthopedics by partnering the company and its distributors.

But in selecting goals, remember to limit the number of goals for variable pay even though other goals can and should be communicated to give a complete picture. Everything that the salesforce should do need not become a measure in the sales compensation solution. Many objectives are issues of leadership, training, and development.

Workforce as Partners to Salesforce

We've talked about the line of sight concerning measures and goals and how it must be lengthened for many in the workforce, to keep the company focused on customers. If sales and customer satisfaction, for example, play a role in the pay of the entire company, this helps clarify the linkage between people and the business strategy. The communications message then is to show how people add value by means of achieving a series of intermediate goals that cascade from the customer. Also, this linkage builds a foundation for developing the core competencies needed to satisfy the customer and for identifying the skills and behaviors that the workforce needs to acquire and apply to gain these ends.

Sales and Workforce Pay Becoming More Similar

We suggest in Chapter 7 (on short-term variable pay) that pay solutions for the rest of the workforce are moving in the direction of more closely matching those of the salesforce. The workforce's increased incidence of variable pay and expanding variable pay opportunity illustrate this. Another way to further similarity is through common goals for variable pay. The salesforce shares some goals with others responsible for selling. Everyone in the company has a role in the selling process, whether this involves effective manufacturing operations, producing quality products and services, handling customer queries, delivering products and services on time, or giving value for the customer dollar. The salesforce is thus likely to have more partners in selling in the future.

This means the possibility of including some measures of growth in the total pay of everyone. Stock options may do this because of the need to educate about what influences stock price. Or short-term variable pay may include goals of company growth, new customers, and the like.

Not Everyone in Same Pay Solution

This is certainly not advocacy for having everyone in the same pay solution. It's a strong suggestion, however, that the salesforce needs closer alignment with the overall business strategy. This clearly starts with the responsibility for growing the company revenue base, getting new customers, keeping excellent customers, introducing new products, ensuring profitable sales growth, and all the rest. In addition, the salesforce increasingly partners with others to make sure that a solid combination of business-aligned goals is achieved. This makes the selling process even more powerful than it is and permits the salesforce to become increasingly valuable to the company.

BUILDING THE CASE FOR CHANGING SALES REWARDS

Often the impetus for reviewing sales compensation is that, in some people's minds, it's not paying off. Another important inducement may be that the salesforce is operating in a different direction from where the company needs to go. The reasons sales compensation isn't paying off should be explored to determine if it's something the salesforce is or is not doing, or if there's a problem in the product or service, marketing mix, or sales compensation design. Developing an effective sales compensation solution starts with the business process and extends to the solution, as it does in developing all effective reward solutions.

Much of the success of the sales compensation change process may come from what's done even before the sales reward strategy is developed:

- *Situation analysis.* How is sales performance? What factors are contributing to the present state of sales? The factors influencing selling and the variables shaping the company's business environment are essential determinants of the role of the salesperson and sales compensation. It's possible that things other than sales compensation are strongly influencing selling performance and need attention. Products and services being offered are of course critical and may be the problem. Identifying these influences is important because otherwise a company could delay addressing the real selling problem, if it spends time and effort on sales rewards and this isn't a major contributor to any lack of sales performance. Asking questions and evaluating the market and selling process are clearly elements of situation analysis.
- *Selling goals.* Have the selling goals changed, or do they remain the same? Have marketing strategies, product and service strategies, and other elements of the business process caused course corrections in the sales plan? For example, the goal may have changed from maximizing sales to a few customers to expanding sales to multiple customers. Another change could be to focus on a few profitable products and services instead of emphasizing the entire product and service line. Compare expectations in terms of outcomes to what the current sales compensation plan accentuates. This is a good test of whether or not messages about objectives are being communicated to the salesforce through sales compensation.
- *Organization design.* What's the most effective way to sell to different types of customers: through distributors, territory sales representatives, or telesales representatives? Does salesforce organization design center around some combination of geography and product or service, or does it center around the customer (as a growing number of businesses have started to do)? What kind of contact do customers want with the sales organization? For example, a large

customer may be tired of receiving calls from many salespeople working for the same company because of poor coordination. What's the most productive way for the company to generate sales?

- *Sales role.* After revisiting the selling goals, ask yourself what role the salesperson plays in getting the sale. Have expectations for the role changed? For example, has the role of the salesperson become that of an account manager, responsible for getting more sales from large and important customers, rather than trying to get many first sales from multiple customers? Some sales compensation solutions focus on initial sales, some on sustained sales. The role of the salesperson influences sales reward design and communication.
- *Competitive practice.* What other companies are paying for similar levels of performance is important to the pay design process. Not only the absolute levels of sales compensation but also the levels of compensation in terms of competitor sales performance matter. Competitors with successful selling records are a good source of competitive pay information; are they getting more or less mileage from sales compensation than your company is? The goal is to see whether designing a new pay approach can result in more mileage from sales compensation expenditures; one standard is what competitors are paying for the value they receive.
- *Strategic direction.* Once all the information is in, develop a sales reward strategy (part of the total reward strategy of the company). Address measures, goals, roles, competitive position, mix of base and variable pay, type of pay design, and the like; and go further, to address the strategic relationship between sales compensation and the pay approach in place for the rest of the company. For example, are there any shared goals? Do functions such as marketing and sales support participate with the field salesforce in any element of sales compensation? What measures and goals reward performance? What's base pay for—should it emphasize any new skills and competencies?
- *Sales compensation design.* At last, prepare the sales compensation design. Consider alternatives that match strategy and develop a solution for implementation and communication. Subsequently, consider continuous improvement to keep the sales compensation approach aligned and refreshed.

Strategy counts, and being prepared to develop the sales reward strategy makes successful implementation more likely. The preparation process need not be time-consuming, but it should chart the direction of the role the sales organization plays in making the company a success.

CONCLUSIONS

Sales rewards are an important part of the business alignment message. Sales compensation design differs from the pay designs of the rest of the workforce, but sharing goals with others in the company is essential. This is fundamental to business-aligned goals. It means more than sales volume determines salesforce pay and that measures and goals may change periodically as the role of the salesforce adapts and adjusts to competitive business realities. More people than the sales professionals are responsible for selling products and services, and they must become stakeholders in sales success as well.

The salesforce has the most customer contact in a typical company and is in many ways the thermometer of its success. So long as the company designs sales rewards effectively, then the better that it does, the more pay the salesforce should receive. It's part of the win-win partnership we've been talking about all along.

CHAPTER 13

Rewarding Executives

What makes a good leader? All successful leaders have one thing in common: willing followers. Although experts disagree about the characteristics of a leader, and even whether leaders are made or born, all memorable leaders are able to marshal a dedicated legion of followers.[1] The legion may be small or large, but success without help from valued followers is tough sledding. Herb Kelleher and Jack Welch have become legendary business leaders. Although both have widely contrasting styles and approaches, they're clearly successful leaders with strong cadres of dedicated followers.

We hope to enlist leaders in helping make everything in *Pay People Right!* work. During World War I, a popular recruitment poster showed a picture of Uncle Sam pointing and saying, "I want YOU." We want a recruitment poster pointing to executives saying, "We *need* you to pay people right!" We believe that good leaders should want this as well.

IMPORTANCE OF LEADERSHIP

Why is executive reward leadership so important? Throughout *Pay People Right!* we call for champions to get out front and lead total reward change. We talk about the importance of having role models with the grit to do the tough things required to make a new reward approach work. We believe executive compensation is a leadership opportunity. How executive compensation is composed tells everyone in the enterprise whether the bosses are walking the talk. It's hard to get people to do something you don't do yourself. Try to get your kids to be on time when *you* are consistently late.

Executive Rewards and Leadership

In this chapter, the word *leaders* includes not only the executive group but also senior-level managers. Although leaders are found anywhere in an organization, executives occupy especially influential roles because what they do has a major impact on the success of the enterprise. They can tie the workforce to the company's game plan for success through pay. They can set a positive tone to rewarding and recognizing the workforce. Leaders are the coaches of the total pay process. And they teach best by example.

Leaders at the top can energize their following by influencing shareholders and the board of directors to design executive pay (and thus indirectly everybody else's pay) properly. We summarize the essential leadership issues surrounding executive rewards in Exhibit 13.1.

Executive Compensation Is Visible

The *Wall Street Journal* and *Business Week* dedicate considerable space to executive compensation. It's often sensational and newsworthy. Overpaid executives concern the press more than business alignment of the pay of the entire workforce. We think the press is missing the target on the biggest pay issue. The more important challenges and opportunities involve pay and other rewards for the entire workforce—not just executives. Unless the workforce actually participates in helping make the company a success, it's unlikely the enterprise can sustain itself in the long run. This makes a far less dramatic story, but a more important one.

Exhibit 13.1. Leadership Issues for Executive Rewards.

- Reflects the six reward principles
- Communicates sponsorship of total pay aligned with the business
- Serves as a role model for pay throughout the organization
- Reflects integrated top-to-bottom total reward strategy
- Reinforces important future-focused, financial, customer, people, and operational goals
- Validates new strategic directions, values, and performance initiatives

The workforce and shareholders have more access to executive compensation information now than ever before. Proxy and 10-K statements tell enough about the pay of the top leaders so anybody in the workforce can determine whether executive pay is similar to or vastly different from everyone else's pay in concept and alignment. Increasing workforce involvement and the advent of team-based organizations also encourage questions of members of the top team. Cascading goals and strategic alignment increase communications about where the company is going and how people can help. This is part of the better workforce deal.

Applying the Reward Principles

Executive rewards should embrace *all* the reward principles—in fact, executive compensation should serve as the foundation of the principles. Principle 1 seeks to create a positive, natural reward experience. It's a leadership role of senior executives to make the reward experience positive for the workforce. Knowing executive rewards follow the same tenets is important to gaining trust and commitment. Principle 2 builds the business case and provides the win-win measures and goals to make it real. Business-aligned goals and development and performance feedback are essential to executive rewards. Creating a partnership throughout the enterprise is what leading effectively is about.

Extending people's line of sight to goals that make the company a bottom-line success, as suggested in Principle 3, starts with executive goals set for executive pay. Information about where the company is going comes from here and cascades to others. Executives set the pace by making the how-to of business success transparent from top to bottom. Principle 4 proposes using each element of total executive rewards for what it does best. This means base pay, variable pay (cash and equity), recognition and celebration, and benefits combine to give an integrated message to executives.

Principles 5 and 6 involve paying for individual ongoing value with base pay and rewarding results with variable pay. These constitute a solid foundation for executive rewards. Principle 5 encourages leadership growth and development to ensure executives serve as role models for the values and behaviors of the company. Executive rewards has and will continue to emphasize Principle 6 to reward both short-term and longer-term results the company needs to grow and prosper.

Aligning Executive Pay

The principles call for alignment of executive pay. In a nutshell, here's what we suggest executives do to demonstrate leadership and act consistently with the reward principles:

- *Communicate through executive pay.* Make your executive pay solution help the company build trust and commitment everywhere. It's a powerful message to tell everyone that we're all in this together and to prove it by having an integrated total reward strategy for everyone.
- *Add strategic goals.* Tie executive rewards to actual measures of company performance in addition to the price of common stock. Because we've suggested that the goals of executives should cascade to everyone and the line of sight to company goals should be more transparent, some future-focused, people, customer, and operational goals must count.
- *Strengthen the relationship between pay and performance.* Create greater variation in rewards based on difference in the level of results achieved. This applies to both the upside and the downside.
- *Improve performance management for the CEO.* Have the board formally evaluate chief executive performance according to established goals in addition to financial measures—for example,

strategic goals and how the top leader serves as a role model for everyone else in the enterprise.

- *Continue remixing total pay.* Transition aggressively to a total pay mix of less base pay and more variable pay. This affords a better chance for tying executive pay to a combination of strategic and financial goals.
- *Balance short-term and long-term rewards.* Change executive pay to make both sustained growth and profitability necessary. Make sure that quarter-to-quarter numbers don't intercept the long view of the business.
- *Make options more stakeholder-friendly.* Add strategic success measures as features of vesting and the number of options available. If it's necessary to reload and reprice options to keep essential talent below the executive level, avoid including executives in this bailout.
- *Pay for ongoing value.* If the core competency of the business is found in its people, this includes the executive team. Base pay should change as a result of executive capability growth; it should be part of succession planning and honing leadership skills.
- *Require ownership.* Create the same stakeholdership as shareholders. Stock ownership signifies the faith leaders have in their company.

Exhibit 13.2 outlines these points. Companies that do these things well are well positioned. For those who aren't already doing all these things, read on.

Exhibit 13.2. Overview of Changes to Executive Pay.

- Stronger link between pay and performance
- Formal evaluation of performance with established goals
- Change in total pay mix to less fixed (base) pay and more variable pay (cash and equity) based on performance
- Balance between short-term and long-term variable pay
- Greater emphasis on and rigor in stock options
- Stock ownership to build confidence in investment community that leaders are stakeholders in company's future

HOW STRATEGIC IS EXECUTIVE PAY?

The concept of *strategic executive pay* isn't new. We don't know of anyone who isn't in favor of this approach. Though there are several definitions, the typical description of strategic executive pay involves a pay solution that in some way parallels the business and financial progress of the company. Executives are successful from the standpoint of rewards only if other stakeholders of the company—most often the shareholders—are successful.

Alignment with Shareholder Interests

The concept of *alignment with shareholder interests* is generally interpreted as the use of stock options to reward executives. In addition, company performance is commonly evaluated for annual variable pay purposes in large part by financial measures such as profit, sales, return ratios, cash flow, or economic value-added. Companies often contend that their shareholders can better relate executive compensation to measures of stock performance than to internal measures that may or may not align the executive with the shareholder in real terms. Sometimes financial measures move contrary to stock performance as a result of positive or negative market views of the industry, resulting in the market ignoring performance of a particular company as judged by conventional financial indicators.[2]

Importance of Stock Options

A review of *Business Week*'s annual executive compensation issues for the last decade suggests base pay and cash variable pay are not the "strategic" elements of executive compensation. Rather, the performance of the company's stock and the number of options granted to the executive team define the primary total pay element. Although companies often expend considerable effort to establish a reasonably competitive level of base pay and to align annual or long-term cash variable pay to important measures of success of the company, stock options are considered the primary strategic executive pay element for publicly traded companies.

As a result, if you accept the suggestion that the stock performance of the company represents the key strategic element for compensating the few at the very top of the company, then the contention that strategic pay exists at the executive level seems sound. However, if you define strategic executive pay more broadly and delve deeper into stock options, executive pay may begin to look less strategic.

Improving Strategic Alignment of Executive Pay

To put solid meaning into the concept of *strategic executive pay,* we suggest actions to match it more closely with the principles we advocate for effective companywide rewards.

LINK EXECUTIVE PAY TO STRATEGIC INITIATIVES. The definition of strategic executive pay needs to broaden. For instance, it's much more common to modify the pay design of the top executives as a result of changes in tax code or new accounting regulations than for changes to be in concert with major company developments and performance initiatives. If executive compensation is strategic, the timing of changes in executive compensation should match movement in the company's business direction and strategy rather than tax and accounting changes. This is an important message to the workforce.

Pay for the executive team should more clearly reflect business strategy. Some companies completely redesign and restructure themselves to become more effective and contemporary yet never change executive compensation in the process. If we look at executive compensation before and after major renewal, we sometimes find that it's still determined as it was prior to the revitalization efforts. This is changing. For example, companies that change to a new measurement approach, such as a balanced scorecard or business-aligned goal-setting process, often use the resulting goals for executive variable pay to accommodate new directions and priorities.

EXTEND LINE OF SIGHT. The top management team, including executives of a major operating unit of the company and those responsible for managing the company's business portfolio or financing, are well positioned to directly influence stock price. Their line of sight is close and direct. However, the best that most managers and others in a company can do is influence operating results and thus perhaps stock price. This means other strategic measures and goals are necessary to tie those things they directly influence to the more distant measure of stock performance. This is why we argue so strongly for communicating the influence on shareholder value of what people do. Stock isn't a perfect measure of company performance, although it improves if other goals and measures are added.

But other factors influencing stock price may be beyond the control of anyone in the company. Often, just being in the right business at the right time (or the wrong business at the wrong time) can influence the price performance of common stock.

STRESS STOCK OWNERSHIP There's little evidence to suggest that companies are likely to perform consistently with shareholder interests when executives or others in the workforce have stock options in the company. There is evidence, though, that executive stock ownership is related to measurable gains in shareholder value.[3]

Because many people who exercise options sell the stock immediately afterward through cashless transactions, it's questionable whether stock and stock options without any holding requirements have lasting value in connecting the company and those granted options. But sustained ownership of stock creates a clear strategic executive pay linkage with shareholders.

STRENGTHEN THE RESULTS-REWARD RELATIONSHIP. A small but positive correlation exists between total CEO pay and performance of shareholder return. There's some alignment of executive compensation with shareholder interests because the top people generally make more when the company does well. The correlation is lost, though, for companies in the bottom half of performance.[4]

In *crystalreport.com* are dramatic examples of unaligned executive pay. It seems that the pay-for-performance relationship works better on the upside than on the downside when performance is lacking. Part of this is due to the propensity of companies to provide more stock options to executives when performance is lagging.[5]

In some instances, executive pay is designed such that if company performance improves moderately (moving, say, only from the 50th to the 70th percentile of performance as compared to peers), the pay of the CEO escalates significantly—and in many instances quadruples. However, if company performance drops from the 50th percentile to the 30th percentile, the decline in executive total pay is often only minor. If pay is to be strategic, aligned with shareholder interests, and consistent with the right workforce message, the pay differentiation must occur both on the upside and on the downside.

ACCEPT UPSIDE AND DOWNSIDE. Because executive compensation is outstripping the stock market, corporate profits, inflation, and general wages, its strategic alignment doesn't seem strong. In 1998 earnings of the companies listed in the Standard and Poor's 500 stock index fell 1.7 percent, overall U.S. wages and benefits increased 3.5 percent, and consumer prices increased less than 2 percent. The

S&P 500 stock index rose 26.7 percent. But chief executives' total pay increased by 36 percent (including exercised options).

Chief executive annual total cash is decreasing and becoming a small part of total pay. Options and other long-term pay amounted to 80 percent of total pay in 1998, compared to 40 percent in 1995. The pay gap continues to widen—the chief executives in this analysis earned 419 times the average wage of a blue-collar worker.[6]

The important strategic question here is whether companies will permit executive pay to fall when the Dow "meltdown" eventually occurs. In most instances, the design of executive rewards doesn't take into account this inevitability. If it truly reflects shareholder interests, it should accept both the upside and the downside.

BE CONSISTENT. Boards and chief executives advocate the use of stock as the primary measure of senior leadership success. But during periods when the stock market in general isn't performing well, some businesses move to cash variable pay and away from the use of stock. As soon as the market turns for the better, they move again to stock-based awards. In contrast, strategic executive pay means the total reward strategy, not the stock market, integrates the pay elements.

ACKNOWLEDGE ECONOMIC COST OF OPTIONS. The major contention around stock options has been that they're "free" to the company and have positive tax and accounting benefits for the enterprise and the recipient. But companies must get the most mileage possible from the options they award because stock options have an opportunity cost. If someone's offered an option to purchase a share of stock at $10 and the stock subsequently appreciates to $20, we believe the company has lost the opportunity to sell the stock at $10 to a satisfied shareholder. Alternatively, the company could hold the stock in the treasury, to have the share for sale at the higher price.

In Chapter 8, we talked about the economic cost of options if a company considers that the cost of repurchasing shares to prevent dilution keeps the company from investing the dollars elsewhere or returning them to shareholders. This supports the argument that options do have a hidden economic cost and the company must deploy them strategically to gain the most value from them.

REQUIRE PERFORMANCE BEFORE EXERCISING OPTIONS. The price at which options can convert to stock is often set low so that they aren't strategic in encouraging people to increase the value of stock to make their options grow. Few companies grant options with a conversion price above the market price on the grant date. At a major company in a recent year, a $2 rise in a $70 stock price increased the value of the CEO's options by $10 million. One solution, taken by Du Pont, is to allow cashing in options only after the stock price exceeds a certain level.

PUT PERFORMANCE REQUIREMENTS ON MEGAGRANTS. Options are easy to issue—easier than pay increases—because competitiveness is difficult to measure objectively at the time of grant. The worth of options isn't measured only by how much the stock increases in value but rather by the increase in value multiplied by the number of options granted.

Megagrants are options with a face value of more than three times an executive's base pay and annual cash variable pay, or restricted stock with a face value of more than 100 percent of cash pay. When an executive receives a large option grant, a small increase in share value leads to a disproportionate award. For megagrants to be more strategic, they should have a performance requirement, such as a premium exercise price that's set above the market price on grant date or a performance hurdle that requires satisfaction of performance conditions before exercising options.

ELIMINATE OPTION REPRICING FOR EXECUTIVES. An example of nonstrategic use of options is repricing underwater options for executives. As we discussed in Chapter 8, some companies argue that they need to do this to retain scarce talent who have options. Repricing has fallen out of favor, though, because of the need for alignment with shareholders, who don't have the opportunity to reprice their stock. Many companies are eliminating the practice for executives because these people are in the best position to influence stock price.[7] Also, repricing brings into question whether the top executives are in reality paying themselves. Athletes' high salaries receive considerable attention, but athletes don't manage or own the business that pays them, as the primary executives of a company do.

Is Executive Pay Competitive and Aligned?

Executive compensation is typically positioned competitively, but it isn't always consistent with the broader strategic directions of a company. Nor is it frequently a good role model for designing rewards from top to bottom in the organization, or have strong enough variability based on performance. An opportunity exists for improving the situation, and the time is ripe for change.

Our research of pay in Fortune 100 companies indicated that while major U.S. companies were changing their workforce pay approaches to better align with key company directions and messages, executive compensation was lagging.[8] When we followed up on the study participants five years later, we found the transition to business-aligned workforce pay had accelerated dramatically but executive compensation had realized less change. Even so, executive compensation is improving. What needs to be done now is to accelerate the improvement process.

REDEFINING EXECUTIVE REWARDS

Prescribing new total pay for the executive team is most important for the message it transmits. The cost of executive pay is minor compared to the overall cost of total pay for everyone else, but its symbolic importance is critical. This is the leadership point we've made.

Workforce Concern

If the level of executive compensation dissatisfies the workforce, their concern may be mitigated if everyone's pay is business aligned. Statements about greater accountability of the executive team, the need to have quality executive talent to ensure the company's viability (and hence workers' careers), and the reasonableness of executive compensation when compared to its respective labor market only go so far, especially if the benchmark comparison also seems out of line to workers. Alignment of pay practices at least gives everyone the same focus.

Pay alignment means executives and the rest of the workforce share in both the upside and downside. Workers and executives share in organizational success; similarly, if the workforce takes a pay cut during bad times, so do executives. Pay alignment is one of the reasons for granting stock options to people below the executive level. (The bull market is another reason.)

Time for Change

Businesses are well positioned to improve on executive reward design, and some positive change is under way. Boards play a primary role in this by addressing the strategic issues of executive pay, which Exhibit 13.3 outlines. Most important, boards determine the strength of the message that pay sends for performance by defining the results-reward relationship, setting performance expectations, and determining the degree of leverage in pay depending on different levels of outcomes. Their formal evaluation of the CEO sets a performance management example for the rest of the company.

The rest of the chapter discusses ways to improve executive rewards in more detail. The pressure is on to improve it, and enterprises have started to respond.

Organizationwide Total Reward Strategy

We believe that there should be one total reward strategy across the organization, applying to executives and everyone else to impart a consistent message. Total pay should be comparably competitive on the basis of performance, although the emphasis on pay elements may vary among workforce groups. But the key principles apply to all levels in the company. The most important consistencies are what the company pays for. The objective is to create a shared destiny and stakeholdership. This is already happening in including everyone in

Exhibit 13.3. Strategic Issues for Boards Concerning Executive Pay.

- Extent to which measured performance is the basis of total pay
- How performance and results are measured and when the board sets and revisits targets
- Performance management process for CEO
- Pay mix (base pay, annual and long-term cash variable pay, stock options, and stock) and extent to which performance leverages pay
- Competitiveness and reasonableness of pay, including definition of comparison group for pay levels and performance
- Stock option and stock awards, and link to shareholder value
- Stock ownership guidelines or mandates
- Employment terms (for example, implications of change of control)

variable pay and stock options to share in the financial future of the business.

Business-Aligned Goals

In Chapter 4, we discussed the importance of business-aligned goals that come from the business strategy and the business case for changing rewards. Executives communicate these goals and performance expectations and extend line of sight for the workforce to the goals by discussing and involving people in the business. But unless the communicated goals strongly influence executive total pay, it's difficult to make these goals credible and gain acceptance, commitment, and alignment.

Goals communicated to the workforce must necessarily include more than the series of financial measures of company performance and stock performance that typify executive pay. Generally the goals are not the same for executives and the workforce, but the goals used for executive compensation cascade to the workforce. For instance, a financial goal of the executive team translates into a goal the workforce can influence, one that has an impact on the financial goal. If executive compensation uses a customer goal, find a way to use a supporting customer goal for others as well.

Whatever the essential strategic measures may be, consider them for executive compensation and also translate them for other members of the workforce. Leaders are more likely to gain acceptance of pay alignment from the workforce if the executives' own pay reflects the goals.

Feedback on Development and Performance

The importance of face-to-face feedback in the performance management process was the other critical element we introduced in Chapter 4. Development and growth for the leadership team are not only important from the standpoint of shareholder interests but also critical in setting an example for everyone. To facilitate direct and honest feedback, and to have managers redefine their role to become teachers and coaches, executives need to set an example. It's not the communication of the results of executive feedback but the knowledge that executive leadership receives and gives feedback that's important.

We see leaders of major companies giving and receiving feedback on development and performance. The board often participates, and the chief executive works with direct reports. Performance management at the top of the organization still has major gaps, but change is under way.

Base Pay for Ongoing Value

Paying for executive value is shareholder-critical. Base pay is becoming a less important component of executive rewards; at some point enterprises, particularly publicly traded ones, may reduce it to a minimum level and replace it with variable pay (both cash and equity devices). Still, an individual's ongoing value is important, but it may be rewarded in various ways, such as being a determiner of the number of stock options granted to the individual.

IMPACT OF THE THREE DIMENSIONS. Ongoing value is made up of a combination of skills and competencies, consistent track record of performance, and the labor market, as we described in Chapter 5. The labor market is less important for executives regarding base pay than it is for variable pay or total cash since the former pay is a smaller component, and many companies are choosing to limit executive base pay and build larger performance-based variable pay opportunity.

Sustained performance, however, is still a relevant component for base pay. Boards and CEOs of great companies set clear, high standards of performance for the business and the executives because they want to bring the company to the next level of excellence. Performance feedback occurs regularly to close the performance-management loop.

SKILLS AND COMPETENCIES. Skills and competencies are particularly important when a company wants to reinforce its core competencies and when senior leadership intends to improve its own capability to impart new directions to the workforce. Executives are often the first to have multisource performance feedback as guidance on development and succession planning. However, pay also needs to acknowledge executives role modeling the desired skills and competencies and demonstrating the company's values as they accomplish results.

A company is in business to make profit, but *how* it does so counts —as does citizenship and reputation. No one wants to do business with a company that can't be proudly identified as a partner or provider. We see many awards for being a "preferred supplier" displayed in prominent business locations. Hewlett-Packard, IBM, Motorola, Wal-Mart, Intel, and others choose partners not on how much profit they make but rather on what type of customer support and care they provide. The executive team is important in role modeling these relationships.

If a company has core competencies but doesn't interpret them in terms of pay for the executive team, we think it's unlikely that the message about acquiring and applying the right skills and competencies is going to get through to the rest of the company. To ensure this, for example, Covey Leadership Center (now Franklin Covey Company) implemented pay solutions for the entire workforce, including executives, based on the core competencies of the company as articulated in *The 7 Habits* and on business results.

Annual and Long-Term Cash Variable Pay

Cash variable pay offers a chance to reward success compared to the company's operating and strategic plans and relative to comparisons with peer companies or industry standards. Thus it plays a complementary role to equity awards.

MEASURES. Cash variable pay can reward more than performance on financial measures; it can reward performance on crucial future-focused, customer, people, and operational measures such as successful new products and services, new markets, market share, innovation, organizational redesign, workforce satisfaction, and customer satisfaction. Exhibit 13.4 shows examples of executive variable pay measures.

Other categories of variable pay measures in addition to financial—particularly future-focused (strategic), people, and customer—reward executives for a more complete picture of performance than financial measures alone provide. Operational goals may be used for executive variable pay measures. But it's often the case that they're most useful in communicating to the workforce how to achieve financial goals and thus attain the alignment between the workforce and executives that we discussed earlier in the section on business-aligned goals.

Exhibit 13.4. Measures for Executive Variable Pay.

- Financial:
  - —Accounting: EPS, operating income, net income, cash flow, EBITDA
  - —Return ratio: ROE, ROCE, ROS, ROI, ROA
  - —Value-based: EVA, profit in excess of cost of capital
- Customer: satisfaction, retention, penetration, brand awareness, market share
- People: workforce satisfaction, retention, and productivity; reskilling; value-added from workforce development
- Future-focused: new products or services, product or service line expansions, breakthrough innovations, new markets, acquisitions, mergers, globalization
- Operational: quality, efficiency, cost, delivery, process improvement, safety, environment

LONG-TERM CASH VARIABLE PAY. We believe long-term cash variable pay will enjoy an increasing role in the future to reward achievement of specific goals related to progress on the strategic plan and long-term business performance. It fits with the long-term nature of executive decisions, where it takes time to determine whether the changes that executives endorse have value. As base pay continues to play a smaller role in the total cash mix, attention will move to long-term cash variable pay.

VARIATION BASED ON PERFORMANCE. Variable pay opportunity should create considerable variation or leverage based on performance. Total cash opportunity should relate to the performance level achieved: competitive if performance is competitive, in the top quartile if performance is in the top quartile, and in the bottom quartile if performance is in the bottom quartile. The comparison group is the same for both pay competitiveness and performance. Performance levels for cash variable pay constitute a reasonable stretch.

More About Stock Options

We go into more detail on stock options since they're a central element of executive compensation. We're clearly in favor of using stock options as *one* important element of executive total pay. Even so, we suggest that some conditions of stakeholdership control their use. The goal of effective option design is to make gains, or the lack of gains, more a result of what people accomplish. In this way, companies need not rely on the luck-of-the-draw stock market as it relates to stock performance. The number and availability of options should depend on something of value to the company, in addition to time with the company or reporting level. For example:

- *Institute a holding period.* If the goal is alignment and linkage, and if stock devices are long-term pay tools, options may be the right vehicle for acquiring stock. But companies should require executives to retain at least a portion of the stock after exercise; otherwise it's difficult to argue that stock price is a good measure of company performance. The objective is to keep executive eyes on how the shareholder is faring; this is impossible if stock is sold right after exercising options.
- *Vary the number of stock options available for grants according to company performance.* One solution for disagreement about the appropriate dilution level is to vary the number of stock options (as a percentage of shares outstanding) that are available for granting during a specific year, depending on a core measure of company performance. The better the company's financial performance, for example, the more options available for grants, and vice versa.
- *Base the size of individual grants on individual performance more than reporting level.* Individual results, skills, and competencies should be the primary determiners of the number of options granted, rather than reporting level. Option allocation is often rather automatic according to a hierarchical formula that starts with the top leadership level receiving the most options. Guidelines should differentiate the number of options granted according to an individual's results and value added to the company. This represents a change from current typical practice, where the formula for option eligibility is a mirror image of the actual options granted.
- *Lengthen vesting periods.* Longer vesting periods help improve the retention value and long-term incentive nature of stock options, although they have negative implications since options held longer continue to exert an effect on dilution. Longer vesting periods allow stock options to serve the retention role currently played by restricted stock.
- *Add performance requirements to option plans.* Add something other than time to the prerequisites for exercising options. There are several types of performance-based options, notably these four:

1. Premium-priced, or out-of-the-money, options have a higher exercise price than the market price on the grant date. They may also have service-vesting requirements. No value is realized until stock price exceeds exercise price. These options don't require a charge to earnings, and they permit rewards only after shareholders have achieved some minimum price for their shares.
2. Performance-vesting options vest only after achieving specific performance hurdles such as financial goals or stock price. As an example, a specified percentage of options vest for each year that EPS (earnings per share) increases by at least 10 percent. There's a charge to earnings with this design.
3. Performance-accelerated options are similar to performance-vesting options, but they avoid the charge to earnings by having all options eventually vest regardless of performance at a specified point in the future. Although this alternative doesn't have the performance emphasis of performance-vesting options, where options are lost if hurdles are missed, the earlier vesting based on performance is advantageous to the executive.
4. Indexed options tie the exercise price to a standard such as the Dow Jones Industrial Average, the S&P 500, or a relevant peer company comparison. For example, if the Dow increases 10 percent, then the exercise price increases by 10 percent. Indexing can go up or down. Indexed options entail a charge to earnings.

• *Address shareholders' legitimate concerns about dilution.* Stock option design that more closely reflects shareholders' interests can mitigate their concerns. Stock ownership, performance-based stock options, and longer vesting schedules are the trade-off for greater dilution. Rather than being automatic or indiscriminate, stock option grants reward performance. Executives should not be eligible for swapping or repricing options. Companies should use fewer full-value awards (restricted stock). Repurchasing shares can neutralize dilution.

Monsanto is an example of a company adding performance requirements to its stock options. It rewards the shareholders before the top executives since stock options become valuable only if stock price surpasses targets. The price executives must pay to exercise an option is set at 150 percent of the market price at grant, and they forfeit their options if the stock doesn't increase the requisite 50 percent within five years of the grant date. In addition, they must pay half of the present value of the option at the time of its grant; they can do this through deferring up to 50 percent of their salary.[9]

Sustaining Stock Ownership

Guidelines give executives a period of time to attain a position where they own and hold onto a specified minimum amount of company stock; guidelines also discourage or prohibit sales for the purpose of diversification if remaining ownership is below an appropriate level. Some enterprises reduce future stock option grants until executives meet the requirement.

SETTING OWNERSHIP LEVELS. With the bull market and large stock option grants, executives have met typical ownership guidelines (four to seven times base pay, for CEOs) fairly easily. Guidelines should set ownership levels according to the number of stock options granted; the more options granted to executives, the more executive stock ownership required.

What happens to executive stock ownership in a bear market remains to be seen, especially for companies that set guidelines as a multiple of base pay, because they're then asking their executives to purchase more shares. Requiring executives to own a specific number of shares rather than predicating ownership on base pay level may better serve the business. How companies monitor ownership is another issue.

EMPHASIZING OWNERSHIP INTENT. True stock ownership means the executives invest their own capital in the stock, for example, by receiving variable pay awards as stock instead of cash or retaining stock acquired by exercising options. By extending loans to executives to purchase shares and forgiving these loans for reasons other than performance, a company doesn't create the true stock ownership that the shareholders expect.

The enterprise should emphasize the ownership intent of stock options. The expectation is for executives to hold onto some of the shares obtained through options for the long run, particularly the shares that represent after-tax gains from option exercises. Alignment between executives and shareholders means that executives can't cash in all options at high prices while shareholders incur the losses if stock price declines. Unless stock ownership goes hand in hand with stock options, it becomes more and more difficult to justify option dilution levels to shareholders.

Employment Agreements

Globalization, M&A activity, tougher competition, and improved boards are placing executive jobs at risk. Executives and the company are negotiating employment agreements that serve to protect both the executive and the company in the event of a parting of the ways. The outcomes are likely to prevent companies from embarrassment as it relates to excessive termination agreements and the executives from becoming unemployable in the future as a result of termination.

Exhibit 13.5 outlines our view of effective executive pay. Alignment is critical and characteristic of total pay that will add value in the future.

Stronger Link to Performance

As we move forward, rewards for executives will emphasize the expected performance to be delivered rather than just competitive practice. Increasingly, executives are paid not merely for taking risks but for stabilizing company performance over time. Beyond improving company performance compared to the prior year's, comparative shareholder value will determine variable pay awards. This is because a shareholder's decision to invest depends on comparative investment alternatives and not just how well a company is doing compared to prior years. Better investor understanding of executive pay will lead to stock option changes.

Executives will have to share in potential performance decline even though stock options afford protection from the risks stockholders assume if company performance fails to meet expectations. Because executives don't share in dividends as option holders, executive compensation has to encourage payment of dividends to shareholders. If the company retains dividends for growth and investment, executives must be accountable for the performance results of money directed from dividends to investment in the company.

Exhibit 13.5. Effective Executive Pay Guidelines.

Pay Element	Present State	Recommended State
Base pay	Competitive or above, with increases generated from competitive practice and board or CEO review of individual performance	Less emphasis; moderately competitive, reflecting individual's ongoing value based on track record of outcomes, individual's competencies related to company's core competencies, and labor market
Cash variable pay	Primarily annual, based on goals related to financial, return, or value-based measures	More emphasis; annual and long-term, based on business-aligned goals that cascade to workforce goals and support communication of key measures to extend workforce line of sight
Equity	Strong emphasis on stock options; options granted based on reporting level, time, and competitive practice	More emphasis on and more rigor in stock options (performance-based options, no repricing, performance-based grants, etc.)
Ownership	Some guidelines	Guidelines related to the number of options granted
Executive benefits and perquisites	Supplemental executive retirement plan (SERP) to make up for government limitations	Less emphasis; focus on wealth-creation opportunities based on performance
Competitiveness	Competitive with questionable concern for performance	Competitiveness contingent on performance; greater pay variation based on performance

Executives will share in the downside as well as the upside of company performance thanks to strengthening of the results-reward relationship. In the future, institutional investors will be more influential than the federal government in making this a reality because they're major business partners with the business enterprise in which they invest.

What Cost Growth?

Growth at all cost needs close monitoring. Some executives are now rewarded for continued company growth even if it merely results in yo-yo company performance and stock price and bloating the workforce if they didn't plan growth well. Cutbacks and downsizing stemming from poor long-range strategizing are not in the interests of investors or the workforce. What are the implications for the better workforce deal we've discussed? It often costs more to cut back in light of wrong business decisions. Cutbacks create a disenfranchised workforce, which results in expensive and time-consuming trust-building exercises that better planning could avoid.

It's becoming increasingly necessary to separate the size of a company, in terms of assets and revenues, from the amount of executive pay. Since the size of the company is currently the primary determinant of executive compensation, they're "paid to bloat" rather than rewarded to grow only at a profitable, sustainable rate.

CONCLUSIONS

The basic principles of the total reward strategy should be consistent throughout the company at both the executive and the workforce levels, to facilitate pay alignment throughout the company. Pay is increasingly aligned partly because of outside pressures and partly because executives are coming to believe strategic alignment makes better sense for them and their company. This means a stronger tie between total pay and performance, and a meaningful performance management process that influences pay. Executives also need alignment with shareholders, which means more long-term variable pay and actions that help build shareholder confidence.

Executive rewards are an increasingly positive opportunity for total pay innovation. We believe that variable pay in cash and forms of stock will become an even larger percentage of total executive pay than it is today. Continuing refinements to measurement for variable pay awards will better fit key business goals. Because of the shift from base pay to variable pay, there will be more dollars allocated to performance pay, thus permitting inclusion of measures for important strategic goals other than financial. Stock ownership by executives will occur across the board, since this ownership carries the same benefits and risks as for other shareholders.

CHAPTER 14

Merger-and-Acquisition Rewards

We were touring a helicopter assembly and manufacturing facility. An engineer said, "If you spent all the money possible to build a machine to test the strength, durability, and flexibility of metal, no matter how long you worked or how much money you spent, the testing machine would still end up looking like a helicopter." A helicopter so strains metal that if anything's going to break, it'll break with the helicopter under power.

Mergers and acquisitions are the helicopters that can make or break total reward effectiveness. A merger or acquisition opens up business opportunity, but it also takes a toll on companies and people. Businesses combine to obtain value and new capabilities. People want to know how, or even if, they fit in. Total rewards are a major source of information for people about how they'll fare in the newly formed company or acquired entity. Pay can help unite and focus, or discourage, the talented people who are the source of company competency and outcomes. We believe mergers and acquisitions are golden opportunities to improve total pay and total rewards for both the company and the workforce.

Each year increases the chances you'll be involved in a merger or acquisition. In 1998, 11,655 U.S. deals were realized, with a value of $1.6 trillion. This is more than double the 5,654 deals that were reported in 1990.[1] Worldwide, the number of deals was about 29,000 in 1999, approaching $3 trillion in value.[2]

The stakes are high for all parties in a deal. Experts suggest that many mergers and acquisitions, even those undertaken by some of the world's banner companies, aren't living up to expected business results—often because of cultural or people issues. Companies are trying to assure themselves that a costly and time-consuming merger or acquisition will work. Leaders are trying to turn the tide in their favor.

PEOPLE COUNT—ESPECIALLY WHEN MERGING AND ACQUIRING

The most common reason companies merge and acquire is to leapfrog the need to develop a business capability internally. Mergers and acquisitions have talent consequences. The workforce spends time worrying about whether it will stay or go; the company hopes to keep the people it wants. Usually, people with the most market value and those performing closest to the company's core competencies are in the best position to leave. The scarce-talent discussion in Chapter 11 addresses this challenge. It's essential to emphasize securing the talent needed to make the postmerger or postacquisition bottom line meet expectations.

We've spoken about the better workforce deal. Every merger or acquisition forces creation of a workforce deal of some sort, good or bad, ready or not. Some of the companies with the best workforce reputations are being acquired, and outcomes may be less than expected. With people of value in short supply, we argue for preserving rather than decimating people value. Research suggests that companies dealing promptly with workforce total pay are more satisfied with the M&A results than are companies that delay.[3] A parallel study, however, indicates that only senior executives receive timely attention to total pay.[4] The stuff of which great companies are made involves promptly treating the people who go or stay so that they can retain their self-esteem.

OPPORTUNITY FOR COMMUNICATIONS AND CHANGE

Members of M&A teams know it can get hectic. They must often make sound decisions expeditiously. In Chapter 16, we provide advice on how to make the process for changing rewards work. The four stages summarized in Exhibit 16.2 apply to mergers and acquisitions no matter how accelerated the process.

Applying the Reward Principles

The reward principles serve to expedite the M&A process because they identify the essential success factors. For example, reaching a positive total reward solution is critical and should occur as fast as is reasonable (Principle 1). Obviously, total pay and total rewards should relate to the new company's directions, goals, and values. People want to know the new rules of the game, and the company wants to communicate expectations quickly. Otherwise rumors and incorrect information rapidly fill the information gap.

Mergers and acquisitions often result in new definitions of team, business-unit, and company success; they need to be communicated as promptly as possible. Will the new entity be team-based? Will new business units be formed? What are the goals for the new company or entity that are important to total pay? All of these issues relate to Principle 2 and must be addressed to develop a win-win partnership. A merger or acquisition also gives the company a chance to move to a pay approach based on rewarding individual ongoing value (Principle 5) and results through variable pay (Principle 6). A merger or acquisition is an excellent time to start fresh with a total pay and total reward solution to help ensure the value of the new association.

Principle 4, integrating total rewards, is key. This includes not only total pay but also the other three reward components: positive workplace, individual growth, and compelling future. The last one is critical; people want to know the new company's vision, values, and the type of future it foresees to determine whether it will be rewarding to them. The company also needs to reassure people about their role in its future. Culture is part of the positive workplace. Cultural differences are cited as one of the reasons for lack of success in mergers and acquisitions (that, as well as paying too much in the deal and integrating too slowly or poorly so value is not realized). It all calls for sensitivity to cultural differences, but this shouldn't stop things from moving forward. A company needs to decide whether to reinforce or change existing culture. But understanding the implications of the present culture is the place to start.

Our suggestions in this chapter about the issues to address help alleviate some of the cultural concerns: understanding the differences during due diligence, acknowledging the differences, communicating honestly with the workforce, and involving people in solutions of total pay and other rewards. Address culture if it's not supporting the directions, values, and goals that are part of the vision of the new company or entity. For example, if the culture rejects rewarding performance and this is what the company believes is necessary for growth, then it must educate and involve the workforce in what to do so both people and the company can win. If the company is unwilling to educate to secure needed workforce groups, perhaps this is a deal breaker.

Key Deliverables from Total Pay

Here are the primary deliverables from total pay in a merger or acquisition:

- *Securing talent.* Keep the people the company needs for the new association to achieve its business goals. Show people they're important to the new business.
- *Communicating new business directions.* Associate the workforce with the business-aligned goals of the new company or entity. Help people understand where they fit and how they add value.
- *Getting the new company or entity moving.* Focus attention on new goals and priorities. Resolve pay issues and retain momentum. Move past obsessing about who "won" or "lost"—make everyone a winner.
- *Creating collaboration and shared values.* Help people understand the vision of the new company or entity. Unify the workforce, and ensure that everyone is in the same boat. Communicate frequently, honestly, and openly; address issues of the merger or acquisition quickly; and promptly turn negative noise into positive noise.

- *Managing human resource costs.* Total pay can be a major business cost, so it's essential to get the most value from total pay dollars in terms of positive people alignment.

All of these objectives are achievable and afford new opportunities for tying people to the business as the merger or acquisition is realized.

Example from the Entertainment Industry

A major entertainment company entered the Internet business as the result of a combination of internal growth and a number of acquisitions of smaller technology enterprises. Its pay approach comprised stock options and employment contracts for the executive team and highly competitive base pay, but little variable pay and no options for everyone else.

The Internet business required that the company adapt the pay solution for IT professionals in the new business to include a combination of both stock options and variable pay based on project completion. The company was somewhat resistant to this change, thanks to years of tradition founded on matching competitive practice as defined by the entertainment industry. Adopting a pay solution for the Internet talent that introduced variable pay and options to the professional ranks created two types of pay solution in the company, based on competitive practice and business needs. One matched the entertainment business for people in that business, and the other matched a scarce-talent Internet market to acquire and keep people with the needed skills and competencies.

FITTING REWARDS TO THE SITUATION

We believe in addressing, balancing, and integrating total rewards. This chapter, though, emphasizes total pay. Progress may not always be predictable, but having an action plan for total pay design at the start is imperative. We categorize two phases that integrate into the four stages in Exhibit 16.2 to make rewards work:

1. *Phase 1: due diligence and initial planning.* This is the courtship stage of the merger or acquisition, when the parties exchange

information to see if the situation is as expected. It's also the time to decide on a workforce strategy and plan the role of total rewards in securing talent.

2. *Phase 2: moving forward.* Once the deal is done, the focus shifts to solidifying the total reward strategy, securing key talent, and integrating and designing pay solutions consistent with the total reward strategy. The honeymoon period is the time to begin communicating new business-aligned goals, the total reward strategy, and the business case for changing rewards. Typically, by the time the newly joined parties are back from the grace period, they must put the new total pay solution into effect. They must make a single business out of what was once two or more companies or entities. It's time for the initial test of total rewards when the new entity makes them part of its business and cultural fabric.

Exhibit 14.1 summarizes the two phases. The plan for the entire process of reward integration is best put in place at the start of the merger or acquisition undertaking. We suggest that an M&A team address total rewards collaboratively. A lot of critical M&A issues influence pay design, and pay in turn influences many of these same issues.

Phase 1: Due Diligence and Initial Planning

Some companies merge, acquire, or are acquired for products, services, or R&D; others for some part of the workforce; others for market share, new markets, new customers, or geographic or customer penetration; and still others for cost reduction through productivity gains and economies of scale. In each of these business strategies, the workforce role varies. If workforce skills and competencies are a reason for the merger or acquisition, it's critical to retain that workforce and consider the investment costs of keeping it (such as added pay costs and training).

Terminating talent only makes sense if those people aren't needed, duplicate other talent pools, or can readily be replaced at lower cost. The cost of terminating talent includes severance; outplacement for certain people; and such support structures as counseling, résumé writing workshops, and job banks. The decision about workforce retention affects the total reward strategy and the attractiveness and cost of the merger or acquisition.

Exhibit 14.1. Reward Design and M&A Phases.

Characteristic	Phase 1: Due Diligence and Initial Planning	Phase 2: Moving Forward
Objective	Explore viability of joining forces from rewards perspective	Develop total reward strategy; implement transitional solution to secure key talent; design reward solution; communicate and implement; unify workforce
Business case	Expedite workability of new venture to add value	Move quickly to make merger or acquisition positive; align workforce with shared goals; build business momentum
Activities	Evaluate pros and cons and cost/benefit; do "detective" work; plan transition if result is a go; identify key talent and develop initial securing approach	Link total reward strategy to business strategy and business case for changing rewards; design specifics of base pay, variable pay, recognition and celebration, and benefits; communicate and educate; implement top to bottom
Alternatives	Go or no go; if go, what to do?	What is the extent of change? What form does involvement take? How will communications be sustained? What is the timing?
Tangible outcomes	Determine degree of fit; if go, know upside and downside; set approach for primary issues	Secure necessary talent; communicate goals; transition to new reward solution; put merger and acquisition in past; celebrate new venture

WORKFORCE RETENTION STRATEGIES. A number of workforce retention strategies are possible:

• *Secure the leadership team.* The goal is to keep leadership talent because it's valuable in itself, or because keeping it is critical to realizing the value from the merger or acquisition. This alternative focuses only on senior management of one or more of the partner companies.

• *Secure key talent with core competency.* The objective is to stay attractive to people who are the repository of skills and competencies that the merger or acquisition targets. This may or may not include executives and managers. The emphasis is most commonly on knowledge workers or other scarce talent who are valuable and costly to replace.

- *Secure a supplemental workforce.* This strategy usually partners with one of the first two alternatives. It emphasizes making it attractive, in the short or long run, for those with skills that supplement or complement others in the company to remain and support members of the leadership team or those with core competency that the company needs.
- *Secure the entire workforce.* In some instances, the company encourages everyone, or most everyone, to remain. This may mean different levels of securing, offering some parts of the workforce more than others, ranging from merely being able to keep a job to inducements to stay past a specific date or occurrence.

The workforce retention strategy directs the due diligence effort for total rewards. Due diligence is a bit of detective work concerning the joining of businesses. It tests the assumptions of the business venture and is commonly a time for further discussion and negotiations. The two companies exchange, review, analyze, and discuss information about areas such as financial performance, customers, products, services, and human resources to determine the value of the transaction. It's essentially time for a go or no-go decision on joining the two. Unless it's been a hostile takeover, there's still a possibility of parting, depending on these results.

PROBING QUESTIONS. It's the time to ask and answer the right questions about total rewards. The objectives are to determine the compatibility of the two entities' total reward strategies and reward designs and whether there are any problem areas that are going to affect the purchase price. The acquiring entity or merging businesses evaluate how difficult the transition will be and if it's worth the potential effort compared to the results expected. They assess strengths and weaknesses. They probe to determine if there are any surprises on the horizon. Due diligence is the time for problem identification and evaluation during the total reward transition.[5]

TRANSITION TEAM. As due diligence relates to total pay and other matters of human resources, HR and finance often address it principally from a cost perspective. We suggest that a merger or acquisition transition team be formed at the time of due diligence and that it comprise a combination of staff and operational people. Because pay is primarily a business tool of communications, it's important that those responsible understand the issues. This team can become the core of one eventually assembled to manage the transition and perform as the primary communications team throughout the transition. During due diligence, a company can do integration planning but can't implement the results of the plan. Companies should be sensitive to this important difference.[6]

Exhibit 14.2 poses sample questions that help the due diligence process relative to rewards. It targets issues such as implied or expressed promises, pension funding liabilities, management style and strategy regarding total pay issues, global reward commitments, union pay, and core competencies. The rewards integration team is looking for differences and similarities in total pay and other rewards and trying to determine what messages are transmitted and whether rewards need changing in the company being acquired, the one doing the acquiring, or both. The questions suggest the extent to which pay messages are clear or ambiguous and the implications of this fact.

SEARCH DEFINITIONS. To avoid misunderstanding, go beyond the answers to questions, to explore the meaning of the words. Phrases such as *pay for performance, investment in people,* and *self-funding variable pay* mean quite different things to various people and companies. For example, *pay for performance* may mean automatic merit increases that are really disguised cost-of-living adjustments, or a large component of variable pay with wide variation in awards based on levels of performance. *Self-funding variable pay* may mean sharing the profit dollars above the target or operating plan profit level, or it may mean sharing a percentage of the cost savings over a historical baseline. Probe beyond the words for examples of what they mean.

IDENTIFICATION OF KEY TALENT. Due diligence involves seeking the source of the capabilities for which the merger or acquisition is being executed and making sure a pay solution secures them during a change of control. Determine the essential core of executives, managers, and key individuals to be retained, and ensure their retention. Essential individuals have a significant business impact, as in product innovation or critical customer account management.

PARACHUTES. Parachutes for essential talent can have a positive impact on a merger or acquisition, or they may be negative if they

Exhibit 14.2. Questions About Rewards During Due Diligence.

Total Reward Strategy

1. What are the strengths and weaknesses of the total reward strategy in terms of the four components: total pay, individual growth, a compelling future, and positive workplace?
2. What are the key messages that total rewards, total pay, and total cash send to the workforce?
3. What is the culture regarding flexibility, formality, autonomy, risk taking, importance of people, results orientation, communications style, and values?

Competitive Practice

1. What are the competitive comparisons, and what is the conclusion about total pay competitiveness?
2. How competitive is each element: base pay, short-term and long-term variable pay (cash and equity), benefits, perquisites, and cash recognition?
3. How does competitiveness vary based on company performance?
4. How long has the competitive pay position of the company been what it is? Is it recent, or historical? Did some major adjustment occur recently? What was the reason for this adjustment?
5. What is the level of competitiveness by workforce group (same or different): executives? sales? professional? administrative? scarce talent? people with the company's core competencies? nonexempt salaried? nonexempt hourly? union? global? What are the reasons for any differences?

Costing

1. What are the average base pay rates for exempt workers, nonexempt workers, executives, managers, and salespeople?
2. What is the cost of pay and benefits compared to the costs of business competitors?
3. What are the liabilities under pensions and other retirement, and are they fully funded? What is the liability of retiree medical benefits? What is the ratio of workers' compensation claims to number of workers? What are health care costs and the level of ongoing claims?
4. What possible cost surprises are on the horizon, such as those caused by eliminating pay and benefits to make the company look more attractive as a merger or acquisition partner?
5. What is the upcoming cost of union contract settlements during the term of the contracts?
6. What is the cost of employment agreements, severance agreements, and parachute clauses, and what is the cost as a percentage of the company's income?
7. What are internal costs of pay and benefit management? What are any outsourcing costs of managing pay and benefits?

Measuring and Managing Performance

1. Describe the goal-setting process.
2. To what extent do measures and goals focus on the individual, team, group, site, business unit, or company?

Exhibit 14.2. (*continued*)

3. What are the core competencies of the company? How do they relate to the business process? How are they measured in the performance management process?
4. Describe the individual performance management process; how does the company measure individual performance and encourage development?
5. What is the relationship between business goals and the performance management process?
6. To what extent is feedback multisource?

Total Cash Mix

1. What proportion of total cash results from base pay? From variable pay?
2. How does the total cash mix vary by workforce group or job or role?
3. How does the mix of base pay and variable pay change based on performance?

Variable Pay

1. Where does the money come from to fund variable pay? If variable pay is self-funding, what does this mean?
2. What people and roles are eligible for variable pay, and what are the types of variable pay?
3. What are the measures for variable pay?
4. What is the average variable pay award for each approach? What is the variable pay opportunity? What is the spread in awards? What variation in performance results in the award spread?
5. What percentage of eligible people actually receive variable pay awards?
6. Which cash variable pay approaches have deferred payouts? What amount has been deferred?
7. Who is eligible to receive stock option grants? What is the average grant level by workforce group? Describe any change of control clauses that will accelerate vesting.
8. What has been the experience in awarding variable pay?
9. What are the reasons for giving financial and nonfinancial recognition? What is the budget for recognition?

Base Pay Adjustments

1. What has been the average base pay increase in each of the last three years? What base pay adjustments will occur before the anticipated close of the merger or acquisition?
2. What is the relationship between the performance management process and pay increases? What determines base pay adjustments?
3. What automatic base pay adjustments has the company granted?
4. What has been the variation in size of base pay adjustments among people? What is the reason for this variation?
5. What are the reasons for awarding lump-sum payments? What has been the budget for lump-sum payments in each of the last three years?
6. What are the reasons for base pay adjustments as compared to the reasons for variable pay awards?
7. What have been the base pay adjustments for people with key competencies? For people with scarce talent?

(*continues*)

Exhibit 14.2. *(continued)*

Benefits

1. Does the company have a flexible benefit program or PTO program? If so, what is the core level of benefits?
2. For each specific benefit (for example, health insurance, life insurance, short-term and long-term disability, vacation, sick leave, retirement, savings), what is the level of benefit? What is the cost? How is cost shared?
3. As the costs of benefits increase, what happens to cost sharing between people and the company?
4. What levels of tax equalization, allowances, and premiums do expatriates and third-country nationals receive?

Pay Communications

1. What have been the communications of pay and benefits in the past?
2. What is the understanding of the workforce about pay matters?
3. What is the level of communication with unions, and globally?
4. What are some examples of pay communications materials?
5. What does the workforce believe will occur concerning total pay as a result of the merger or acquisition?

Involvement in Pay Process

1. Who has been involved in pay matters? What has been the result of this involvement?
2. What has the experience been with workforce involvement in pay and benefit issues? What is the history of pay design teams or focus groups?
3. What is the overall attitude toward workforce involvement?

Postmerger or Postacquisition Promises

1. Who are the key people who need securing during the merger or acquisition?
2. What written and unwritten promises has the company made? To whom has it made them?
3. What legal commitments exist that encourage staying beyond the merger or acquisition?
4. What kinds of parachutes or severance agreements exist? Who has received them?
5. What has changed about pay and benefits just prior to the merger or acquisition?

trigger for the wrong reason. Single-trigger parachutes, which "open" merely as a result of change of control, deny the acquiring or merged company important talent. However, rather than making the company less valuable, double-trigger parachutes, which require not only a change of control but also a negative action (such as firing without good cause, pay cut, major demotion, or significant relocation), give the acquiring company the chance to keep the talent for which it buys the business.

So too do severance agreements that stipulate payments if one of the negative actions occurs regardless of a change of control. Double-trigger parachutes or severance agreements that protect key talent rather than serve as a defense against takeovers are tools that help make a merger or acquisition work. Parachutes for everyone beyond the critical core group tend to be more of a takeover defense than a talent retention tool.[7]

RETENTION AWARDS. Retention awards keep people during the transition and after the deal. These are often granted for accomplishing certain goals over a specific period of time; the monetary amount increases or decreases depending on performance. It's important to establish performance goals and measurement derived from the direction of the new business so people remain focused and productive during this time of change.

Retention awards not only help retain people to complete a process but also buy the company some time to determine the new pay solution. For example, give IT professionals who are needed for a special project retention awards that increase or decrease according to project performance to help ensure that they stay on to complete the project. Even so, simply getting people to stay isn't enough. It takes the better workforce deal we've been talking about to focus them on a career rather than just a job.

STOCK AND STOCK OPTIONS. Stock and stock options are not always limited to executives and managers. In fact, prominent companies are extending options to people other than members of the management team. We discussed this in Chapter 8 (long-term variable pay) and Chapter 13 (executive compensation). Restricted stock and stock options may be used for retention until after the deal is closed, if the conditions of the options and restrictions focus on keeping people beyond the date on which the merger or acquisition becomes a reality.

Restrictions and option requirements may also be defined in terms of knowledge bounties, which describe specific requirements for transferring and documenting important knowledge relevant to the acquired company that's critical for the acquirer in operating the new business. Another alternative is cash variable pay for debriefing on issues of technology, strategy, products, or customers. Recognition and celebration also support building the new culture and reinforce integration successes.

Phase 2: Moving Forward

What's learned in due diligence can be applied to total pay and other rewards only after completing the merger or acquisition deal. This phase uses the integration planning of the due diligence phase to solidify a total reward strategy and secure key talent. Subsequently, the company develops pay approaches for the entire workforce that correspond to the total reward strategy. One essential decision here is whether to gear the total pay solution toward moving the company past some critical time period or whether to put a long-lasting solution in place. In most cases, a workforce doesn't become dedicated to a postmerger company merely because of inducements to remain long enough to give the new entity a chance to prove itself. A total reward strategy must make the picture clear and bright for an extended period.

REWARD INTEGRATION TACTICS. A number of possible tactics exist:

- *Continue talent-securing tactics.* The company institutes a series of time-spanning pay solutions that require talent to leave something on the table if they depart. This approach can't be the primary one over the long run because of the anxiety and stress that uncertainty about the future creates.
- *Implement the total reward solution of the dominant company.* Once talent is secured, whatever the degree, the total pay solution of the dominant company in the merger or acquisition is universally implemented.
- *Retain the acquired company's preacquisition reward practice.* In addition to whatever time-sensitive talent-securing actions are taken, the acquired company retains basically whatever total pay approach existed before the combination. This may occur if the acquired business is in a different industry that has different pay practices or if it functions autonomously and has a total pay philosophy consistent with that of the acquirer.
- *Blend practice under a minimal-innovation scenario.* This involves taking some practice from one partner and some from the other. It means integrating a total reward strategy in large part from what exists. Sometimes this involves filling gaps among practices, and in other instances cost plays a role.

• *Design a new total reward solution.* This means developing a solution for total pay and other rewards based on the business strategy of the new company. In this case, nothing that existed in either premerger business is sacred, and new directions are explored and followed.

PAY AS COMMUNICATOR. Mergers and acquisitions constitute a unique window of opportunity that's easily lost. Too many mergers and acquisitions miss the boat by paying only lip service to total pay designed to help make everyone a partner in the new venture. Although it's hard to change pay, it's even harder to gain strategic alignment of the workforce with the new business once alignment is lost through the disruption of being acquired or merged. Instituting positive total pay change aligned with business direction and goals can lessen this problem. That's why pay is such a good lead change element.

Few opportunities are as good as they are following a merger or acquisition. The workforce members want clarity and a message about how important they are. The company wants a workforce that's positively disposed to help make it a success. Rather than patching something together to get the merger or acquisition behind them, organizations can fill the information gap with new directions and information. It's an excellent time for realignment of total pay.

Pay can effectively help bring clarity and put some of the uncertainty to rest during a merger or acquisition by reinforcing the signals about business direction, values, and desired culture. This is an excellent opportunity for the new executive team to demonstrate leadership and secure the company's important talent. Here's a chance to communicate company goals and clarify people's roles and responsibilities—a chance to emphasize cohesion and collaboration and convert potentially negative energy into positive, in support of the new association. But all of this requires ongoing and honest communications—in fact, so much communication that people start to say "Enough, already!"

MAKING THE MENTAL BREAK. Psychologists sometimes deal with the acceptance of dramatic change in terms of unfreezing existing behaviors, instituting the needed change in behavior, and subsequently freezing the postchange behaviors. Sometimes it's difficult for the acquired entity to make the mental break from its former self, particularly if that identity was as an employer of choice.

To make the break and show appreciation of the former culture, managers of one acquired company declared a day to acknowledge and honor the past, where people used mugs and wore hats and T-shirts of the former company and grieved the past. The next day, they handed out mugs, hats, and T-shirts with the acquiring company's logo at a meeting to celebrate the new entity and discuss the future. Leadership articulated the business strategy, goals during the next 12 months, the values and behaviors regarding how people would work together, and how leadership would communicate with the workforce. They also shared the entity's business opportunities and new products. This was not a one-time communication, but the kick-off to continued communications.

TRANSITION MANAGEMENT. The acquiring company must assess its ability to manage the transition and communicate effectively, as well as the time and energy required. Many companies that do a good job of acquiring another don't do so well in managing the new company into the fold. One opportunity to address is how the actual pay transition is led. It's one thing to say that leadership commitment is critical, and quite another to make this a reality. In fact, transitions are sometimes led and made effective without the direct involvement of those at the very top of the organization. It's good if the top executive is involved; however, some pay changes during mergers and acquisitions need to be managed by leaders lower in the organization.

IMPACT OF ORGANIZATION DESIGN. Several factors play a role in what the total pay of the new entity looks like. The more centralized the operating style is, the more likely total pay reflects the pay practices of the stronger centralized organization. Also consider the similarity of the two businesses and their degree of integration.[8] If the two businesses are in different industries and have dissimilar competitive labor markets and total pay practices (for example, in a conglomerate), converting the acquired company's total pay approach to the acquirer's pay practices may not make sense. If the two businesses play similar roles in the same industry and are being integrated, then the answer may not be to adopt the dominant partner's pay solution or what prevailing practice suggests, but instead either adopt the most strategically aligned total pay solution or change to one that yields improved competitive differential advantage through business alignment.

Major opportunities to use pay to reinforce business direction may be lost in a merger or acquisition. In many instances, the pay practices of the acquiring company replace those of the business being bought. If the acquirer has variable pay, the acquiree probably inherits such solutions. If pay is market-based or emphasizes internal equity in the acquiring company, guess what solution to base pay the acquired entity is likely to get? In other words, the company doing the buying typically prevails without concern for the style, business needs, or culture of the one being acquired. Not that this is all bad; it's just that often the logic of the acquiring company's pay solutions lacks strategic orientation or a powerful and understandable business case relative to the acquiree.

COST AS A FACTOR. Costs are important in making a good merger or acquisition deal. An organization generally doesn't want to increase pay costs unless it's meeting the business objective of the merger or acquisition because it wants to realize value from the association. For example, benefit costs are usually not performance-related. As with other total pay elements, merging benefits also depends on the diversity between the two businesses, the degree of business integration, autonomy of the business unit, and the dominant operating style. The less diversity between the businesses (and the more integration, the less autonomy, and the more centralization), the more impetus there is to integrate benefits and other total pay elements.

Averaging benefits in two merging organizations usually doesn't make either former workforce happy. A flexible approach that allows choice in selecting benefits may make the consolidation easier. Particularly in situations with widely differing levels of benefits, it enables everyone to keep the former approach even if individuals need to pay more than before.

INTEGRATING TOTAL PAY. Pay represents an existing and important obligation. The acquiring (or new parent) company usually assumes the outstanding stock options and restricted stock of the former company. It converts them to its stock options and restricted stock based on a conversion factor that reflects stock price at purchase. It commonly maintains vesting requirements.

If the company being acquired has broader stock option participation than the acquirer has, then deciding participation in the acquirer's stock option program depends on the business case for changing rewards; competitive practice; and issues of business diversity, integration, autonomy, and operating style. If the decision is not to continue participation, the dominant partner may need to consider special cash variable pay for individuals who would be excluded after acquisition, or find trade-offs in other pay elements to make up for the change.

If the acquiree provided long-term cash variable pay that the acquiring company does not have, usually long-term cash variable pay is cashed out because it's difficult to continue to measure performance. This is done at the current performance level if it can be meaningfully determined, or at the target award opportunity prorated according to the time elapsed during the performance period. Another long-term cash variable pay solution can replace it to reward making the new entity a success in terms of growth in profits, value to shareholders, or revenue if this is consistent with the total reward strategy and the business case for changing rewards.

EXAMPLE OF INTEGRATED PAY. Consider integrated total pay, not just each element in isolation, during the merger or acquisition. A consumer products company with competitive base pay and performance-based variable pay acquired a business with highly competitive base pay and a small discretionary bonus. The acquirer adopted a strategy for the acquired workforce to hold base pay and build variable pay opportunity over time consistent with specific performance goals. Expectations about skills, competencies, and performance required to continue to earn the base pay were clearly communicated.

Communication of goals for variable pay occurred immediately to facilitate understanding of and focus on goals; the transition of the total cash mix took two years. The transition of pay for the workforce happened over time, but the communications message about pay went out immediately, to shorten and lessen the dip in performance that usually occurs after an acquisition.

ENSURING LASTING BUSINESS VALUE FROM A MERGER OR ACQUISITION

Leaders are often tired after the transition. They've dealt with issues such as who stays and who goes, who gets what role and which responsibilities, where people work, who reports to whom, and what people's new titles are. Also, because executives are involved in making the new entity a successful reality, executive compensation is usually the first pay issue in the minds of those responsible for the merger or acquisition. It often requires time-consuming negotiations. Senior executives have normally expended so much energy getting their own total pay into place that they lack the energy to begin to address pay solutions for the entire workforce.

However, the new business must expend the effort to deal with total pay and other rewards for the workforce early. This gives leadership the opportunity to move beyond the merger or acquisition and get on with business. If the new pay solution links to business-aligned goals, it focuses people on the business sooner. It also reduces the uncertainty, fear, and anger that people may have and allows them to make intelligent decisions about their future and get back to being productive workers. Swift and proper handling of pay issues can energize a workforce.

Involvement

If total pay change is a team sport, we believe this in spades in the case of a merger or acquisition. The people involved in designing the pay solution should also be active in the actual implementation process. We suggest that the transition team comprise people from both the acquirer and the acquiree. Also, if a merger involves relatively equal parties, the M&A transition team should represent both parties similarly. Again, the most important things are what gets done, how it gets done, and how the result transitions into something that the combination can sustain.

Implementation follows the action plan that results from due diligence. Successful implementation involves:

- *Timing.* Once it's decided what'll be accomplished, the enterprise must determine when it will be done and implemented. This depends in part on how significant the changes are to be (for example, adopting the acquirer's total pay solution requires less time than creating a new solution). It also depends on the trade-off between getting the change accomplished quickly with loud noise over a short period of time, or over an extended period of time (perhaps with softer noise that lasts longer).
- *Communications.* Starting communications early is important. Repetition is essential to getting the message across. Communicating

the total reward strategy and the new entity's specific business case for changing rewards and linking the business case to the reason for the merger or acquisition are a start for gaining workforce understanding and acceptance.

- *Involvement.* Implementation must be spelled i-n-v-o-l-v-e-m-e-n-t if it is to be successful. People like to influence and get their hands around something they can understand, and this is critical for a pay change—the more so if you believe that our reward principles (particularly the first one) make sense. The objective is for the workforce to help the new pay solution become operative in as short a time as possible. Marshaling forces by means of involving people in the process is a logical way to accelerate the change and make it stick.

A Story of Success

Dealing effectively with total pay is not only humane but also the best path from an objective business perspective. The track record on addressing pay effectively during mergers and acquisitions is clearly mixed. On the positive side, one large biotechnology company merged two important entities to form a new business unit. The pay approach of one entity, which had been acquired a year earlier, was more formal and less flexible, as exemplified by a point-factor job evaluation plan and merit increase grid. The other had a highly unstructured pay approach. The potential for conflict and a lose-lose was significant.

The business unit chartered a diagonal-slice pay design team representative of both former organizations to execute a pay strategy in between the solutions of both former companies. In six serious work sessions, the team designed a new pay approach, including a combination of variable pay and a market-based framework for paying for skill and competency, that the design team members could champion to their colleagues. Even though the dialogue and work sometimes became heated, the solution was innovative, business-focused, and something everyone could implement and manage as an example of a new company working on a complex and controversial topic from the bottom up rather than only from the top down.

Without involvement and a sense that everyone was in it together to develop the best business solution to a reward solution, the odds of total pay becoming a source of separation, not unification, would have been significant at the business unit. As it was, a concept of shared destiny was created; change was hard, but it was understood and addressed as a mutual opportunity to add value. At the completion of the process, the business unit president was both pleased and surprised that a team of people, with no experience working together to address an issue as challenging as combining total pay in a newly merged organization, had developed a solution that was so reflective of the needs of the new business.

A Story of Woe

Then there's the tale of poor implementation following an acquisition in the financial world. A large bank headquartered outside the United States acquired a major American commercial business bank. The acquiree's regional business units had an excellent client portfolio of medium-sized businesses. They were organized in "customer teams" that included a business developer, a credit analyst, an account management professional, and perhaps one or two other professionals depending on the business base they served in the region.

Team incentives paid awards according to a combination of such measures as credit quality, loan production, profitability, growth in business, and customer satisfaction and retention. This team pay approach balanced the efforts and shared goals such as loan quality and profitability. Members optimized performance at the level of the team rather than the individual, where representatives of credit and sales could have conflicted over what good business is or where loan profitability creates credit problems by encouraging loans to higher-risk customers willing to pay more interest to borrow.

Once acquired, the big bank eliminated the team incentives and implemented individual incentives that rewarded team members according to competing measures. For example, business developers selling loans are paid only for sales performance, but credit analysts are paid for making only the most secure loans possible. Within a year, poor-quality business loans and drooping product sales riddled the organization.

The company eventually eliminated these teams with a business-banking, customer-focused design because it viewed them as "dysfunctional." The bank lost significant market share. Only acquisition of a primary rival by another large bank and the ensuing disruption of that poorly managed acquisition at the competitor's put the banks on equal footing. Neither acquisition seriously considered people issues. The saving grace was that the competitor was equally ineffective in M&A activities related to human resource matters.

Reward Reminders

In Exhibit 14.3, we outline a few reminders in each essential area for implementing rewards associated with a merger or acquisition. You can obviously expand on these, depending on your specific situation. Thus far, we've suggested the need to address some very important

Exhibit 14.3. Checklist for Making the Merger or Acquisition Reward Change Work.

1. What measures and goals will determine the success of the merger or acquisition?
2. How dramatic is the change implied by the total reward strategy? Does the change involve:
   - Implementing the dominant company's approach
   - Retaining most of the acquired company's preacquisition reward practices
   - Integrating or blending the two entities' reward solutions under a minimal-innovation scenario
   - Designing a new reward solution based on the business strategy of the new entity
3. How will total pay and other rewards integrate?
4. What is the time period for implementing any new reward solution?
5. Who will be the sponsor of the reward change process? Who will be the champions?
6. Who will be on the team to design and communicate reward change?
7. What are the cost parameters for changes to total pay and other rewards and the range of variation based on performance?
8. What will the base pay approach be like? short-term and long-term variable pay, including cash and stock? benefits? recognition?
9. What is the communications strategy regarding reward changes?
10. Is there any opportunity to automate any element of the reward process?
11. How will total pay and other rewards be managed and administered in the future?
12. What measures will evaluate the success of the reward change design and implementation process?
13. How will reward solutions be subject to continuous improvement over time?

questions about pay as a result of a merger or acquisition. It might seem we believe a company is on its own to choose the best solution and that what it chooses matters little, but this isn't true. We believe the reward principles provide direction. How and when the change is made also count.

The two issues we feel most strongly about are (1) whether the company should keep what exists or make needed changes, and (2) whether any changes should be made fairly quickly or gradually over time. It's been our experience that many mergers and acquisitions tend to make only minimal changes to avoid rocking the boat and make those changes over an extended time period to lessen the blow. This is not the most business-effective way to proceed in many instances, though. A merger or acquisition is a prime opportunity for total pay alignment. The chance may not come readily again.

It makes the most sense to communicate the total pay solution and begin implementation of any needed changes as quickly as possible, although in some cases a transition period may be needed to complete the implementation. Pay change is difficult to swallow at best, and dragging communication of pay change over the years keeps the workforce waiting for the other shoe to drop. Thus it makes sense to communicate and begin implementing the needed changes as soon as practical, with involvement and understanding of the reasons for the changes. This takes advantage of the merger or acquisition and shapes a foundation for moving forward with things as they should be in the future. Strike while the iron is hot; get it over with and move on to forming a cohesive organization.

Pay solutions must by their very nature be agile and adaptable as businesses, customer expectations, goals, and work situations change. Build a straightforward foundation that can adapt as the organization's needs change. For example, if variable pay is to support or supplant a merit base pay program, put a direct and simple variable pay approach in place throughout the company, and build on it from there as needed.

CONCLUSIONS

Doug French, now COO of Daughters of Charity National Health System, understood what workers were thinking when he said, "You can mess with anything but my kids and my pay."[9] When he was CEO of one of its entities, St. Vincent Hospitals and Health Services in Indianapolis, the organization was growing and acquiring a wide variety of enterprises that were long-term investments for its parent. French was moving forward to reinvent pay and apply it to their new acquisitions correctly and with concern for the workforce. Mergers and acquisitions are challenging from a human resource perspective. Rewards are critical; address them not only at the executive level but also throughout the organization.

Once your company is involved in a joining of forces, it may be the start of a continuous series of organizational changes and associations. Instead of being a challenge, pay must become the cement that helps bind the new company or entity together effectively. This means developing an active strategy to implement without delay a total reward solution that solidly communicates the new directions, goals, priorities, and emphasis that the resulting organization will take. How quickly an enterprise integrates pay approaches after a merger or acquisition varies, and flexibility is needed in the pay solution; but paying for results is a necessary goal. This is because of the economic pressures stakeholders place on the new enterprise to meet the financial expectations for which the merger or acquisition was undertaken.

CHAPTER 15

Global Rewards

Companies large and small are going global and growing globally. Those in the United States are growing faster globally than locally and must evolve a proactive global business strategy. Those headquartered in other countries are also globalizing by acquiring U.S. businesses. Global mergers and acquisitions complicate the formula. The United States has six time zones across which companies must communicate. Globally, they communicate across 24 time zones and face a host of unique cultural complexities and country challenges. Someone said addressing global human resources and pay challenges is much like trying to train an army of cats to write an opera. But at least cats speak the same language!

Global reward design needs clarity, flexibility, alignment with the business, local accountability for results, and reward for the skills and competencies essential for global success. This often means changing total pay practice. Those hesitant to do so locally are even more concerned when change involves people in far-flung organizational units with which they have less contact.

To adapt a familiar slogan, "Strategize globally, act locally." But this is meaningless unless the workforce understands the win-win of goal achievement and the better workforce deal applies to a company's worldwide business operations.[1] This means applying the six reward principles we suggest as well as the four total reward components.

Too often, global rewards substantially lag globalization initiatives. We believe globalizing rewards should at least parallel globalizing the organization. This prevents having to repair pay solutions driven more by what others do than by what the company needs to do to achieve global workforce alignment.

GLOBAL TOTAL PAY

The opportunity exists to have people unified around global business goals. The concepts of business-aligned goals and feedback on development and performance discussed in Chapter 4 (on measuring and managing performance) are important here.

Business Logic

This is the business logic for changing rewards:

- *Implement performance pay everywhere.* Aligning rewards makes the entire workforce a stakeholder in the success of the global enterprise. If total pay is to communicate, the message must be that the performance of the business matters in rewarding people.
- *Communicate business-aligned goals.* How global workers fit with company goals is important. Capitalize on the fact that it's hard to communicate across the world; let total pay help.
- *Begin to define global talent.* Through individual development and performance feedback, invest in preparing global talent to add value to the business. Pay for individual ongoing value. Emphasize the skills and competencies needed to make a local business successful.
- *Choose global leaders for the right reasons.* Select global leaders because they're the best for the role, not because they're bribed by guarantees and income protection. Put the best into global roles and rotate talent as needed. Coach and develop to build workforce value.

- *Match to stage of business globalization.* Every company has its own approach to global business. Design total pay to accommodate the differences, and let it evolve as the company changes how it addresses global markets.
- *Support new organization designs.* Improve global organization designs to match the streamlining efforts in the headquarters country. These new designs can have major implications for total pay communications.

Businesses communicate and translate global, transnational regional, and country measures from the financial, customer, operational, people, and future-focused categories into goals relevant to the specific business situation. They communicate competencies, defined as organizational, strategic, technical, and behavioral, in the context of the global worker.

Issues of culture, readiness, or tax are frequently thrown up as barriers for changing pay to match your business strategy and business case. But our experience is that few barriers to strategic total rewards are impossible to address. We address cultural issues later in this chapter. Imperfect solutions that can be fine-tuned as you go keep a focus on strategy and still avoid trouble.

Two Global Workforce Groups

In this chapter, we discuss two types of worker. The first, global talent, is a subset of expatriates (those who relocate from their home-country headquarters to work abroad) and third-country nationals (those who aren't citizens of the headquarters country and who work in a host country that's not the individual's home country). The second is the global worker, someone employed by a global company; this includes local nationals (those who are citizens of the country in which they work).

GLOBAL TALENT

Global talent is our term for people whose career is based globally rather than in a home country, who've worked successfully for an extended period of time in, typically, more than one location besides the home country, and whose next assignment is likely to be outside the home country.

Characteristics of Global Talent

Although global talent has no hard definition, a handful of guidelines characterize this workforce group:

- *Achievement of business-aligned goals.* People in these roles can achieve business-aligned goals and participate in development and performance feedback to grow as their role expands, changes, and adapts to match business circumstances.
- *Matching organizational needs.* Global talent has the ability to learn differing approaches to the business depending on the situation: entrepreneurial start-up or growing, rebuilding, reorganizing, merging and acquiring, rejuvenating, or even exiting the business. It's important to know how to work globally in good times and bad.
- *Assimilation in the local culture.* Global talent becomes immersed in the local culture, develops contact with local people, and doesn't isolate themselves in the expatriate compound. The home country is no longer the financial reference point for global talent.
- *Career learning.* Global talent is willing to put energy into learning and growing throughout a career with the company. These people represent a significant investment for the company and eventually may grow to receive more pay for the total package of capabilities they bring to the table than for the role they occupy. They can be in problem-solving and challenging situations according to skills, competencies, and results rather than simply the level of job they last held.
- *Flexibility.* Global talent must have the flexibility for pay based on results and growth rather than entitlement, tenure, and factors unrelated to the success of the enterprise. They must be business people who see the win-win of aligning pay with the company's objectives.
- *Skill and competency growth.* Global talent acquires and applies the skills and behavioral competencies required of a global assignment, such as flexibility and adaptability to new circumstances; managing complexity, uncertainty, and ambiguity; building trust; and working comfortably with people from different cultures. This is in addition to knowledge of local business culture and practice, language facility, and other skills and competencies crucial to success in

the locale. It's not one set of skills and competencies but those that are relevant to the specific business situation.

- *Focus on total rewards.* Global talent is interested in global assignments for reasons related to all four components of total rewards, not just the total pay provided. The concept of the better workforce deal must be attractive to people who can produce overall value. Career opportunity in the (global) growth area and personal development are reasons for taking global assignments, not overcompensation.

This represents an evolution to a different type of worker—global talent—that will likely include some or many expatriates and third-country nationals and eventually some local nationals.

The Business Case

The objective is a universally valuable workforce. The goal is to facilitate integrating the individual into the host country rather than to have a total pay solution that creates separatism and isolation, as is characteristic of the balance-sheet approach. What people accomplish and what they have in their skill and competency bag, rather than simply where their work is done or where they originally came from, combine to determine their total pay value.

Getting the Right Global Talent

Filling roles globally requires more than putting someone into a job. Many enterprises believe the failure rate for global staffing is excessively high. Failure costs, both direct and indirect, are significant. As more earnings derive from sources other than home-country business, global talent fills essential roles. This translates into increased expenses for development, training, placement, and coaching. But the investment cost counterbalances the potential expense of global staffing failures.

Global talent can assume executive, management, or nonmanagement roles. We suggest that executives should lead the way in moving toward the characteristics outlined for global talent. They can serve as role models for the change process to reduce failure rates that are painful to both the individual and the company.

The value and importance of global talent vary from company to company, depending on the type of role required for implementing the business strategy. In some instances, people who negotiate effectively in a global environment are critical; people capable of starting up new global ventures are key elsewhere; and still others skilled at working with global partners may be important. Managers who develop global workers also possess a valued competency. Changes of this nature require a holistic and flexible view of what makes an individual valuable.

Global Talent Objective

One primary objective of global talent is to prepare the workforce to operate at a higher level of performance, skill, and competency. Often, expatriate or third-country national managers develop next-level local nationals to perform at a higher organizational level. Unless the company can translate effective operations of a global business in some part to local nationals, the cost of managing only with expatriates and third-country nationals continues to escalate.

Businesses are seeking ways to maximize advantage not only from expatriates and third-country nationals but from local talent as well. One human resource strategy is to eventually place nearly every critical role in the global business network in the hands of local nationals. The objective is to do what's required to create workforce bonding with a global company, which realistically is best done at the individual level. This also requires the company to do a gap analysis to evaluate what the business needs are relative to people and to use this to close the preparedness gap. Global talent facilitates this process.

Changing Role of Expatriates

A major change is under way for the expatriate and third-country national workforce. These people have been the engine driving the business boom of global companies. They will continue to be important. Their new role will be as developers of global workers and global talent (and some will become global talent themselves) and establishing a transglobal business presence for an enterprise.

From a performance perspective, expatriates in particular are often protected from the ups and downs of running a global business. Seldom are they viewed as having pay at risk, even to the same extent as comparable local nationals. Some suggest that the cost of a poor-performing expatriate in a leadership position can be up to $1.2 million in pay, training, development, orientation, relocation, and termination cost alone. This says nothing about the negative influence an ineffective person has on the business process as a result of bad morale, lost market share, upset customers and suppliers, and missed strategic business goals for which the individual was accountable.[2]

The balance-sheet approach to expatriate total pay was not designed to support what's needed to be an effective global business. It equalizes pay and protects the individual who works outside the home country. This must change, because total pay should help show global talent where they fit as members of a global business team. Although traditional expatriate pay works for some assignments, there's increasing need for a more flexible total pay approach that makes global talent stakeholders in business success.[3] Companies are already redefining what equalization and protection are. The trend is clearly more toward doing what is "fair and reasonable" than guaranteeing to keep "everyone whole."

Rewarding Global Talent

Companies need to give special attention to certain elements of the total reward components for global talent.

INDIVIDUAL GROWTH. Development involves not only understanding of and assimilation into the culture of the host country but also enhancing the behavioral skills and competencies required for a successful global career. The company must be prepared to develop global talent in a broader context than only the specific role they presently occupy. This means more investment in people; it translates into more emphasis on salvaging and developing global talent and better preplacement planning to improve the chances of success. It also means having a way to make midcourse career corrections to keep people satisfied, challenged, and aligned with the business.

COMPELLING FUTURE. Global talent want a company with a reputation that enables them to be successful and values that support their own. They want to know the global growth strategy and the steps to make this achievable and understand how they fit in the company's future. They don't want to be left stranded. They want to understand their career path and coordinate it with the company's human resource forecasting and succession planning processes. They want to understand where they fit in the success formula and what's in it for them to stay with the company—what's the win-win for them as well as the company.

POSITIVE WORKPLACE. A leader must be clear about the outcomes expected from global talent on an assignment and provide support and the tools they need to be successful. This component also includes sensitivity to the family's adjustment to the new location and culture, to reduce the possibility that life problems will distract the individual's attention. Orientation and family support programs help speed acclimatization.

TOTAL PAY. The company needs to be flexible in developing reward packages for global talent. Total pay reflects the value they bring to the company relative to local nationals. Global talent brings more value than local nationals only so long as the former attract good people among the latter; develop them so they can take the place of the global talent; impart the vision, values, objectives, and technical expertise of the company; and accomplish the objectives that were the reason for the assignment. However, if global talent decides to stay in the host country after accomplishing these objectives, they lose some of their value to the company because in most cases they're more costly than local nationals. This case requires a move to a local total pay solution.

INTEGRATING TOTAL REWARDS. This is why it's so critical to coordinate the reward elements, particularly total pay and development and career planning. The level of total pay takes into account a variety of factors: the unique value that the global talent brings to the assignment, the specific environment faced in the new assignment, how local nationals are paid in the global talent's new location, and the market value of the role and the lifestyle it supports in the new location as well as in the previous location. For the long-term interest of the individuals (to avoid downsizing or being without an assignment), it's important not to price them out of the labor market for their level of value.

- *Base pay.* This reflects individual ongoing value—the global skills and competencies the individual possesses, consistent performance over time, and the individual's value relative to the labor market. The labor market is a combination of the local labor market for talent and the labor market globally for this talent. As global talent grows in global skills and competencies, these people subsequently become more valuable and are considered for additional pay treatment. This implies migration to paying the person, not the job or role.

- *Short-term variable pay.* This is localized to the host country or region's goals and gives global talent and the local national workforce the same direction. It rewards achievement of goals related to the reason for the global talent's assignment—for example, grow the business, introduce new products into the market, improve profitability, reposition the business, or open or upgrade a manufacturing facility. Both the local workforce and the global talent can share in the success of meeting these objectives.
- *Long-term variable pay.* This can be useful in rewarding long-term performance of the local business relative to the objective of the global talent's assignment. More often, this reflects broader-based performance than the specific assignment, so corporate headquarters may manage it.
- *Benefits.* Health insurance is generally local. Retirement, savings benefits, and life insurance tend to be based on the home country. Retirement increasingly shifts from defined benefit to defined contribution plans.
- *Recognition.* This rounds out any total pay package, including that for global talent.
- *Allowances, premiums, equalizations, etc.* Depending on the global talent's situation, and with the exception of home leave allowances, enterprises are reducing these payments, making them transitional for a brief period of time before assimilation, or moving away from them entirely because they send the wrong message—entitlement and an internal emphasis on keeping the person whole, rather than an external, performance focus. Premiums and allowances are a fixed cost that, when inflated by cost-of-living adjustments and housing prices, prompts the company to question, sooner rather than later, the value of the global talent relative to local talent.

The Balance-Sheet Approach to Pay

The balance-sheet and tax-equalization approach to compensating expatriates and third-country nationals intends to equalize total pay and related living costs on the basis of a comparison with the home country. Expatriates and third-country nationals are equalized from one global location to another according to home-country practice, to maintain a home-country style of living. Premiums and allowances make accepting these assignments more attractive from a financial perspective. These people normally have less performance-based pay than home-country counterparts. Thus many believe expatriate assignments with a balance-sheet approach to pay attract a more risk-adverse individual to run things globally than do assignments in a home country. The balance-sheet approach to pay and income protection often makes it difficult for the expatriate to move back to the home country.[4]

Expatriate pay often has a counterpoint. A firm may extend very limited opportunities to return to a better job when people repatriate to their home country. This ignores the total reward approach we're suggesting.

LACKING BUSINESS ALIGNMENT. The balance-sheet approach with tax equalization doesn't reflect the business processes we believe are essential. Instead, it creates a pay-to-buy mentality that causes people to focus on pay more than on the career opportunity and performance. It's also inconsistent with the approach of thinking globally, acting locally. The more expatriates are paid differently from local nationals, the less likely alignment with business goals is, and the more probable are equity concerns of local nationals. The global talent pay concept we propose intends to level the playing field within a country by treating people according to a common total reward strategy. An analogy to the balance-sheet approach is the internal-equity, point-factor job evaluation system, which doesn't have an external business focus so it no longer fits most businesses and has rapidly declined in usage in the United States.

USE IN SPECIFIC SITUATIONS. Companies may choose to continue to use a balance-sheet approach for development, temporary assignments, and situations where the individual's career is really in the home country and the person isn't expected to assimilate into the local culture. They may also use it if their businesses are in the early stages of globalization. The balance-sheet approach may be useful in the export stage, where products manufactured in the headquarters country are sold in other countries by a functional, centralized international sales unit. It may also be appropriate in the next stage of globalization, the international stage, where a decentralized international sales function in major international markets sells products produced in the headquarters country and elsewhere.[5]

The balance-sheet approach becomes less appropriate when the headquarters country is no longer the primary frame of reference for all operations. In the multinational stage, multicountry manufacturing, R&D, and decentralized functions such as sales and human resources are characteristic. Here total pay becomes more localized based on the host country; however, we suggest that there be an overriding total reward strategy from which customization occurs. The global stage, with its borderless management and global product line groups, has a global total reward strategy customized to the business case for specific situations. In any of these stages, headquarters typically handles executive compensation.

GLOBAL TALENT AND GLOBAL WORKERS

Total pay must unite global talent and global workers. Even though global talent may move among global assignments, global workers are more likely to be citizens of the country where they work. Some differences exist in total pay design, but we believe consistent messages about rewarding achievement of business-aligned goals and individual ongoing value are necessary. Exhibit 15.1 summarizes rewards for the global workforce.

Although total rewards must be integrated, our focus in the remainder of this chapter is on total pay. Building global total pay guidelines founded upon the company's total reward strategy can best address total pay integration from a global perspective. We now turn our attention to unifying global talent and global workers.

GLOBAL REWARD GUIDELINES

The more mature the stage of globalization, the more a global total reward strategy and global pay guidelines are needed for global talent and global workers. However, in any globalization stage, the company needs to articulate a total reward strategy. Guidelines give leaders specific information about the implications of the strategy, so pay solutions consistent with the strategy can be developed locally. The guidelines start with the strategy and may include both general and specific assistance on developing pay approaches, depending on the company and circumstances.

Exhibit 15.1. Rewards and the Global Workforce.

Characteristic	Expatriate and Third-Country National	Global Talent	Global Worker
Career perspective	Home country with short to intermediate global assignment	Global career outside home country with next assignment likely global	Local career in home country and limited global movement
Business case	Temporary talent injection to global enterprise	Universal talent with flexibility to integrate into local situation to apply advanced business tactics and to develop people	Locally valuable talent applying global business goals to a local situation
Individual growth	Limited goal of local assimilation	Global development with local assimilation and adaptable to numerous locale changes	Local development with emphasis on adapting needed skills to local application
Talent sources	Expatriates and third-country nationals	Expatriates and third-country nationals with potential local participation	Local nationals
Reward solution	Modified balance-sheet approach	Total rewards (all four components) emphasizing business alignment and targeting and encouraging total career in global business environment	Total rewards (all four components) emphasizing business alignment, local practice, and competitive realities

Total Reward Strategy

Global companies start with a total reward strategy that spells out the basic principles or philosophy that the company believes is fundamental across the organization. It may document brief philosophical points, such as outlining what the company means by creating a stronger link between pay and performance. Or it may be more specific, addressing some key issues such as how conservative or leading-edge the company wants to be on pay design, where consistency and variation across countries are acceptable, which pay elements headquarters determines and which are in the local purview, and basic competitive position.

USING THE REWARD PRINCIPLES. The reward principles apply to the total reward strategy. Principle 1 is critical because it's important to establish pay as a positive, natural experience in a global enterprise. Principle 2 is vital in making "strategize globally, act locally" more than a slogan by rewarding results on business-aligned goals that cascade from the company's goals to create a win-win partnership. Our argument for global talent and global workers supports Principle 3 because at the core of the total pay solution we're suggesting is extension of the line of sight to the team, group, business unit, and company.

It's also important to integrate the four components of total rewards, Principle 4, to ensure the necessary people for global success and to be responsive to the local country's situation in terms of business needs and what people value. Principles 5 and 6 are central because they suggest that, rather than entitlement or merely matching local practice, individual ongoing value and variable pay are the best ways to encourage skill and competency improvement and performance.

EXAMPLE OF LESS DETAILED STRATEGY. Let's look at two sample strategies. A pharmaceutical company's total reward strategy encourages variable pay, significant differentiation in rewards based on performance, and positioning pay design on the leading edge to add business value. The company determines executive compensation and long-term variable pay (cash and equity) at headquarters. Benefits are locally determined according to local laws and competitive practice. Relative to the relevant labor market, the company pays at the median for base pay and median total cash for meeting expectations, and higher total cash for exceeding expectations.

EXAMPLE OF MORE DETAILED STRATEGY. A consumer products company gives detailed guidelines regarding total pay. Bands with broad role descriptors help clarify organizational levels across the company. Band range minimums and maximums vary with local competitive practice. The company's four primary competencies—customer service, teamwork, communications, and technical skills—are factors in determining everyone's base pay. Locally, other skills and competencies in addition to these four can stress important capabilities needed to be successful locally.

Variable pay rewards results based on business-aligned goals. For managers, it centers mainly on the performance of the individual's primary organizational unit but also extends one organizational level higher. For example, a country manager's variable pay includes rewards for the country's performance but also is partially based on group performance (the group is an organization unit with more than one country working under the next higher level of management).

For other people, the firm encourages variable pay, which should include rewards for performance of the most pertinent organizational unit, to stimulate stretching the individual's line of sight and teamwork (for example, the team, factory, or region within a country). It holds managers across the company accountable for recognition and celebration customized to the local culture.

Business Case for Changing Rewards

After the total reward strategy is developed, business units or groups typically construct their own specific business case for changing rewards. Business units may differ in performance management and pay depending on the specific business situation they face. For example, a unit starting up in a country is different from an established one with a more mature market. The former may emphasize revenue growth while the latter seeks profitability or profitable growth. Skills and competencies may also differ. In the start-up, the emphasis may be on risk orientation and innovation. The more mature market may demand leadership and people skills.

Cultural Differences

Cultural differences play a role in the business case for changing rewards.[6] But our view is that they shouldn't play a major role in the reward strategy because it's already reflected in local labor market practices.

ASSERTION. One dimension of cultural differences—assertion—involves values being more materialistic or relationship-based. Countries favoring relationship-based values typically offer more benefits and have a smaller total pay difference between the highest and lowest organizational levels. If the global company's position is to use locally competitive benefits and total pay, it's already reflecting the culture. If the country is relationship-based, the company discusses pay as a communications vehicle more than as a driver of behavior.

POWER DISTANCE. The company's organization design and position on workforce involvement drives its position on the cultural-difference dimension of power distance (equal or unequal societal structure). Incidence of perquisites and emphasis on (or number of) hierarchical levels often reflect cultural differences on this dimension. If the company decides to position itself less competitively relative to the labor market on perquisites and visible status symbols, and to deemphasize job titles, then it makes up for this in other total reward elements.

AVOIDING UNCERTAINTY. The cultural difference of avoiding uncertainty reflects the ability to deal with rules, among other things. The more rigid the country's culture, the more rigidly defined or detailed the business case for changing rewards and the resulting pay plans are. Also, individual ongoing value and variable pay may have very clearly defined criteria with less room for judgment by the manager. Because variable pay isn't fixed pay, some may see it as being on the end of the continuum that embraces uncertainty. But countries that are on the inflexible end of the continuum may use variable pay; for example, Japan has profit-sharing plans and France requires them. These examples show that there may be more leeway in the impact of cultural dimensions on rewards than some propose.

COLLECTIVISM-INDIVIDUALISM. The continuum of collectivism to individualism reflects another cultural difference. U.S. businesses have felt tension as they moved along this continuum by adding emphasis on the team or the larger organizational unit to the focus on the individual alone. This tension creates healthy dialogue about the organizational levels where performance should be rewarded to focus people most effectively and to optimize performance. The same healthy dialogue can happen globally on this or other cultural dimensions.

LONG-TERM ORIENTATION. The cultural dimension of long-term-orientation reflects the degree to which a culture has a future-orientation perspective. Like the collectivism-individualism dimension, the United States has experienced tension as it moves toward a longer-term focus. This has not stopped U.S. companies from making the change within their own country; rather, it shows the kind of tension businesses experience as they move workforces in other countries along continuums that make sense for the business.

EVOLUTION. If global companies base their pay design on an understanding of local labor market practices, they're incorporating cultural differences. The global company should be sensitive to these cultural differences but also move pay plans further along the continuums as needed to reflect the company's way of doing business. The process is an evolving one, not a dramatic move. For example, if people have had no variable pay, the company may not move initially to high variable pay opportunity with base pay reductions but instead start the process toward more variable pay. The objective is business effectiveness while transitioning in a manner that acknowledges and respects the culture of the workforce.

IS THE CULTURAL ARGUMENT SOUND? The cultural argument is often made regarding total pay implementation. We suggest that considering culture is important, but not to the exclusion of business alignment. From a global perspective, no cultural difference should preclude moving to total pay driven by a combination of needed capabilities plus performance. The issues and opportunities, from a communications perspective, must be consistent for global talent and global workers alike. Unless a company can initiate a developmental perspective in the workforce and hold the workforce accountable, global alignment of people to the business isn't possible.

The balance between culture and high performance is important. A way must be found to accommodate cultural diversity globally and still be an effective business. It's unacceptable to sustain a workplace culture if it rebukes the move to total pay that communicates and is consistent with the company's objectives. Attaining results in some cultures is a competency that must be nurtured and significantly rewarded.

MOVING FORWARD TO WIN-WIN. At a work session in Buenos Aires, we were discussing the cultural implications of moving a company to a pay approach based on a combination of performance, skills, and competencies to match its global business goals. Maggi David, head of human resources for Perez Companc, a large South American company based in Buenos Aires, suggested cultural differences are commonly used as an excuse for inadequate alignment of global pay with the business strategy. He believes companies must overcome cultural challenges that make it difficult to implement pay strategies aligned with business objectives.

In the contest between culture and business alignment, David would clearly favor adapting culture to match business alignment, because in the long run this facilitates the company's success, which in turn has an impact on workforce success. He was especially focused on pay design and how he believed pay could encourage a focus on business results.

Global Guidelines

It would be a major error to design one-size-fits-all global total pay for global workers and global talent. Thus we suggest developing guidelines that assist local managers and business unit leaders concerning total pay management. The guidelines may include the elements of base pay, short-term variable pay, long-term variable pay, benefits, and recognition and celebration. They address issues of the kinds of goals to be used and the skills and competencies needed to measure performance.

Some companies have found advantage in developing a global pay workbook, with guidelines for managing and implementing total pay consistent with the total reward strategy. It supports implementation of specific plans throughout groups, business units, and countries around the world. National Semiconductor used guidelines for a large-scale team pay solution they developed and implemented. The materials suggested how business units could design variable pay to follow some consistent strategic guidelines the company had developed.

A STARTING PLACE. Guidelines make it easier for groups, business units, and countries to develop total pay approaches because they don't have to start with a blank sheet of paper; they also understand what's consistent with the company's total reward strategy. Guidelines are useful as long as they don't overly restrict an organizational unit, given its specific business case for change. Units differ, in some cases substantially. The challenge is to support the unit but not force it into a format that fails to match its business situation.

Sales compensation is an example where guidelines frequently facilitate local design, especially when there's cross-geographic selling. The company either identifies acceptable measures or lists possible measures to select for various selling opportunities, based on differences in market share, market maturity, sales strategy, and organization design. It may specify or provide guidelines regarding weightings of measures and payout formulas, while local management determines total cash mix and performance ranges.

ELEMENTS OF GLOBAL TOTAL PAY GUIDELINES. A guideline approach is useful in determining what issues are globally uniform and what can be localized depending on the unique business circumstances. Exhibit 15.2 presents areas where guidelines may be of assistance.

Some elements of pay planning are readily offered from a company perspective, and some derive from the local level with guidance on form and substance. Flexibility is essential.

TOWARD THE GLOBAL WORKFORCE

Some companies transcend culture and local practices to make pay reflect the business and create a unified workforce of global workers. In Brazil, an IBM manager told us that the reason IBM implemented variable pay for everyone throughout the world was to tie them to the key priorities and deliverables that the business needs everywhere. He said this was effective everywhere they have a global operation.

In Asia, a major consumer products company confronted an opportunity to use team pay to address a combination of cultural differences and the need to emphasize forming a high-performance manufacturing workplace. It implemented team pay and new technology at a manufacturing facility that had just been purchased. The result was local workforce alignment with the business, something that hadn't existed before.

Exhibit 15.2. Elements of Global Total Pay Guidelines.

Mix of total pay

- Assessing local strengths and weaknesses relative to the total reward components
- Guidance on positioning total cash and each pay element with respect to the labor market and determining the range of competitiveness based on variation in performance
- Examples of changing the total pay mix to fit the company's total reward strategy more closely

Base pay

- Range of emphasis for individual ongoing value regarding skills and competencies, consistent performance over time, and value relative to the labor market
- Identification of core competencies and skills
- Guidance on basing the atom of work on the job, role, or person and how to design the organization in terms of staffing and accountabilities
- Basic design issues and sample alternatives for determining base pay consistent with the total reward strategy

Exhibit 15.2. (*continued*)

Short-term variable pay

- Guidance on what types of variable pay may be used, who can and should participate, and what the various sources of acceptable funding are
- Examples of alternative designs and results-reward relationships for what's likely a local-country opportunity

Stock options

- Acceptable uses for options and where not to use them because of tax or expense issues in the specific country
- Guidance on eligibility criteria for participation
- Suggestions on determining the size of grants

Long-term cash variable pay

- Guidance on design if stock options aren't available or the company wants to use long-term cash variable pay to link local pay solutions to a global business plan or to reward long-term local results
- Examples of key long-term business goals and measures, eligibility for participation, the mix of short-term and long-term variable pay, and funding sources

Benefits

- Compliance with local law and government regulation
- Guidance on integrating competitive practice with legal and governmental requirements according to the company's strategy for total pay mix
- Possible reasons for variation from competitive practice for benefits

Recognition and celebration

- Using recognition to parallel other pay elements
- Role of celebration and fun in creating a collaborative workplace
- Basic tenets of effective recognition and how to determine it for a given workforce, since the specifics vary with the country culture and individual preferences

Measures, goals, skills, and competencies

- Where goals and competencies come from, use of financial and nonfinancial measures, how to determine the organizational levels for rewarding performance
- Role of goals for the individual, team, group, and business unit in the performance management process

Performance management

- Basic tenets on coaching, developing, and providing feedback
- Guidance on how to associate performance management with the pay process, who may be involved in the performance management process, how often the process occurs
- Foundation for developing the skills and competencies of global talent and global workers

Another consumer products firm, Gillette, is a truly global company. It continues to use expatriates and third-country nationals for many global assignments, but local nationals are increasingly rising to positions of importance and recognition. The value of this was proven by success in China and the rest of Asia, using primarily Asian workers in both leadership and support positions. The key to paying global talent and global workers is total pay guidelines that flexibly offer assistance and examples of the important concepts, measures, and principles that are to be elements of pay localization.

EVOLVING GLOBAL TRENDS

If companies respond appropriately to globalization, flexible and business-focused solutions of total pay and other rewards developed for global expansion could strongly influence those in the headquarters country. Increasingly, a company's global reward strategy drives how it determines total pay. It ultimately has to set pay by how effective performance is; whether goals are missed, achieved, or exceeded; and how the workforce grows and applies the skills and competencies needed to perform in a global business environment, rather than setting pay by where people work or what their home country is. Talent shortages of a global nature, rather than where people come from or where they work, strongly determine what they're paid.

Greater Reward Globalization

A strong influence on reward globalization is the fact that executive pay is becoming progressively more global. It's become necessary to assign leadership responsibilities that span country boundaries and to select the best person to fit the role according to prior results and capabilities. This influences the design of rewards for the rest of the workforce.

Total reward strategies are becoming more global and less industry-specific. Rather than determining pay according to whether the company is in one industry or another, the era of the global trans-industry leader is evolving. Global talent can migrate from company to company because of their success in a global business, rather than industry-specific success. Global rewards increasingly must communicate what's necessary in terms of paying for individual ongoing value and for results the company needs if it's to be successful. This is possible if consistent global guidelines for total pay and other rewards integrate local pay translations, while taking into account the business case for the specific location, local culture, and local laws.

Strategic Priority

Some suggest that the globalization of total rewards should depend on the importance of people to the business strategy. For example, oil companies would place less emphasis on globalizing total rewards because oil is a commodity and labor-to-capital cost ratios are low. Financial services companies have entirely different ratios, so total rewards are more essential. We believe that total rewards are universally essential, as in an oil company where a dollar spent on rewards has the chance to leverage the performance of large capital assets. Thus global total rewards need a close look everywhere.

CONCLUSIONS

The same messages must get through to the workforce no matter where they come from or where they work. Because communications challenges are so great (for a range of reasons we've discussed in this chapter), businesses must design rewards to help accelerate and strengthen the messages. This means some dramatic changes in pay design as it applies to both global talent and global workers.

We're closer to the beginning of globalization of total pay and other rewards than we are to the end. Pay will increasingly align global talents and workers with the business. In the future, there'll also be a truly global talent pool, moving from country to country and able to understand and assimilate each local culture to enhance the business. The balance-sheet approach to expatriate pay may be grandfathered for a declining population, or else it will have ever more limited allowances and equalizations.

The pay solution for the new generation of global talent combines global value with pay localization; in exchange global talent will enjoy career opportunities that may no longer be available to traditional expatriate or local workers. Becoming a global company helps a business become increasingly creative and aggressive about how pay aligns with business goals.

PART IV

Moving Forward

The Six Reward Principles

1. Create a positive and natural reward experience.
2. Align rewards with business goals to create a win-win partnership.
3. Extend people's line of sight.
4. Integrate rewards.
5. Reward individual ongoing value with base pay.
6. Reward results with variable pay.

The Four Components of Total Rewards

- Individual growth
- Compelling future
- Total pay
- Positive workplace

CHAPTER 16

Making Rewards Work

Stephen R. Covey says, "Begin with the end in mind."[1] Yogi Berra said, "It ain't over 'til it's over." These concepts apply to implementing total pay. Remember that we measure the value of total pay in terms of its long-term positive impact on the people and the company. The test of strength for total pay is whether the company can both start strong and finish strong. Sometimes Indianapolis 500 cars that are out in front through much of the race drop out in the last lap because of mechanical or electrical failure. Some potentially effective pay solutions also stall near the finish. This chapter addresses the importance of effective design, communications, implementation, and refinement to the pay development process and suggests how to get buy-in, sponsorship, and continuing value from total pay.

ELEMENTS OF SUCCESSFUL IMPLEMENTATION

Exhibit 16.1 shows some factors to consider in determining how ready your company is to implement reward change, and what it can do to improve readiness and thus the likelihood of success.

Exhibit 16.1. What's Necessary for Reward Change to Work.

- Top management support and championing
- Workforce trust
- Consistency with total reward strategy, business case, and work design
- Challenges that people can help address
- Belief that workforce can enhance organizational performance
- Adequate communications with people
- Willingness to share information with people
- Current measurement of results on key initiatives
- Accounting and information systems to support reward solution

At the top of the list, company leaders deliver the total reward strategy and the business case for changing rewards to give direction to the process and champion the design and implementation process. Without this support and championing, success is probably not within reach and your company should ask why it's doing this anyhow.[2]

Communications

Communications start at the beginning of development, intensify during implementation, and continue strongly once the pay change is operational. If the entire pay solution must wait to be sold on the back end, to the senior leadership team or the workforce, the risks of lack of understanding and failure are high. Communications during the design process are critical to ensure acceptance. We believe workforce involvement is an essential ingredient of success, but alternative levels of participation are possible. (We touch on some of the choices here.) It's becoming increasingly difficult to implement an acceptable pay solution with little or no workforce participation and support.

Straightforward Message

Even though the pay solution needs to be complete, it must also be as straightforward as possible. It's harder to develop a simple solution that satisfies business strategy than a complex one. If an in-process design effort can stand the elevator-speech simplicity test in a focus group conducted by a design team member, it may stand the test of workforce implementation. Pay change is a business process, not an administrative undertaking. Effective pay emphasizes performance issues, rather than administrative issues. It reflects the business case for changing rewards and the goals the company needs to achieve.

Speed Matters

How often have you heard it said that time is money? Great companies make business decisions quickly and get the benefit of positive change sooner than others do. Once they decide that total pay should be consistent with their business, they want to get it done as soon as they can. If they come to realize the communications value of pay and the fact that current pay processes may even have a negative impact on the workforce's business understanding, they want to make changes and gain advantage. They want to match the speed with which they do their homework and deliver results, in all other business areas, to the reward design, implementation, and communications process. This is often news for reward designers. Even those who have earned their way into the company business process find the velocity accelerating. This also applies to obtaining workforce acceptance and to the transition to the better workforce deal.

Why is speed so important? From the standpoint of the workforce, pay is crucial. It represents people's economic tie to the company. It's important to their family and self-worth. They want to know where they stand and what the win-win is that the company is seeking. People want to know how they fit in the company's future, what their role will be, what changes are in the works, and what they can do to ensure their future.

The company wants to align rewards with the business and get on with improving effectiveness. As we've said, pay is a noisy change process, and the sooner the company can get the noise working positively for it, the better. Once leadership understands that total pay can extend workforce line of sight to crucial business goals; help put customers in the limelight for everyone; and help people identify their individual future with the team, group, business unit, or company they're a part of, then leaders realize they want these benefits quickly.

Importance of Positive Change

Many sweeping and dramatic pay transitions are going very well. People and managers report value, performance improvement, growth and development, and a sense of fairness. In some cases the hottest pay change goes very well, while some fairly cold changes go less well. From time to time things go awry with pay implementation.

Interestingly, the technical aspects of what's working and what isn't are often similar enough to suggest that issues of process and communication are at least as important as technical design. When failures in cold-change elements such as training or staffing go awry, they're often ignored. When total pay change goes awry, it becomes a major issue.

GRIT REQUIRED. The differences between great companies and others becomes visible to people like us, who've spent an entire career in other people's organizations. One major difference is that the excellent businesses differentiate themselves from the rest by having the grit to implement their solutions. Yes, they plan and strategize, do their homework, and explore alternatives; they do all the necessary preparation. But they do it faster, and then they implement their decisions and follow through. During follow-through, they still fiddle with their people-based solution so that it improves—but they do so while the change process is in motion. Indecision doesn't immobilize them.

Determine where your company is on a continuum from inaction to action in the area of human resource strategy—and, more important, in total pay. Indecision and confusion communicate to the workforce as well as do action and clarity. The former communicate the wrong messages and make it potentially much more difficult to ever get back to a serious total pay revitalization process.

TRUST IS ESSENTIAL. Trust is a powerful issue in the area of pay. Total pay must build trust such that once the transition is under way, workers and leaders feel confident about the results. We see situations where fairly minor changes create major negative noise that doesn't abate. In other situations, the company turns major change and extensive noise into a positive force that enhances its ability to apply what it's learned to other problem areas. A reasonable level of workforce trust is a prerequisite. If it's low, the company should start with frequent, honest, direct communications about the business and management-workforce relations until the trust level improves so that pay can be meaningfully addressed.

STAGES TO CHANGE REWARDS SUCCESSFULLY

Making rewards work involves several stages:

1. Develop the total reward strategy and the business case for changing rewards

2. Develop the reward solution
3. Conduct communications and rollout
4. Continue refinement

All four stages are important to achieving Principle 1, making pay change a natural and positive event. The objective is lasting value for both the company and the workforce. Exhibit 16.2 outlines these stages.

STAGE 1: DEVELOP TOTAL REWARD STRATEGY AND BUSINESS CASE

The process starts with the total reward strategy, followed by the more specific business case for changing rewards.

Total Reward Strategy

The senior leadership team plays the central role in developing the total reward strategy. This may be the senior leadership of the company or that of a business unit, depending on the company's size and how it's organized. The elements of the total reward strategy vary from one company to another, but the four reward components in Exhibit 1.2 offer a start.

Because it represents one of the four reward components, the total pay strategy is a subset of the total reward strategy. The leadership team sticks to high-level policy issues. It articulates reward principles based on the business strategy, organization design, and human resource strategy. Business strategic direction is often a 30,000-foot view of where the company is going; the task of the leadership team is to translate this strategy into goals and to interpret them for the workforce.[3] They're accountable for a number of issues:

- The fundamental messages that total pay and total rewards impart to the workforce (for example, emphasis on results or development)
- The workforce deal (better, new, or old)
- Key measures and goals that the company uses to determine success

Exhibit 16.2. The Four Stages to Make Rewards Work.

Characteristic	1: Develop Reward Strategy/ Business Case	2: Develop Reward Solution	3: Conduct Communications and Rollout	4: Continue Refinement
Objective	Develop total reward strategy to reflect business concept and strategy; prepare business case for changing rewards	Design total pay or total rewards to reflect strategy and business case	Implement new reward solution to gain understanding, acceptance, and commitment	Evolve reward solution to maintain business effectiveness and sustain the better workforce deal
Business case	Leadership accepts total reward or total pay concept on front end; no selling on back end; provides champions and sponsors; builds trust and commitment	Design reflects strategic direction; high involvement builds trust based on leadership championing	Meet commitment to workforce on communication and education; start of benefit to business and better workforce deal	Be nimble and responsive to business change; make reward solution part of the "way things are done here"; gain the benefit from aligned rewards
Who's involved	Leaders and champions, owners of business strategy, authors of business case for changing rewards, human resources	Representatives of strategy and business case designers, high-involvement design team, human resources	Leaders, strategy and business case designers, managers, high-involvement design team, human resources, and all workforce enlistees	Representatives of strategy and business case designers, managers, high-involvement design team, human resources, and all workforce enlistees
Actions	Provide direction to design process on elements and requirements that new reward design must meet; define link between rewards and realities of business; begin communication and education	Develop solution with true involvement, real input, and leadership support; continue communications and education	Accelerate communications and education; meet promised delivery dates and implement; champion; celebrate; prepare for continuing refinement; keep the course	Gather information on solution; evaluate; fine tune, adjust, modify; sustain communications and education; administer

- The mix of total reward components as well as the mix of total pay elements
- Competitiveness, and the relationship between competitiveness and results
- The source of variable pay funding (for example, defining what self-funding means)
- The availability of stock options and other equity vehicles
- Differences in total pay strategy among workforce groups

The Business Case for Changing Rewards

Using the total reward strategy as the framework, the leadership team of a business unit or group in a large company develops the business case for changing rewards for the business unit. For a small company, the senior leadership team concurrently develops the total reward strategy and translates it into the business case for changing rewards. The business case is more detailed and specific than the overall total reward strategy and is customized to the specific business situation faced by the organization. (Chapter 2 described some examples of the business case for changing rewards.)

DESIGN PARAMETERS. The business case addresses the reasons for changing rewards, outlines the win-win for the company and people and what value should result from the change, and articulates such key issues as the measures and goals that need to be communicated, funding, and workforce involvement in pay design. The leadership team defines whatever parameters are necessary to give the design team the go to develop and recommend a pay approach: financial parameters, cost constraints, critical messages to deliver, competitiveness, mix of base pay and variable pay, or relationship between results and rewards.

Leadership also assesses how ready the workforce is for reward change. The results of this assessment don't stop forward movement. Rather, the assessment clarifies strengths and weaknesses so that the organization can design and implement a plan to make the process go more smoothly.

The leadership team defines a plan for development and implementation, including selecting champions for the design process and guiding the overall strategy for workforce involvement and communications. They subsequently turn over the business case for changing rewards, with their sponsorship, to a design team (including in most instances a senior sponsor and champion).

STREAMLINED APPROVAL PROCESS. Having the leadership teams develop the total reward strategy and the business case is important for reasons beyond the fact that in most companies strategy is their job. Of primary importance is that it changes the tactics from a leadership posture of saying "We'll know it when we see it" to a cascading process that adds value. In addition, their involvement in strategy and the business case up front avoids having to sell the entire solution on the back end—not knowing whether the solution is a go until a presentation, down the road, to convince an unsuspecting leadership team of the appropriateness of the strategy and the business case. Leaders are very effective at championing what they own and are committed to. Championing is important in design, implementation, and communications, as well as in refining rewards to match changes in business direction.

Having the leadership team develop the business case is also an opportunity to set a calendar for delivery of the final pay work product. If leadership sets the schedule for completion, deadlines will probably be met. Leaders also set some measures and milestones that can be useful in monitoring the progress of the undertaking, while keeping the focus on key deliverables.

STAGE 2: DEVELOP REWARD SOLUTION

In the next stage, the design team is responsible for developing a reward solution to recommend to the leadership team—in this case, a pay solution. The recommendations should be consistent with the total pay strategy, which is a subset of the total reward strategy, and the business case for changing rewards; they should also fit within any parameters identified by the leadership team.

The design team may comprise people representing major functions and a diagonal slice of the organization, including management and the workforce levels that feel the impact of the pay change. Or it may be a management team. We don't recommend constituting a design team only of human resource people because pay is a management communications tool to improve business success. If the company uses an HR team, though, its members have to engage others through conducting focus groups or holding periodic meetings with line managers to get their perspective on the design. The role of HR should be to facilitate the pay change process and do background work, not to own the process. Line management must own and support it. Pay is foremost a business tool.

Workforce Involvement

We've found that enlisting the people affected by pay change in the actual process of making the change not only adds value but is also significant in bringing about acceptance and success of the pay solution. It's important to make sure that involvement is a key factor in the pay change process, and equally important that the involvement be meaningful.[4]

A range of opportunities for workforce involvement in reward design are possible. Exhibit 16.3 describes involvement opportunities based on how extensively the workforce participates in reward design, from focus groups to diagonal-slice design teams. Across the continuum, however, the responsibilities of the latter teams are not the same. Some may work with a detailed reward strategy and business case that limit the design issues they address; others may receive few parameters so they'll have considerable design freedom to propose recommendations for approval.

INTERVIEWS AND GOAL SETTING. On the left side of the continuum is less involvement, which occurs before or after the pay design. It happens before, for example, in sales compensation designs when salespeople are interviewed to gather their opinions on the effectiveness of pay and performance measures, on selling opportunities and challenges, on how they direct their selling effort and spend their time, and on what makes them successful in selling. Subsequently, management in sales and marketing, finance, and human resources design the pay solution.

Workforce involvement may occur after the pay design, perhaps during the goal-setting process. For instance, at UCLA Medical Center, a design team composed of directors and managers developed, implemented, and communicated the major change to team variable pay that we described in Chapter 7. The workforce is involved because a workgroup within each team is actively involved in setting the goals

Exhibit 16.3. Options for Involvement in Reward Design.

Less	Moderate	Considerable			Extensive
• People are interviewed for their perspective on pay, performance measures, and performance management to provide background information for the design process • People participate in goal setting after the design process	• Focus groups comment on design developed by leadership • Focus groups play continuing role by giving "how it is going" feedback periodically	• Design team receives key elements of pay design—for example, type of solution; variable pay funding formula, performance period, goals from operating plan or business-aligned goals; ongoing value specifications and base pay adjustment methodology • Design team develops and recommends some elements such as variable pay eligibility and basis for award sharing, examples of determining individual ongoing value and the logic for base pay decisions; details review process to make it workable; communicates, trains	• Design team receives very detailed design parameters—for example, type of solution, variable pay funding formula, definition of individual ongoing value dimensions, and base pay budget • Design team develops and recommends additional variable pay measures, goals, how these goals earn awards, basis for award sharing, eligibility; designs and recommends specifications of ongoing value dimensions, criteria for determining base pay adjustments, and review process; communicates, trains, implements	• Design team receives strategy—for example, self-funding gainsharing and individual ongoing value base pay that emphasizes the skills dimension • Design team develops and recommends variable pay funding formula, measures, goals, performance period, basis for award sharing, eligibility; defines the applicable ongoing value dimensions; develops and recommends base pay methodology and review process; communicates, trains, implements	• Design team receives broad philosophy only—for example, variable pay rewards results and aligns with operating plan and base pay rewards individual ongoing value to the business • Design team develops and recommends entire pay solution for approval, communicates, trains, and implements

for its team. A subset of the original design team continues to meet to refresh the design periodically.

FOCUS GROUPS. As you move from the left end of the continuum, you find focus groups offering input on design issues. Solectron California, described in Chapter 10, is an example. The workforce gave input on a selection of variable pay design issues the final design incorporated. This is a chance to make design course corrections as necessary. A review of the current literature suggests that focus groups are an important way to enlist involvement; they offer an opportunity to communicate pay change while it's still in the design process.

DESIGN TEAMS. Move further along the involvement continuum and you find the workforce participating on a design team that develops and recommends performance criteria and the pay distribution methodology but doesn't determine funding. ARCO Marine (now part of BP Amoco) developed a major new pay approach for masters of oil tankers with the involvement of a design team that included ship's captains, who developed the performance criteria and the base pay and variable pay allocation methodology. Masters were the people most knowledgeable about the technical aspects of their role; management brought in the behavioral skills and competencies that represented the culture shift they were implementing.

Another example is dj Orthopedics, having developed a new distributor sales compensation approach by using a design team of distributors, sales and marketing managers, and the head of finance. The company had determined the financial parameters before the design team met. Including distributors on the design team created a win-win partnership between distributors and the company so both sides understood one another's issues; the design of the pay solution achieves the company's needed business objectives and focuses the distributors' business to position them for success.

COMBINATION OF DESIGN TEAM AND FOCUS GROUPS. Involvement can include both a design team and focus groups. The Monsanto business we discussed in Chapter 2 is an example of this combination. Between meetings, the design team gathered input from the workforce.

Another example is the medical group mentioned in Chapter 7. A design team comprising mainly physicians was responsible for a major redesign of physician compensation. Three sets of focus groups were held to communicate and obtain input. The first gathered feedback from physicians on the existing pay program and what they thought pay should reward; the second communicated and gathered feedback on the new pay strategy; and the third did the same on the preliminary pay design. The involvement level was necessarily high to gain acceptance of a major change in pay that was closely attuned to contemporary medical practice as well as customer needs.

DESIGN TEAM OF UNION, NONUNION, AND MANAGEMENT PEOPLE. An example of involving management and union and nonunion workers is PeaceHealth Oregon Region. A diagonal-slice design team representing the workforce of this large health care organization worked together to develop and communicate a major new pay solution. The approach involved a performance management solution based on growth in competencies and skills, base pay anchored in the labor market and focused on the individual as well as the job, and variable pay that unified the organization with shared measures and goals.

Several union members and the business agent joined the high-involvement pay design team to help make the change in pay a reality. For PeaceHealth Oregon Region, this was a revolutionary move that helped to bind union and nonunion workers and allow an exchange of perspectives and views in open dialogue. The entire pay solution was implemented for nonunion workers, and union workers adopted the performance management sections in contract negotiations.

INVOLVEMENT AT SATURN. At Saturn, union workers are actively involved in designing pay and setting performance goals. Total cash includes an hourly wage below that of the rest of General Motors, as well as variable pay based on measures of Saturn performance and other objectives. At a recent negotiation, the union had a chance to end variable pay based on performance. The timing would have been right, because Saturn sales were slumping on account of customer preference favoring larger cars. But the union stuck with the variable pay solution and emphasis on paying for performance. Encouraging more of such active workforce involvement and positive relationship between union and management as it relates to pay is critical.

Design Process for a Diagonal-Slice Design Team

We've found that when workforce members are involved to a meaningful extent in designing, implementing, and communicating a pay solution that's well aligned with the business, experience with a high-involvement process has important transfer value to other business decisions in the company.

DESIGN TEAM MEMBERSHIP. Design teams vary in number. Some diagonal-slice design teams may have as few as five members to as many as 40, but a representative team of 10–16 members who work seriously on the project can serve the process well.

Members frequently have a specific skill or technical knowledge that helps the process, and they also meet criteria such as satisfactory communications skills, respect from peers, reasonable intelligence to generate ideas, and willingness to commit to the process. In other instances, a design team comprises qualified volunteers, as long as they too represent a diagonal slice of the organization overall. Design team members should have experience in high involvement, or be interested in receiving training in participation and collaborative decision making.

TIME COMMITMENT. We find that if the company wants workforce acceptance and commitment, basically it spends the same time and effort in implementing pay change, regardless of involvement. It chooses whether to emphasize high involvement so that it expends more energy during design than on communications and implementation, or, if it wants less workforce involvement, it expends more energy on the back end.

Generally, diagonal-slice design teams work about four months from the design to the communications phase. The time period depends on the priority of the pay design, the amount of time people can regularly devote to it, and the scope of the pay design.

In a typical high-involvement design process of four months, the first month involves orientation, education, planning the task, and beginning the design process. The second and third months are for design. The fourth month attends to approval and preparation of communications materials. The design team meets in half-day, one-day, or two-day sessions depending on the extent of required travel. There may be two or three weeks between meetings, depending on how much members communicate and get feedback from the workforce and on the amount of homework between sessions.

DESIGN TEAM PROCESS. The design team typically starts its work by adopting the ground rules that other quality or continuous-improvement teams in the company use, such as listening to understand, respecting others' opinions, participating actively, leaving job titles and roles at the door, and honoring individual confidentiality. They also determine the decision-making process, as in matters of voting or consensus.

The design team comes to understand the total reward strategy and the business case for changing rewards. The team members may put the business case into words that are meaningful to the workforce.

During work sessions, they often break into subteams to address specific issues of communications, measures, and pay distribution, and then regroup to report on subteam work and make decisions. The team usually spends the last part of each meeting deciding homework, what they'll communicate to the workforce, and what information they want to gather from the workforce.

HOMEWORK. Between work sessions, members gather input from the workforce, communicate on progress, and do homework on pay design. One major role is expanding involvement—a "scoop" (more on this in a moment) that increases the constituency for the business case for change and the corresponding pay solution.

It's important to focus not only on the technical aspects of the pay transformation but also on the process by which the change is executed. Usually at the beginning of the process design team members are just learning, so the initial communications have more to do with the process than content. Then the members communicate (or support the communications related to) the business case for changing rewards. As they relay progress on the design, they make clear that it may change and that these are preliminary ideas.

They also gather feedback and questions from the workforce. The design team spends part of its next meeting resolving the issues raised at update meetings or focus groups, and answering questions. Some design teams then publish the answers on the intranet or in a newsletter. Others offer a hotline that allows the team to communicate periodically to the workforce and is a medium for the workforce to leave questions and comments.

SPONSOR RELATIONS AND ROLLOUT. The design team periodically touches base with its sponsor, who represents the leadership team for guidance and feedback from the top of the organization—again to avoid having to sell the pay solution to senior management on the back end. This makes it easier to communicate progress to the workforce with confidence that what they design will actually be implemented.

The design team manages the communications and rollout. Once things are operational, some members remain to ensure that the solution is fine-tuned and to keep the communications and championing process active and strong.

LEGAL ISSUES. In involving the workforce in developing pay approaches, the company needs to be sensitive to the National Labor Relations Board ruling (1992) in the case of Electromation, a company that had a workforce design team develop a pay plan during an attempt at union organizing. We don't recommend involving the workforce in developing pay recommendations as a last-minute stance against a union; it should be part of an ongoing effort of workforce involvement in solving business issues. We know many organizations that involve the workforce to gain commitment, understanding, and a better solution. Consult legal counsel if there are concerns about this.

We also believe that the government's view of teams needs to change so that a company with a high-involvement pay design team helping it develop a viable pay solution isn't judged to be "negotiating" with people in a unionlike bargaining session. Labor law and regulations should encourage rather than discourage teams and workforce involvement.

The Involvement Scoop

Involvement and communications start early in the process. The best time to begin involvement is after the business case has been developed and when it's ready to be communicated. Communications have a much better chance of being accepted if they're championed by the people affected by the pay change.

How does a company get people to accept the business case for change and become "storytellers" for a positive message about their role in eventual success? For many years, organizations developed expansive communications processes geared toward getting the message through by overpowering worker resistance to change. How often have you participated in a communications effort where everyone is paraded into a large room and a leader thanks people for coming and then launches into "a brief introduction"? During the next hour or more, the lights are dimmed, and everyone dozes through an elaborate, professionally developed slide or video show telling them how good the new pay approach is. On their way out, they get a multicolored pamphlet that they keep until they get back to their work area. The results are:

- No dialogue
- No understanding
- No retention
- No involvement
- No acceptance
- No storytelling

Here, the absence of involvement is significant. For communications really to be accepted, there must be involvement of a representative sampling of the workforce in designing, communicating, rolling out, and refining a pay solution consistent with the business case for change. We call the process of encouraging involvement from the start and growing constituency for the result a *scoop*.

The leadership team builds the strategy and business case "box" that defines the parameters within which the involvement process develops a pay work product. The scoop begins with the design team working to understand the need for change, starting from the total reward strategy from the leadership team. The design team uses this to develop and recommend a responsive pay solution; it's responsible for helping leadership sponsor the solution by getting out front on the continuing communications process and telling the story.

STAGE 3: CONDUCT COMMUNICATIONS AND ROLLOUT

Often, the only thing that makes change attractive is the comparative unattractiveness of what's being left behind. This is never truer than in the case of pay. Most of the benchmarking, piloting, and surveying eventually comes down to making the decision to move forward to communicate and roll out the new solution because it's no longer possible to stay in the past.[5]

But for many people, the known past is always more attractive than the unknown future. In the words of one executive: "If we waited until everyone was ready to change pay, it would never happen. We need to start the transformation process, show we're serious, and enlist support as we go." Thus, it's important to ready the company and people for change once it's deemed necessary. This means giving a strong push to communicate, roll out the pay solution, and move forward. It means enlisting the help of the people who are change-friendly to move the fence-sitters into accepting the change, and neutralizing the impact of those who resist the change or try to make the change process fail.

The Big Push

How can companies push most effectively? It begins with workforce involvement during design and continues during communications and rollout of the solution. This is applying the scoop process beyond the design team to the rest of the workforce. As the design team develops alternatives, they're described to small groups for input and consideration. At the same time, people are educated on the total reward strategy, the business case for reward change, design solutions under way, and what this means to people. The scoop grows: gathering input, answering questions, and sharing information. The concept is two-way communication that permits the pay design team and the workforce to learn, consider, and continue the process.

Everyone on the Same Page

An objective of communications and rollout is to get everyone moving in the same direction. Acceptance of the pay change by managers is especially critical because they're the primary communications link to the workforce. They must be made to feel part of the change process and an important factor in the future of the company.

A consumer electronics company was struggling with a pay-for-skills plan for one major reason: the frontline managers weren't supporting it. They viewed themselves as losers in the process. The pay solution supported increased workforce involvement and resulted in pay decisions being moved lower in the organization by peer assessment; decisions would be more objective by being based on skill certification, not management judgment. Managers needed to understand that their new accountabilities were more important than those they felt they'd lost. The new accountabilities included performance planning, coaching, training, developing, facilitating, and serving as a role model. Dealing with noise not only from the general workforce but also from managers is part of effective communications and rollout.

Communications Choices

There are a number of successful communications possibilities. The most powerful is face-to-face communications with the workforce, led by members of the high-involvement design team and managers. Managers participate actively and show support for the change. The concept for successful communications is to use every effective means of communication to get the message across. This varies by company but may entail small-group meetings, one-on-one meetings, an intranet site, bulletin boards, e-mail, brochures, newsletters, videos, audiotapes (for salespeople on the road), and hotlines.

Because repetition is critical, each member of the design team must get out and communicate the story—moving to the positive from negative communications noise. We like to have the design team prepare answers to the 10 to 15 most frequently asked questions and use the Q&A in the communications process. The list in Exhibit 16.4 is a beginning, but the questions quickly become more specific depending on the type of pay solution and the company's unique design.

Exhibit 16.4. "Most Frequently Asked" Communications and Rollout Questions.

1. Why is the company doing this? Why must pay change now?
2. What does the pay change mean to me? How will my pay change? What's in it for me?
3. We hear a lot about "total rewards and total reward strategy"; what are they, and can we see the strategy?
4. Who was involved in this pay design? How were they selected?
5. Will any elements of current pay be reduced? When, how, why, and how much?
6. How does the new pay plan work specifically?
7. What do I need to do to be successful under this new pay plan?
8. What role does my manager play in this new program?
9. Where can I go to get more of my questions answered?
10. What plans have been made to keep us informed on how the organization is doing compared to the goals you discussed?

Keys to Acceptance

Although written communications are important, involvement and sharing afford face-to-face communications and the opportunity to learn from one another. It's really a go-for-broke process that gets the message through, repeats it, and then goes on repeating it as needed. Here are the tenets of effective understanding and acceptance:

- *Overcommunicate.* Even if you think you've communicated enough, you probably haven't. Wait until most people are saying "Enough already!" before shifting from initial to ongoing communications. The latter engage the workforce in what it can do to be successful under the new pay approach.
- *Train managers.* Enhance managers' understanding of the design and implications of the new approach. Prepare them to answer questions. Help them be coaches, trainers, facilitators, and leaders of the change process.
- *Train people.* Help everyone understand the business, the business case, the vision for the future, and the business goals being pursued. Give them the skill and competency to work in a company with a total pay solution such as yours. Set the stage for acceptance and commitment.
- *Stay goal-focused.* Provide milestones and ongoing communications on progress toward goal achievement. Coach on how to achieve goals and how to correct course. Orient people on the importance of the goals to the business as well as to the workforce.
- *Celebrate.* Follow all of our suggestions in Chapter 9 regarding celebration and helping everyone understand what's going on and why. Make it fun. Use celebration and recognition to make the total pay transition positive. Don't be defensive; be confident, and keep sponsor visibility high. This is a good thing that's happening; if it isn't, it shouldn't happen at all.

Art or Science?

Pay design is an art form, not a scientific process. The process of how pay changes is just as important as the actual substance of the changes to pay elements. How a company develops, implements, communicates, and rolls out pay solutions matters. This sets the atmosphere for attending to and managing them in the future. Exhibit 16.5 summarizes the factors associated with a successful pay change process.

Exhibit 16.5. Getting Started on Successful Pay Change.

Most Associated with Problems	Most Coupled with Success
Selling on back end	Leaders champion
Little or no involvement	Involvement
Little dialogue	Continuous communications
Complex solution	Straightforward solution
No value-added	Business value-added and win-win
Dramatic, radical change	Incremental positive change
Focus on administrative issues	Emphasize performance issues

STAGE 4: CONTINUE REFINEMENT

Some people say that once communications and rollout are completed the real work begins. We like to see some members of the original pay design team remain in place as "resident experts" for at least the first year of the implementation process. This implementation team encourages continuity, remaining in contact with managers and the workforce and continuing the communications and training process. It also prepares others in the company to be involved in making the program a success. Technology transfer and process transfer are important to maintaining the program internally.

Areas for Refinement

There are many ways to refine total pay and total rewards. Here are some areas that allow refinement:

- *Business directions.* Have business goals changed such that pay and other rewards need to deliver new communications messages? How can the line of sight of these goals best be addressed: through business-aligned goals, feedback on development and performance, rewarding individual ongoing value, variable pay, or recognition? Have the objectives of pay changed? Do the specific messages communicated by pay need to change?
- *Design effectiveness.* Is each pay and other reward element accomplishing its objective? Is the business improving or becoming more effective as a result of total pay? Are pay elements being used effectively together with other rewards to create an integrated package? What about performance measurement and management? base

pay? variable pay? benefits? sales compensation? How effective is the company's approach to scarce talent, global rewards, and recognition and celebration? How did rewards work for a merger or acquisition?

- *Communications.* How effectively do pay and other rewards carry the business message? What's the state of noise in the workplace concerning pay? Are successes celebrated?
- *Sponsorship.* Are sponsors and champions out front and visible? Does what they say and do need to be updated? Are new or additional champions needed? Are the champions' messages clear and consistent? Are sponsors and champions approachable and available? Does the sponsorship or championing process need to be refreshed?
- *Managers.* Are managers communicating, supporting, and demonstrating commitment to pay solutions? Are they making effective pay decisions? Are they using all the pay and other reward tools available to them well? Are they effectively measuring and managing performance?
- *Workforce.* Do people understand and accept the business case for changing rewards and the resulting pay solutions? Are they engaged in doing what's needed to be successful in earning awards under the pay solutions? Are they committed to the business and to the win-win partnership with the company?

The refinement challenge is to keep interest high. The temptation, though, is to take a breather once the heavy lifting of design, communications, and rollout is over. But this is precisely the time the process can most easily break down. The first year of a new pay solution tests everyone and everything involved in the new process. New performance measurement and management approaches need consistent communications and reinforcement. Variable pay may involve a host of people who haven't participated in such approaches before. Base pay and lump-sum payments that emphasize individual ongoing value require another view of how people are valued. This requires training of managers and the workforce; it's also why some believe the real work of pay change doesn't begin until the program is in force.

Sponsorship and Guidance

Continued sponsorship and involvement are critical. We like to see a sponsor retained, someone who's out front on continuing communications, addressing questions, and ensuring that training and development remain at a high level. Members from the design team, supplemented with some replacements and a plan to rotate membership at least annually, are the prerequisite for work yet to be done on the pay solution. This supplements internal human resource staff in ensuring that pay approaches are continuously refreshed and kept current.

Some companies like to implement a sunset clause in total pay. This means that after a specific period of time, many or all of the provisions of the total pay approach terminate. We prefer not to do this because it sets a drop-dead date that requires the company to fix something that may not be broken. Rather, we'd like to see a team in place, periodically testing, evaluating, and making changes as they're needed. Or the trigger for the annual review is during the development of the annual operating plan to ensure alignment.

Continuous Change

The examples and case studies we've mentioned in *Pay People Right!* evolve over time. The organizations with the best and most durable applications of rewards to the business process just don't stay still. It's likely that technical solutions and approaches will evolve. For example, the best way to pay strategically for critical skills changes to match the situation. Periodic review is an opportunity to reassemble the parts so that they continue to meet the company's current and future business objectives.

We're all in exciting times. Reward design and effectiveness have come out of the shadows to assume increasing importance for both enterprises and people. Those who are accountable for making pay and other reward changes are becoming the scarce human resource talent. More and more, we see the very best facilitators and change agents applying pay as a tool of positive performance improvement and excellence.

CONCLUSIONS

Companies expending considerable time and effort to realign pay must become marathon runners more than sprinters. Effective process begins with a total reward strategy that the leadership team sponsors and sticks with. It entails a design process that includes involving people who feel the impact of the pay solution. Communications are important not only in the rollout but also early in the process, as soon as the total reward strategy and business case for changing rewards are final and design begins. Partnering members of the design team that developed the pay approach with managers to conduct face-to-face communications is a powerful message.

On top of all of this is the requirement for speed from start to finish—not careless speed, but a commitment to make deadlines and keep promises to both people and the company. This means looking for ways to maximize effectiveness while addressing issues as expeditiously as possible and converting strategy to tactics. The reason for this is the need to gain the promised advantage and to convert from negative to positive noise that supports and helps communicate the business goals.

Epilogue
21st-Century Rewards

ONCE ALICE followed the March Hare down the rabbit hole, an entirely new world opened. Some of it was very pleasant, some was challenging; but the whole thing was different, exciting, and full of opportunities. Her adventure ended positively, and Alice learned a great deal about herself and her world. That's the situation many companies find once they explore total pay and total rewards as a tool of business effectiveness.

The *Pay People Right!* road map shows a new role for total pay and total rewards. As we said, pay is a hot-change tool, which makes it a strong communicator. The trick is to also make pay a positive element in the business formula for improvement. We've suggested how the business case for changing rewards can establish a foundation for effective communication, and how the design of total pay can deliver the business message positively to people and contribute to the better workforce deal. The future for total pay and total rewards is clearly not more of the same. This means change, whether or not the company and the workforce are ready. Our goal has been to help prepare organizations and people for what's at hand.

MOONS IN ALIGNMENT

We predict that the future will foster more positive and enlightened total rewards. The "moons" of economic change and human resource change are in alignment. Total rewards can—and should now—be positively positioned to accelerate alignment of people with business success. This win-win partnership makes sense for both people and the company.

THE REWARD PRINCIPLES

We've suggested that one way to do this is to keep six reward principles in mind as you consider changing total rewards and total pay, with the objective of improving company and workforce effectiveness and sharing success. The first of these principles requires that pay change be a positive and natural experience. This means people must understand, accept, and commit to the logic and outcomes that change produces. Involving people in the pay design process best accomplishes change of this magnitude and importance. It also means the company must provide education, training, development, and coaching to prepare everyone to adapt to and succeed under a new reward solution. Communications are essential concerning the business case for changing rewards, the business goals and objectives, and the skills and competencies necessary for success.

Business goals and a win-win partnership define the second principle. It requires meaningful alignment of rewards with business goals to create a strong and positive company-workforce partnership. This means all stakeholders in the reward transaction need to gain something from the exchange—the company and the workforce as well as shareholders and customers. To have a deal that makes sense, the sharing of results must be balanced among all partners. This can only happen if business success is the primary factor in driving the reward process.

The third principle suggests extending the workforce line of sight to the goals of the business. This is powerful logic because it makes no sense to link rewards to business goals unless people understand how what they do adds value to what the company needs to achieve. The enterprise must educate people and increase workforce involvement to enable them to be knowledgeable stakeholders in its success. This requires that a combination of business-aligned goals and ongoing development and performance feedback be part of the total pay determination process. It means considering what the customer wants and shaping rewards so they match organization design, at whatever levels best set the basis for pay: individual, team, group, business unit, or company. The key is using goals that not only add value to the business but are also within the influence of the people responsible for performance.

The fourth principle suggests that reward design is not one-size-fits-all. Instead, thoughtful integration of rewards takes advantage of which elements best fit the bill defined by the total reward strategy. This permits innovative and continuing customization of rewards according to what each reward element does best. It is the mix-and-match proposition we've been suggesting.

The final two principles emphasize rewarding individual ongoing value with base pay and results with variable pay. The positive development emphasis of performance management requires that base pay link to how people acquire and apply the skills and competencies the company needs, the value of these competencies in an increasingly competitive global talent market, and the track record of measurable results delivered. Variable pay continues to be a favorite of ours for rewarding results. The agility and flexibility of variable pay, coupled with the fact that it can deal with a host of evolving and changing measures of success, make it a powerful accelerator pedal for achieving business results.

THE BETTER WORKFORCE DEAL

Our definition of the better workforce deal is based on four total reward components, with total pay being only one of them. The need to grow the business and compete for talent has amplified the importance of the better workforce deal. This translates into individual growth opportunities, aligned total pay, a positive workplace, and an exciting and compelling future in which everyone wants to share. From the perspective of the workforce, this brings more contemporary training and development, total pay that's better aligned and competitive with value provided, a workplace and work associates that people want to join as co-stakeholders, and the prospect of a good future.

Who gets what out of total rewards as part of the better workforce deal? Why do we say everyone is a winner? The company finds a total pay solution that grows in cost only if people become more valuable and meet business goals. People earn more as they increase their value and meet business goals. The company attracts people who want to add value. If you're an individual who wants to add value, the company makes it worthwhile for you to join. The organization enjoys a total reward solution that retains the best talent possible. The workforce finds a business that's a positive place to be and makes them feel good about the work experience. On any dimension possible, a balanced deal is simply better than an unbalanced one. If the old deal was biased toward the workforce and the next deal—the new deal—was most attractive to the company, the better workforce deal is attractive to everyone.

We leave it at that for now. We'd like to keep in touch with you and exchange information and thoughts as you undertake your total reward and total pay journey in your company. As the book jacket suggests, you can contact us at www.paypeopleright.com; we hope to hear from you.

Notes

Preface

1. Schuster, J. R., and Zingheim, P. K. *The New Pay: Linking Employee and Organizational Performance.* San Francisco: Jossey-Bass, 1996.
2. Cappelli, P. *The New Deal at Work: Managing the Market-Driven Workforce.* Boston: Harvard Business School Press, 1999.

Chapter 1: Total Rewards and the Six Reward Principles

1. Adapted from Zingheim, P. K., and Schuster, J. R. "How to Pay Members of Small, High-Performance Teams." In *Team Pay Case Studies: What's Working in Companies Today.* (Special issue of *Compensation & Benefits Review.*). New York: American Management Association, 1997.
2. Lawler, E. E., III. *From the Ground Up: Six Principles for Building the New Logic Corporation.* San Francisco: Jossey-Bass, 1996.
3. Richter, A. S. "Compensation Management and Cultural Change at IBM: Paying the People in Black at Big Blue." *Compensation & Benefits Review,* 1998, *30*(3), 51–59.

Chapter 2: The Business Case for Changing Rewards

1. Ledford, G. E., Jr. "Designing Nimble Reward Systems." *Compensation & Benefits Review,* 1995, *27*(4), 46–54.
2. Schuster and Zingheim (1996).
3. Covey, S. R. *The 7 Habits of Highly Effective People.* New York: Simon & Schuster, 1989.
4. Zingheim, P. K., and Schuster, J. R. "Dealing with Scarce Talent: Lessons from the Leading Edge." *Compensation & Benefits Review,* 1999, *31*(2), 36–44.
5. Seaman, R. *The Path: A Practical Guide to Improving Your Life on the Job.* Palo Alto, Calif.: Guidance Press, 1999.
6. Adapted from Zingheim, P. K., and Schuster, J. R. "Compensation Strategy: 'New Pay' Deployed to Advance Organizational Goals at Three California Hospitals." *Strategies for Healthcare Excellence,* 1997, *10*(8), 9–12.

Chapter 3: Integrating Total Pay

1. Hammer, M. *Beyond Reengineering: How the Process-Centered Organization Is Changing Our Work and Our Lives.* New York: HarperBusiness, 1996.
2. See, for instance, Branch, S. "The 100 Best Companies to Work for in America." *Fortune,* 1999, *139*(1), 118–144.
3. From "Becoming the Employer of Choice: A Strategic Approach," Human Resource Strategy Forum and Center for Effective Organizations Conference, Los Angeles, Nov. 1998.
4. *Report on the 1999–2000 Total Salary Increase Budget Survey.* Scottsdale, Ariz.: American Compensation Association, 1999.

Chapter 4: Measuring and Managing Performance

1. Kaplan, R. S., and Norton, D. P. *The Balanced Scorecard: Translating Strategy into Action.* Boston: Harvard Business School Press, 1996.
2. Edwards, M. R., and Ewen, A. J. *360 Degree Feedback: The Powerful New Model for Employee Assessment & Performance Improvement.* New York: AMACOM, 1996.
3. O'Byrne, S. F. "EVA and Management Compensation." *ACA Journal,* 1994, *3*(2), 60–73.
4. Schonberger, R. J. *Building a Chain of Customers: Linking Business Functions to Create the World-Class Company.* New York: Free Press, 1990.
5. Hamel, G., and Heene, A. (eds.). *Competence-Based Competition.* Chichester, U.K.: Wiley, 1994.
6. Zingheim, P. K., Ledford, G. E., Jr., and Schuster, J. R. "Competencies and Competency Models: Does One Size Fit All?" *ACA Journal,* 1996, *5*(1), 56–65.
7. Zingheim, Ledford, and Schuster (1996).
8. Flowers, E. W., and Schuster, J. R. "Developing and Implementing Competency-Based Pay at Monsanto." Presented at Performance & Rewards Forum, American Compensation Association, Chicago, Oct. 1996.
9. Zingheim, P. K., and Schuster, J. R. "Supporting Teams with Multi-Rater Performance Reviews." *Compensation & Benefits Management,* 1995, *11*(3), 41–45.

Chapter 5: Rewarding Individual Ongoing Value: Base Pay

1. "Grove Advises Keeping an Eye on Big Picture." *USA Today,* Apr. 28, 1999, p. 7B.

2. Schuster, J. R., and Zingheim, P. K. "'New Pay' Strategies That Work." *Journal of Compensation and Benefits,* May/June 1993, pp. 5–9.
3. Richter (1998).
4. Salokas, L. "Pay for Future Capability." Presented at New Directions in Pay for Performance, Center for Effective Organizations, Los Angeles, Dec. 1996.
5. Lawler, E. E., III. *Rewarding Excellence: Pay Strategies for the New Economy.* San Francisco: Jossey-Bass, forthcoming.
6. Gupta, N., Shaw, J., and Ledford, G. E., Jr. "When Do Pay-for-Skills Plans Survive? A Five-Year Follow-Up to the ACA Study." Presented at Seminar Series Pay for Skills and Competencies: New Research and Practice, Center for Effective Organizations, Los Angeles, Mar. 1998.

Chapter 6: Building Infrastructure for Base Pay

1. Schuster and Zingheim (1996).
2. Gilbert, D., and Abosch, K. S. *Improving Organizational Effectiveness Through Broadbanding.* Scottsdale, Ariz.: American Compensation Association, 1996.
3. Abosch, K. S. "Confronting Six Myths of Broadbanding." *ACA Journal,* 1998, *7*(3), 28–36.
4. Dalton, G. W., and Thompson, P. H. *The Four Stages of Careers in Organizations.* Provo, Utah: Novations Group, 1991.
5. Abosch, K. S. "The Promise of Broadbanding." *Compensation & Benefits Review,* 1995, *27*(1), 54–58.

Chapter 7: Rewarding Performance: Short-Term Variable Pay

1. Turan, K. "The Thrill Isn't Gone." *Los Angeles Times,* Dec. 28, 1998, pp. F1ff.
2. Schuster and Zingheim (1996).
3. Zingheim, P. K., and Schuster, J. R. "Introduction: How Are the New Pay Tools Being Deployed?" *Compensation & Benefits Review,* 1995, *27*(4), 10–13.
4. Schuster, J. R., and Zingheim, P. K. "The New Variable Pay: Key Design Issues." *Compensation & Benefits Review,* 1993, *25*(2), 27–34.
5. Belcher, J. G., Jr. *How to Design & Implement a Results-Oriented Variable Pay System.* New York: AMACOM, 1996.
6. Zingheim, P. K., and Schuster, J. R. "Linking Quality and Pay." *HR Magazine,* 1992, *37*(12), 55–59.

Chapter 8: Rewarding Performance: Long-Term Variable Pay

1. Block, P. *Stewardship: Choosing Service over Self-Interest.* San Francisco: Berrett-Koehler, 1993, p. 178.
2. Schuster and Zingheim (1996).
3. Foulkes, F. K. (ed.). *Executive Compensation: A Strategic Guide for the 1990s.* Boston: Harvard Business School Press, 1991.
4. Staiman, J., and Tompson, K. "Designing and Implementing a Broad-Based Stock Option Plan." *Compensation & Benefits Review,* 1998, *30*(4), 23–40.
5. Staiman and Tompson (1998).
6. "Breathing Underwater." *Wall Street Journal,* Apr. 8, 1999, p. R6.

Chapter 9: Recognition and Celebration

1. Nelson, B. *1001 Ways to Energize Employees.* New York: Workman Publishing, 1997; Nelson, B. *1001 Ways to Reward Employees.* New York: Workman Publishing, 1994; Hemsath, D., and Yerkes, L. *301 Ways to Have Fun at Work.* San Francisco: Berrett-Koehler, 1997.

Chapter 10: Rewarding Teams

1. Drucker, P. F. *Managing in a Time of Great Change.* New York: Dutton, 1995, pp. 89, 101.
2. Lawler, E. E., III. "Creating Effective Pay Systems for Teams." In E. Sundstrom and Associates (ed.), *Supporting Work Team Effectiveness: Best Management Practices for Fostering High Performance.* San Francisco: Jossey-Bass, 1998, p. 189.
3. Mohrman, S. A., Cohen, S. G., and Mohrman, A. M., Jr. *Designing Team-Based Organizations: New Forms for Knowledge Work.* San Francisco: Jossey-Bass, 1995.
4. Lawler (forthcoming).
5. Duarte, D. L., and Snyder, N. T. *Mastering Virtual Teams: Strategies, Tools, and Techniques That Succeed.* San Francisco: Jossey-Bass, 1999.
6. Wellins, R. S., Byham, W. C., and Wilson, J. M. *Empowered Teams: Creating Self-Directed Work Groups That Improve Quality, Productivity, and Participation.* San Francisco: Jossey-Bass, 1991.
7. Zingheim, P. K., and Schuster, J. R. "Best Practices for Small-Team Pay." *ACA Journal,* 1997, *6*(1), 40–49.
8. Zingheim and Schuster, "How to Pay . . .," 1997; and Zingheim, P. K., McKee, L. A., and Rich, J. A. "Rewards in a Small-Team Environment."

Presented at Performance & Rewards Forum, American Compensation Association, San Francisco, Nov. 1997.

Chapter 11: Rewarding Scarce Talent

1. Zingheim, P. K. "Rewarding Hot Talent." In L. A. Berger and D. R. Berger (eds.), *The Compensation Handbook.* New York: McGraw-Hill, forthcoming.
2. Zingheim and Schuster, "Dealing with Scarce Talent . . .," 1999, pp. 36–44; and Zingheim, P. K., and Schuster, J. R. "Rewards for Scarce Information Technology Talent." *ACA Journal,* 1999, *8*(4), pp. 48–57.
3. Wilkinson, S. "How Employee Ownership Makes a Difference at Science Applications International Corporation (SAIC)." Presented at Becoming the Employer of Choice: A Strategic Approach, Human Resources Strategy Forum and Center for Effective Organizations, Los Angeles, Nov. 1998.

Chapter 12: Rewarding the Salesforce

1. Collins, J. C., and Porras, J. I. *Built to Last: Successful Habits of Visionary Companies.* New York: HarperBusiness, 1994.
2. Schuster, J. R., and Zingheim, P. K. "Sales Compensation Strategies at the Most Successful Companies." *Personnel Journal,* June 1986, pp. 112–116.
3. Kearns, D. T., and Nadler, D. A. *Prophets in the Dark: How Xerox Reinvented Itself and Beat Back the Japanese.* New York: HarperBusiness, 1992.
4. Colletti, J. A., and Fiss, M. S., with Wood, W. *Compensating New Sales Roles: How to Design Rewards That Work in Today's Selling Environment.* New York: AMACOM, 1999.
5. Moynahan, J. K. (ed.). *The Sales Compensation Handbook.* New York: AMACOM, 1991.

Chapter 13: Rewarding Executives

1. Boyett, J. H., and Boyett, J. T. *The Guru Guide: The Best Ideas of Top Management Thinkers.* New York: Wiley, 1998.
2. Brindisi, L. J., Jr. "Executive Compensation Links to Shareholder Value Creation." In F. K. Foulkes (ed.), *Executive Compensation: A Strategic Guide for the 1990s.* Boston: Harvard Business School Press, 1991.
3. Kay, I. T. "How Stock Drives CEO and Company Performance: America's Competitive Advantage." *ACA News,* 1997, *40*(9), 19–22.
4. Crystal, G. S. *In Search of Excess: The Overcompensation of American Executives.* New York: Norton, 1991.

5. Crystal, G. "Stock Options in a Bear Market." *ACA Journal,* 1998, *7*(1), 117–118.
6. Reingold, J., and Grover, R. "Executive Pay." *Business Week,* Apr. 19, 1999, pp. 72–118.
7. Cook, F. W. "The Future of Stock Options: What If the Market Doesn't Cooperate?" *ACA Journal,* 1998, *7*(1), 119–120.
8. Schuster and Zingheim (1996).
9. Crystal, G. S. "Fair Play at Monsanto." *crystalreport.com,* Mar. 22, 1999, pp. 1–3.

Chapter 14: Merger-and-Acquisition Rewards

1. Grossman, R. J. "Irreconcilable Differences." *HR Magazine,* 1999, *44*(4), 42–48.
2. Mulligan, T. S. "The New Oligopoly Boom." *Los Angeles Times,* Aug. 22, 1999, pp. C1, C4.
3. Schuster, J. R., and Zingheim, P. K. "Managing Human Resources in a Merger." *Compensation and Benefits Management,* 1990, *6*(3), 230–233.
4. Schuster, J. R., and Zingheim, P. K. "In Hostile Takeovers: Protecting Key Personnel Compensation." *Compensation & Benefits Review,* 1987, *19*(4), 44–53.
5. Galpin, T. J., and Hernden, M. *The Mergers & Acquisitions Handbook: Tools, Templates, and Techniques to Support M&A Integration at Every Level.* San Francisco: Jossey-Bass, 1999.
6. Clemente, M. N., and Greenspan, D. S. *Winning at Mergers and Acquisitions: The Guide to Market-Focused Planning and Integration.* New York: Wiley, 1998.
7. Bickford, L. C. "Mergers and Acquisitions: How Executive Compensation May Affect a Deal." *Compensation & Benefits Review,* 1997, *29*(5), 53–59.
8. Jacobs, W. I. "Combining Compensation Programs." In M. L. Rock, R. H. Rock, and M. Sikora (eds.), *The Mergers & Acquisitions Handbook.* New York: McGraw-Hill, 1994.
9. Presentation at Leadership Forum, St. Vincent Hospitals and Health Services, Indianapolis, Jan. 1998.

Chapter 15: Global Rewards

1. Zingheim, P. K., and Schuster, J. R. "Lessons from Asia in Paying Teams and Rewarding Enterprise." *Journal of International Compensation & Benefits,* July–Aug. 1994, pp. 44–47.

2. Swaak, R. A. "Expatriate Failures: Too Many, Too Much Cost, Too Little Planning." *Compensation & Benefits Review,* 1995, *27*(6), 47–55.
3. Tilghman, T. S., and Hempel, G., Jr. "Alternatives to Tax Equalization: Responding to New Challenges for Multinational Organizations." *ACA Journal,* 1996, *5*(2), 66–77.
4. Sheridan, W. R., and Hansen, P. T. "Linking International Business and Expatriate Compensation Strategies." *ACA Journal,* 1996, *5*(1), 66–79.
5. Tilghman, T. S. "Beyond the Balance Sheet: Developing Alternative Approaches to International Compensation." *ACA Journal,* 1994, *3*(2), 36–49.
6. Thompson, M. A., and Richter, A. S. "Using Culture Principles to Resolve the Paradox in International Remuneration." *ACA Journal,* 1998, *7*(2), 28–37.

Chapter 16: Making Rewards Work

1. Covey (1989).
2. Zingheim, P. K., and Schuster, J. R. "Moving One Notch North: Executing the Transition to New Pay." *Compensation & Benefits Review,* 1995, *27*(4), 33–39.
3. Lawler, E. E., III. *Strategic Pay: Aligning Organizational Strategies and Pay Systems.* San Francisco: Jossey-Bass, 1990.
4. Lawler, E. E., III. *The Ultimate Advantage: Creating the High-Involvement Organization.* San Francisco: Jossey-Bass, 1992.
5. Zingheim, P. K., and Schuster, J. R. "Exploring Three Pay Transition Tools: Readiness Assessment, Benchmarking, and Piloting." *Compensation & Benefits Review,* 1995, *27*(4), 40–45.

Index

S